# The Australian Women's Weekly

## for ALL SEASONS

## cookbook

For more than 50 years, the recipes appearing in the pages of **The Australian Women's Weekly** have encapsulated the spirit of the way we cook and eat in this country. From our parochial English past with its meat pies, warm puddings and Christmas fruit cakes, to our tentative first embrace of the Mediterranean food introduced by the huge wave of post-war immigration, to today's fascination with the vast panoply of homegrown produce as well as an affinity for the flavours revealed by our Asian neighbours, the way we cook and eat has both been determined by and reflected in the pages of **The Australian Women's Weekly**.

So it is with great delight that I introduce you to **The Australian Women's Weekly Cookbook for All Seasons**, a book that brings together more than 250 of the most popular recipes from Australia's oldest, most-respected and much-loved magazine. **The Australian Women's Weekly** Test Kitchen, under the directorship of Food Editor Pamela Clark and her team of experienced and enthusiastic home economists, has always prided itself on the quality, simplicity and originality of all its recipes, and here we've reproduced some of the best recipes that will excite and inspire you the whole year through.

*Happy cooking!*

Nene King
GROUP PUBLISHER

# The Australian Women's Weekly

# Weekly
FOR ALL SEASONS

## cookbook

Food editor: *Pamela Clark*
Assistant food editor: *Alexandra McCowan*
Associate food editor: *Karen Green*
Contributing editor: *Karen Hammial*
Home economists, stylists, photographers and
editorial staff of *The Australian Women's Weekly*
test kitchen

**Home Library Staff**
Editor-in-chief: *Mary Coleman*
Marketing manager: *Nicole Pizanis*
Designers: *Michele Withers, Caryl Wiggins*
Subeditor: *Bianca Martin*
Editorial coordinators: *Fiona Lambrou, Kate Neil*

Managing director: *Colin Morrison*
Group publisher: *Paul Dykzeul*

Produced by *The Australian Women's Weekly*
Home Library.
Colour separations by ACP Colour Graphics
Pty Ltd, Sydney.
Printed by Toppan Printing, Hong Kong.

Published by ACP Publishing Pty Ltd,
54 Park Street, Sydney;
GPO Box 4088 Sydney, NSW 1028;
Ph: (02) 9282 8618  Fax: (02) 9267 9438.
Email: AWWHomeLib@publishing.acp.com.au
http://awwhomelibrary.ninemsn.com.au
Distributed by Simon & Schuster,
20 Barcoo St, East Roseville, NSW 2069;
Ph: (02) 9417 3255.

UNITED KINGDOM: Distributed in the UK by
Australian Consolidated Press (UK),
Moulton Park Business Centre, Red House Rd,
Moulton Park, Northampton, NN3 6AQ;
Ph: (01604) 497 531  Fax: (01604) 497 533.
Email: Acpukltd@aol.com
CANADA: Distributed in Canada by
Whitecap Books Ltd,
351 Lynn Ave, North Vancouver, BC, V7J 2C4,
Ph: (604) 980 9852.
NEW ZEALAND: Distributed by Simon & Schuster,
20 Barcoo St, East Roseville, NSW 2069;
Ph: (02) 9417 3255.
SOUTH AFRICA: Distributed in South Africa
by PSD Promotions, PO Box 1175, Isando 1600,
SA, Ph: (011) 392 6065.

The Australian Women's Weekly
cookbook for all seasons
Includes index
ISBN 1 86396 061 9
1. Cookery. 1. Title: Australian Women's Weekly.
641.5
© ACP Publishing Pty Limited 1999
ACN 053 273 546

First published 1997. Reprinted 1998, 1999.

*Photographs pages 8, 130 and 190 courtesy of Australian
House & Garden. Photography by Rodney Weidland/
Valerie Martin/Neil Lorimer
Photographs page 68 courtesy of Belle
Photography by Simon Kenny*

**Front cover:** Garlic and rosemary chicken with
Roasted tomatoes and green onions
**Back cover:** *clockwise from top,* Chocolate flans with
almond toffee, Baked fetta, Rhubarb souffle with vanilla
bean ice-cream, Bok choy pork and noodle stir-fry
**Title page:** Citrus peppered veal

The Australian Women's Weekly Test
Kitchen has researched, developed,
triple-tested and photographed every
recipe appearing in their 75 cookbooks as
well as all those recipes published in the
pages of The Australian Women's Weekly
magazine for more than fifty years.

# Triple-tested for your success every time!

Food editor Pamela Clark and the Test Kitchen home economists create every recipe then triple-test each one for guaranteed success, ease of preparation, accessibility of ingredients... and fabulous taste.

# contents
## *for all seasons*

**spring** Perfect food for days when the sun is warm, the cold winds of winter a thing of the past and the sight of new season food in the shops awakens dormant appetites *page 9*

**summer** The heat is on, and from the sun-drenched mornings to balmy evenings on the patio, lighter food that's easily prepared becomes one of life's more enjoyable necessities *page 69*

An irresistible invitation to indulge in the change of season and its cornucopia of exquisite fruits and vegetables and the time to enjoy them *page 131*

**winter** A windfall of comfort food offers succour and solace to gatherings of friends and family on the chilliest and greyest days *page 191*

*while burgeoning buds*

claim much of the limelight, spring has a myriad of other fresh treasures.

Delicate shoots of asparagus, buttery new potatoes and the tenderest of peas are just one delectable trio amid the inspired new growth.

Relaxed gatherings are *fresh approaches* a perfect expression of the contagious joy of the season, with food inspired by cultures as diverse as nature itself.

The freshest of spring's abundant produce marries with flavours from both East and West, inviting us to share the spirit of a whole new world.

spring

## Pizza night

ANTIPASTO platter *(page 12)*

Rocket PESTO pizza *(page 51)*

Hot sausage PIZZA *(page 50)*

Spinach, asparagus
and soft egg SALAD *(page 18)*

Vanilla SLICE
with two-tone custard *(page 65)*

SERVES 4 to 6

## Spring picnic

Spicy buttermilk DRUMSTICKS  *(page 49)*

Cheesy BRIOCHE tarts  *(page 48)*

Pasta and fetta SALAD
with artichokes  *(page 50)*

CHINESE cabbage salad  *(page 17)*

Lattice apple PIE  *(page 56)*

Chocolate BUTTONS  *(page 39)*

SERVES 6 to 8

## A hint of Asia

Sweet and sour
PORK tartlets  *(page 14)*

OCTOPUS salad
with coriander dressing  *(page 31)*

Chicken YAKITORI  *(page 20)*

Szechuan pepper beef
with NOODLES  *(page 53)*

Steamed RICE

Fresh FRUIT

SERVES 6

## Tomato and bocconcini SALAD

*Recipe can be made several hours ahead*

8 medium (1.5kg) tomatoes, sliced
250g bocconcini cheese, sliced
$^1/_2$ cup (80g) seeded black olives, thinly sliced
$^1/_4$ cup firmly packed fresh basil

### Dressing

2 tablespoons lemon juice
2 tablespoons olive oil
1 teaspoon balsamic vinegar
$^1/_2$ teaspoon sugar
$^1/_4$ teaspoon cracked black pepper

Layer tomatoes and cheese alternately on serving plate, sprinkle with olives and basil; drizzle with dressing.

**Dressing** Combine all ingredients in jar; shake well.

□ SERVES 6 TO 8

**Storage** Covered, in refrigerator
**Freeze** Not suitable

## ANTIPASTO platter

*Chilli prawns can be made a day ahead*
*Recipe can be prepared several hours ahead*

500g button mushrooms
$^1/_4$ cup (60ml) olive oil
2 cloves garlic, crushed
2 teaspoons sea salt
$^1/_2$ teaspoon cracked black pepper
1 medium (200g) yellow capsicum
1 medium (200g) green capsicum
2 medium (400g) red capsicums
$^1/_2$ small (400g) rockmelon

150g sliced prosciutto
10 slices (125g) salami
$^2/_3$ cup (100g) seeded black olives
$^2/_3$ cup (100g) pimiento-stuffed green olives

### Chilli prawns

1kg uncooked king prawns
1 tablespoon lemon juice
3 cloves garlic, crushed
2 small fresh red chillies, seeded, sliced
2 tablespoons shredded fresh basil
2 tablespoons olive oil
1 tablespoon tomato paste
2 tablespoons balsamic vinegar

Combine mushrooms, oil, garlic, salt and pepper in large baking dish.

Bake, uncovered, in hot oven about 20 minutes or until mushrooms are very soft; cool.

Quarter capsicums, remove seeds and membranes. Roast under grill or in very hot oven, skin side up, until skin blisters and blackens. Cover capsicum pieces in plastic or paper for 5 minutes. Peel away skin, slice capsicums.

Cut rockmelon into 10 thin wedges. Cut prosciutto in half lengthways, wrap around each rockmelon wedge.

Just before serving, arrange mushrooms, capsicums, prosciutto-wrapped rockmelon, salami, olives and chilli prawns on platter.

**Chilli prawns** Shell and devein prawns, leaving tails intact. Combine prawns, juice, garlic, chillies and basil in medium bowl; cover, refrigerate 1 hour.

Heat half the oil in large frying pan, add prawns in batches, cook, stirring, until prawns begin to change colour. Add combined remaining oil, paste and vinegar, stir until prawns are just cooked. Serve warm or cold.

□ SERVES 4 TO 6

**Storage** *Chilli prawns, covered, in refrigerator  Antipasto covered, in refrigerator*
**Freeze** *Not suitable*
**Microwave** *Not suitable*

Tomato and bocconcini salad, *above left*
Antipasto platter, *above*

# SALMON peppercorn puffs

*Recipe can be made a day ahead*

**440g can pink salmon**
**30g butter**
**3 green onions, chopped**
**1 teaspoon drained green peppercorns, crushed**
**2 tablespoons plain flour**
**3/4 cup (180ml) milk**
**2 teaspoons chopped fresh dill**
**3 sheets ready-rolled puff pastry**
**3 hard-boiled eggs, sliced**
**1 egg, lightly beaten**

Drain salmon, reserve 1/4 cup liquid. Melt butter in large pan, add onions and peppercorns, stir over heat until onions are soft. Stir in flour, cook 1 minute, cool slightly. Stir in reserved liquid and milk, stir over heat until mixture boils and thickens; cool. Stir in flaked salmon and dill.

Using 11cm and 12cm round cutters, cut out 6 rounds of each size from pastry. Place 11cm rounds on oiled oven tray. Top with sliced egg, leaving 0.5cm border. Place a sixth of the salmon mixture over egg. Top with 12cm rounds, press edges together with a fork. Using a sharp knife, decorate tops of puffs as desired, brush with beaten egg.

Bake, uncovered, in moderately hot oven 15 minutes or until puffed and browned.

□ MAKES 6

**Storage** *Covered, in refrigerator*
**Freeze** *Not suitable*
**Microwave** *Filling suitable*

# Sweet and sour PORK tartlets

*Recipe best made just before serving*

**3 cups (600g) cooked long grain rice**
**2 eggs, lightly beaten**
**30g butter, melted**

<u>Sweet and sour pork</u>

**225g can pineapple pieces in syrup**
**1 medium (120g) carrot, chopped**
**1 tablespoon soy sauce**
**1 tablespoon tomato sauce**
**1 tablespoon dry sherry**
**1 tablespoon white vinegar**
**4 green onions, chopped**
**125g Chinese barbecued pork, sliced**
**1 tablespoon cornflour**
**1/2 cup (125ml) water**

Lightly oil 6 deep 10cm loose-based flan tins.

Combine rice, eggs and butter in a bowl, press rice mixture over bases and sides of prepared tins to form 1cm-thick shell.

Bake, uncovered, in moderate oven about 30 minutes or until firm; stand 5 minutes.

Run knife around edge of shells, remove from tins; spoon hot sweet and sour pork into shells.

**Sweet and sour pork** Drain pineapple, reserve syrup. Combine syrup and carrot in medium pan, boil, covered, about 3 minutes or until carrot is just cooked. Stir in pineapple, sauces, sherry, vinegar, onions and pork. Blend cornflour with water, stir into pork mixture, stir over heat until mixture boils and thickens.

□ MAKES 6

**Freeze** *Not suitable*
**Microwave** *Not suitable*

Salmon peppercorn puffs, *above left*
Seafood spring rolls, *above right*
Sweet and sour pork tartlets, *right*

# SEAFOOD spring rolls

*Recipe best made just before serving*

8 seafood sticks, chopped
2 tablespoons chopped
    fresh coriander
1 large (180g) carrot, grated
310g can corn kernels, drained
300g can water chestnuts,
    drained, chopped
1 teaspoon sesame oil
8 large (25cm square) spring
    roll wrappers
50g butter, melted

Combine seafood sticks, coriander, carrot, corn, chestnuts and oil in large bowl; mix well.

Spoon an eighth of seafood mixture across corner of spring roll wrapper. Brush edges with some of the butter, tuck in ends, roll up to enclose filling. Repeat with remaining seafood mixture, wrappers and some of the butter. Place spring rolls on oiled oven tray, brush with remaining butter.

Bake, uncovered, in very hot oven about 10 minutes or until browned and hot.

□ MAKES 8

**Freeze** *Not suitable*
**Microwave** *Not suitable*

## Chicken and cheese ROULADE

*Recipe best made just before serving*

200g broccoli, chopped
1 tablespoon vegetable oil
1 medium (150g) onion, chopped
200g chicken thigh fillets, chopped
1 tablespoon plain flour
1/2 cup (125ml) cream
1 teaspoon Dijon mustard
1/2 teaspoon seasoned pepper
2 teaspoons chicken stock powder
60g butter
1/3 cup (50g) plain flour, extra
1 cup (250ml) water
3/4 cup (60g) grated
   parmesan cheese
4 eggs, separated
2 tablespoons chopped fresh basil

Lightly oil 26cm x 32cm Swiss roll pan, line base with baking paper.

Cook broccoli until just tender; then drain.

Heat oil in medium pan, add onion and chicken, cook, stirring, until chicken is well browned. Add flour, stir until combined. Remove from heat, gradually stir in cream, mustard, pepper and half the stock powder, simmer, uncovered, 15 minutes. Blend or process chicken mixture until smooth, return to pan, stir in broccoli; keep warm.

Melt butter in pan, stir in extra flour, stir over heat until bubbling. Remove from heat, gradually stir in water and remaining stock powder, stir over heat until sauce boils and thickens; cool slightly.

Stir in cheese, egg yolks and basil; transfer to large bowl.

Beat egg whites in small bowl until soft peaks form, fold into cheese mixture, in 2 batches. Pour mixture into prepared pan.

Bake, uncovered, in hot oven about 15 minutes or until puffed and browned.

Turn onto piece of baking paper on bench, carefully remove lining paper. Spread evenly with chicken mixture, gently roll up from long side, using baking paper to lift and guide roll. Serve hot.

□ SERVES 6 TO 8

***Freeze*** Not suitable
***Microwave*** Broccoli suitable

Chicken and cheese roulade, *above*

Combine cabbage, onions, celery, nuts and seeds in large bowl.

Just before serving, add noodles and sweet soy sauce dressing; toss well.

**Sweet soy sauce dressing** Combine all ingredients in jar; shake well.

□ SERVES 6 TO 8

*Storage*  Covered, in refrigerator
*Freeze*  Not suitable
*Microwave*  Not suitable

# Crunchy THAI chicken rounds

*Chicken mixture best prepared a day ahead*
*Assemble just before serving*

- **250g minced chicken**
- **2 tablespoons coconut milk**
- **1¹/₂ tablespoons mild sweet chilli sauce**
- **2 teaspoons finely chopped fresh lemon grass**
- **1¹/₂ tablespoons lemon juice**
- **2 tablespoons chopped fresh coriander**
- **1 clove garlic, crushed**
- **2 medium (600g) green cucumbers**

Add chicken to medium heated non-stick pan, cook, stirring, until browned; cool slightly. Process chicken until chopped finely. Combine chicken, coconut milk, sauce, lemon grass, juice, coriander and garlic in medium bowl. Cover, refrigerate several hours or overnight.

Cut cucumbers diagonally into slices 1cm thick. Top each slice with chicken mixture.

□ MAKES ABOUT 25

*Storage*  Airtight container, in refrigerator
*Freeze*  Not suitable
*Microwave*  Not suitable

# CHINESE cabbage salad

*Recipe can be prepared several hours ahead*

- **¹/₂ medium (750g) Chinese cabbage, shredded**
- **12 green onions, chopped**
- **2 sticks celery, chopped**
- **³/₄ cup (60g) flaked almonds, toasted**
- **¹/₃ cup (55g) sunflower seed kernels, toasted**
- **100g packet fried noodles**

Sweet soy sauce dressing

- **¹/₂ cup (125ml) vegetable oil**
- **¹/₄ cup (60ml) white vinegar**
- **¹/₄ cup (50g) brown sugar**
- **2 teaspoons soy sauce**

Chinese cabbage salad, *top*
Crunchy Thai chicken rounds, *above*

## Spinach, asparagus
## and soft egg SALAD

*Croutons can be made a day ahead*
*Dressing can be made a day ahead*
*Salad is best assembled just before serving*

**¹/₂ x 500g loaf unsliced white bread**
**125g butter, melted**
**2 teaspoons seeded mustard**
**250g fresh asparagus**
**4 eggs**
**¹/₂ bunch (250g) English
   spinach, rinsed**

### Blue cheese dressing

**100g blue vein cheese**
**¹/₂ cup (125ml) vegetable oil**
**1¹/₂ tablespoons lemon juice**
**1 egg yolk**
**¹/₂ teaspoon Dijon mustard**
**¹/₄ cup (60ml) water**

Trim crusts from bread, cut bread into
2cm cubes. Toss bread in combined
butter and mustard in medium bowl.
Place bread cubes on oven tray in
single layer.

Bake, uncovered, in moderate
oven about 30 minutes, turning once
during cooking, or until croutons
are browned.

Cut asparagus into 5cm-long
pieces, boil, steam or microwave until
just tender; drain, pat dry.

Place eggs in pan, cover with cold
water, bring to boil, stirring
constantly, boil, uncovered, 4 minutes.
Drain, rinse under cold water; cool.
Shell eggs, cut into halves lengthways.

Combine croutons, asparagus and

spinach in large bowl, top with eggs, drizzle with blue cheese dressing.

**Blue cheese dressing** Blend or process all ingredients until smooth.

□ SERVES 4

*Storage* Croutons, in airtight container
*Dressing* Covered, in refrigerator
*Freeze* Croutons suitable
*Microwave* Asparagus suitable

## PRAWN salad with hazelnut dressing

*Salad can be made several hours ahead*

2 tablespoons sugar
1 tablespoon water
1 tablespoon brandy
3 medium (540g) oranges, segmented
1kg cooked medium prawns
2 medium (400g) green capsicums, thinly sliced

### Hazelnut dressing

1 tablespoon vegetable oil
2 teaspoons curry powder
$1/3$ cup (40g) chopped toasted hazelnuts
$1/3$ cup (80ml) vegetable oil, extra
$1/4$ cup (60ml) white vinegar
1 teaspoon sugar

Combine sugar and water in medium pan, stir over heat until sugar is dissolved, stir in brandy and oranges; cool.

Shell and devein prawns, leaving tails intact.

Combine prawns, capsicums, undrained oranges and hazelnut dressing in large bowl.

**Hazelnut dressing** Heat oil in small pan, add curry powder, cook, stirring until fragrant. Combine curry mixture, hazelnuts, extra oil, vinegar and sugar in small bowl.

□ SERVES 4

*Storage* Covered, in refrigerator
*Freeze* Not suitable
*Microwave* Not suitable

*Clockwise from top*
Spinach, asparagus and soft egg salad,
Prawn salad with hazelnut dressing,
Minty potato and lamb salad

## Minty potato and LAMB salad

*Recipe can be prepared a day ahead*

25 (1kg) baby new potatoes, halved
2 tablespoons olive oil
600g lamb fillets
2 tablespoons shredded fresh mint

### Minty dressing

$1/2$ cup (125ml) sour cream
2 tablespoons lime juice
2 tablespoons milk
2 cloves garlic, crushed
$1/2$ cup firmly packed fresh mint
1 tablespoon mint jelly

Boil, steam or microwave potatoes until tender, drain; rinse under cold water, drain, pat dry.

Heat oil in large pan, add lamb, in batches, cook until browned and just cooked; cool 10 minutes.

Cut lamb diagonally into slices 1cm thick.

Combine potatoes, lamb and minty dressing in large bowl. Sprinkle mint over top.

**Minty dressing** Blend or process all ingredients until smooth.

□ SERVES 4 TO 6

*Storage* Covered, in refrigerator
*Freeze* Not suitable
*Microwave* Potatoes suitable

## Kumara WEDGES with pesto mayonnaise

*Pesto mayonnaise can be made 1 hour ahead*
*Wedges best made just before serving*

2 large (1kg) kumara
$1/2$ cup (125ml) olive oil
2 teaspoons seasoned pepper

### Pesto mayonnaise

$1/2$ cup firmly packed fresh basil
2 tablespoons olive oil
1 clove garlic, crushed
1 tablespoon grated parmesan cheese
$1/2$ cup (125ml) mayonnaise

Peel kumara, cut into 2cm x 8cm wedges. Place kumara in single layer in baking dish, drizzle with combined oil and pepper.

Bake, uncovered, in very hot oven about 20 minutes or until browned and tender. Serve wedges with pesto mayonnaise.

**Pesto mayonnaise** Process basil, oil, garlic and parmesan until smooth; stir in mayonnaise.

□ SERVES 4

*Storage* Pesto mayonnaise in airtight container, in refrigerator
*Freeze* Not suitable
*Microwave* Not suitable

Kumara wedges with pesto mayonnaise, *below*

stirring, until soft. Add spices, cook, stirring until fragrant. Stir in lentils, tomatoes and stock. Simmer, covered, about 20 minutes, stirring occasionally, until lentils are tender and most of the liquid is absorbed; cool. Stir in half the mint. Divide lentil mixture among toasts, top with teaspoons of hummus and remaining mint.

□ MAKES ABOUT 25

***Storage*** *Toasts in airtight container Lentils, covered, in refrigerator*
***Freeze*** *Lentil mixture suitable*
***Microwave*** *Lentil mixture suitable*

## Spiced LENTIL and hummus toasts

*Toasts can be prepared a day ahead*
*Lentils can be prepared a day ahead*
*Assemble just before serving*

28cm bread stick
2 teaspoons olive oil
1 small (80g) onion, finely chopped
1 clove garlic, crushed
1 teaspoon ground cumin
1 teaspoon ground coriander
$^1/_2$ teaspoon sweet paprika

$^1/_2$ cup (100g) red lentils, rinsed, drained
$^1/_2$ x 400g can tomatoes, undrained, crushed
$^3/_4$ cup (180ml) vegetable stock
$2^1/_2$ tablespoons chopped fresh mint
$^2/_3$ cup (180g) hummus

Trim ends from bread, cut diagonally into slices 1cm thick. Grill slices, on both sides, until browned. Heat oil in pan, add onion and garlic; cook,

## Chicken YAKITORI

*Recipe can be prepared a day ahead*

4 single (680g) chicken breast fillets, sliced
$^1/_2$ cup (125ml) teriyaki marinade
2 cloves garlic, crushed
2 teaspoons grated fresh ginger
1 teaspoon sugar

### Dipping sauce

$^1/_4$ cup (60ml) soy sauce
1 tablespoon mild sweet chilli sauce
1 green onion, sliced

Soak 16 skewers in water for 1 hour or grease metal skewers.

Combine chicken, marinade, garlic, ginger and sugar in medium bowl. Cover, refrigerate, 3 hours or overnight.

Drain chicken from marinade; discard marinade. Thread chicken onto prepared skewers.

Cook chicken skewers, in batches, on heated, oiled griddle pan (or grill or barbecue); until cooked through. Serve skewers with dipping sauce.

**Dipping sauce** Combine all ingredients in small bowl.

☐ SERVES 4

*Storage* Covered, in refrigerator
*Freeze* Uncooked marinated chicken suitable
*Microwave* Not suitable

# Minted lamb and noodle SOUP

*Recipe best made just before serving*

**100g bean thread
   vermicelli noodles**
**2 tablespoons peanut oil**
**1kg lamb fillets, sliced**
**2 teaspoons bottled chopped chilli**
**2 tablespoons chopped fresh
   lemon grass**
**2 tablespoons grated fresh ginger**
**4 cloves garlic, crushed**
**$^1/_3$ cup (80ml) fish sauce**
**1.5 litres (6 cups) chicken stock**
**1 tablespoon sugar**
**500g asparagus, chopped**
**$^1/_4$ cup chopped fresh coriander**
**$^1/_3$ cup chopped fresh mint**
**8 green onions, sliced**
**4 medium (520g) tomatoes,
   seeded, sliced**

Place noodles in small heatproof bowl, cover with boiling water, stand 20 minutes; drain.

Heat half the oil in large pan, add lamb, in batches; cook, stirring, until brown and tender; remove from pan.

Heat remaining oil in same pan, add chilli, lemon grass, ginger and garlic; cook, stirring, until fragrant. Add sauce, stock and sugar; bring to boil. Add asparagus; simmer, uncovered, until just tender. Stir in herbs, onions, tomatoes, noodles and lamb; stir until heated through.

☐ SERVES 4 TO 6

*Freeze* Suitable without noodles
*Microwave* Not suitable

Spiced lentil and hummus toasts, *above left*
Minted lamb and noodle soup, *above*
Chicken yakitori, *left*

## Warm CABBAGE salad

*Best made just before serving*

1 medium (120g) carrot
1 small (150g) green capsicum
40g butter
1 medium (150g) onion, sliced
2 cloves garlic, crushed
1 small (150g) red
 capsicum, chopped
$1/2$ small (600g) cabbage,
 finely shredded

### Herbed dressing

$1/2$ cup mayonnaise
2 teaspoons French mustard
1 tablespoon chopped
 fresh parsley

Cut carrot and green capsicum into thin strips.

Heat butter in large pan, add onion and garlic, cook, stirring, until onion is soft. Add carrot and capsicums, cook, stirring, until just tender. Add cabbage, cook until just wilted. Stir in herbed dressing.

**Herbed dressing** Combine all ingredients in jar; shake well.

□ SERVES 4

**Freeze** *Not suitable*
**Microwave** *Suitable*

22

Combine chicken, torn spinach leaves and remaining ingredients in large bowl. Just before serving, add warm chilli dressing; mix well.

**Chilli dressing** Combine all ingredients in small pan, whisk over heat until warm.

▢ SERVES 4

***Storage*** *Covered, in refrigerator*
***Freeze*** *Not suitable*
***Microwave*** *Dressing suitable*

# Crunchy BLUE CHEESE salad

*Dressing can be made several days ahead Salad best made just before serving*

**100g firm blue vein cheese**
**4 thick slices brown bread**
**30g butter**
**1 tablespoon vegetable oil**
**1 clove garlic, crushed**
**1 cos lettuce**
**1 mignonette lettuce**
**100g cherry tomatoes, halved**

### Dressing

**1 teaspoon dry mustard**
**2 cloves garlic, crushed**
**2 teaspoons sugar**
**1 tablespoon milk**
**2 tablespoons vegetable oil**
**1 tablespoon white vinegar**

Cut cheese into 1.5cm cubes. Remove crusts from bread, cut bread into 1cm cubes. Heat butter and oil in small pan, add garlic and bread, stir over heat until croutons are crisp and browned; drain.

Arrange lettuce leaves in large bowl, top with cheese, tomatoes and croutons, sprinkle dressing over salad.

**Dressing** Combine all ingredients in jar; shake well.

▢ SERVES 4

***Storage*** *Dressing, covered, in refrigerator*
***Freeze*** *Not suitable*
***Microwave*** *Not suitable*

Warm cabbage salad, *above left*
Chicken and coriander salad, *left*
Crunchy blue cheese salad, *above*

# CHICKEN and coriander salad

*You will need 1 large cooked chicken for this recipe  Recipe can be prepared several hours ahead*

**3 cups (450g) chopped cooked chicken**
**1 bunch (500g) English spinach**
**100g snow pea sprouts**
**1 medium (200g) red capsicum, chopped**
**4 green onions, chopped**
**250g cherry tomatoes, halved**
**1 small (130g) Lebanese cucumber, sliced**
**¹/₄ cup chopped fresh coriander**

### Chilli dressing

**¹/₃ cup vegetable oil**
**1 tablespoon soy sauce**
**2 tablespoons mild sweet chilli sauce**
**¹/₂ teaspoon sesame oil**
**¹/₄ cup white vinegar**
**¹/₂ teaspoon sugar**

*Dear Mum —*
*Gone fishing*
*Anne*

## Fish SALAD with lime dressing

*We used ocean perch for this recipe*
*Recipe can be prepared several hours ahead*

**500g white fish fillets**
**8 mignonette lettuce leaves**
**1 cup firmly packed watercress**
**4 small (50g) radishes, sliced**
**2 medium (240g) carrots, chopped**
**1 medium (200g) red**
 **capsicum, chopped**

### Lime dressing

**1 teaspoon grated lime rind**
**1 teaspoon grated fresh ginger**
**1 tablespoon lime juice**
**$^1/_3$ cup (80ml) French dressing**
**2 teaspoons chopped fresh chives**

Cut fish into bite-sized pieces, place in large pan, cover with water. Bring to boil, simmer, uncovered, about 2 minutes or until fish is tender; drain. Combine fish and lime dressing in medium bowl, refrigerate 3 hours.

Combine remaining ingredients and undrained fish in medium serving bowl.

**Lime dressing** Combine all ingredients in jar; shake well.

□ SERVES 4

***Storage*** *Covered, in refrigerator*
***Freeze*** *Not suitable*
***Microwave*** *Suitable*

*clockwise from top left,* Tandoori-style fish cutlets, Fish salad with lime dressing, Mexican prawn kebabs

## Tandoori-style FISH cutlets

*We used snapper cutlets for this dish*
*Recipe best prepared a day ahead*

**$^3/_4$ cup (180ml) yogurt**
**1 tablespoon lemon juice**
**1 clove garlic, crushed**
**1 teaspoon grated fresh ginger**
**1 teaspoon curry powder**
**$^1/_2$ teaspoon ground turmeric**
**$^1/_2$ teaspoon sweet paprika**
**$^1/_4$ teaspoon chilli powder**
**4 medium (720g) fish cutlets**

Combine yogurt, juice, garlic, ginger and spices in small bowl.

Place fish cutlets in single layer in medium dish, top with yogurt mixture, turn fish to coat with mixture. Cover, refrigerate 3 hours or overnight.

Remove fish from yogurt mixture;

reserve yogurt mixture. Barbecue or grill fish until cooked through, brushing occasionally with reserved yogurt mixture.

□ SERVES 4

**Storage** *Covered, in refrigerator*
**Freeze** *Not suitable*
**Microwave** *Not suitable*

# Mexican PRAWN kebabs

*Recipe best prepared a day ahead*

36 (about 1kg) uncooked
   king prawns
3 medium (360g) zucchini, chopped
35g sachet taco seasoning mix
1/4 cup (60ml) lemon juice
1 tablespoon vegetable oil
2 tablespoons chopped fresh chives

Soak 18 bamboo skewers in water for 1 hour.

Shell and devein prawns, leaving tails intact. Thread prawns and zucchini onto skewers. Combine the remaining ingredients in a medium bowl.

Place kebabs in single layer in medium dish, top with juice mixture. Cover, refrigerate for several hours, turning occasionally. Remove kebabs from juice mixture; reserve juice mixture.

Grill or barbecue kebabs until prawns are cooked through, brushing occasionally with reserved juice mixture.

□ SERVES 6

**Storage** *Covered, in refrigerator*
**Freeze** *Not suitable*
**Microwave** *Suitable*

# Cheesy tuna and potato PIE

*Recipe can be made a day ahead*

2 sheets ready-rolled
   shortcrust pastry
1 tablespoon milk
1/2 teaspoon poppy seeds

Tuna and potato filling

2 large (600g) potatoes
20g butter
2 tablespoons plain flour
2/3 cup (160ml) milk
3/4 cup (90g) grated
   cheddar cheese
2 teaspoons seeded mustard
185g can tuna in brine,
   drained, flaked
1 teaspoon chopped fresh dill
2 tablespoons chopped fresh basil

Cut a 20cm round from 1 sheet of pastry, place on oiled oven tray, top with tuna and potato filling, spread over pastry leaving 1cm border. Brush edge of pastry with some of the milk, top with remaining pastry sheet. Press top pastry sheet onto lower pastry sheet around filling, trim and pinch edge. Brush top with milk, sprinkle with seeds.

Bake, uncovered, in hot oven about 30 minutes or until pastry is browned and filling hot.

**Tuna and potato filling** Cut potatoes into 1cm cubes, boil, steam or microwave potatoes until tender; drain. Melt butter in large pan, add flour, cook, stirring, until bubbling. Remove from heat, gradually stir in milk, stir over heat until mixture boils and thickens. Stir in potatoes, cheese, mustard, tuna and herbs; cool.

□ SERVES 4

**Storage** *Covered, in refrigerator*
**Freeze** *Not suitable*
**Microwave** *Filling suitable*

Cheesy tuna and potato pie, *left*

## Potato and corn SLICE

*Recipe can be made a day ahead*

1 tablespoon vegetable oil
1 large (200g) onion, sliced
1 clove garlic, crushed
1 small (150g) red capsicum, chopped
130g can corn kernels, drained
2 teaspoons chopped fresh oregano
2 medium (400g) old potatoes, thinly sliced
6 eggs, lightly beaten
$1/2$ cup (125ml) cream
2 teaspoons chopped fresh thyme
$1/2$ cup (60g) grated cheddar cheese

Oil deep 19cm square cake pan, line base and 2 opposite sides with baking paper.

Heat oil in medium pan, add onion, garlic and capsicum, cook, stirring, until onion is soft, drain; cool. Combine onion mixture, corn and oregano in medium bowl. Layer half the potatoes over base of prepared pan, top with onion mixture then remaining potatoes. Pour combined eggs and cream over top, sprinkle with thyme and cheese.

Bake, uncovered, in moderate oven about 1 hour or until potatoes are tender and top is browned lightly.

□ SERVES 4

**Storage** *Covered, in refrigerator*
**Freeze** *Not suitable*
**Microwave** *Not suitable*

Potato and corn slice, *above*

## Bacon and herb OMELETTES

*Recipe must be made just before serving*

8 eggs, lightly beaten
2 tablespoons water
$1/4$ cup (60ml) milk
1 tablespoon chopped fresh parsley
20g butter

Bacon and herb filling

3 bacon rashers, chopped
2 tablespoons chopped fresh chives
1 tablespoon chopped fresh parsley
1 cup (125g) grated cheddar cheese

Combine eggs, water, milk and parsley in medium bowl. Heat 1 teaspoon of butter in medium non-stick pan, pour in a quarter of the egg mixture, cook until top is almost set and underneath is browned lightly. Spoon a quarter of the bacon and herb filling on one side of omelette, fold omelette in half; slide onto serving plate.

Repeat with remaining butter, egg mixture and filling.

**Bacon and herb filling** Add bacon to heated medium non-stick pan, cook, stirring, until crisp; drain on absorbent paper. Combine bacon with remaining ingredients in medium bowl.

□ SERVES 4

**Freeze** *Not suitable*
**Microwave** *Not suitable*

Bacon and herb omelettes, *above right*
Creamy broccoli and bacon fettuccine, *right*

# Creamy BROCCOLI and bacon fettuccine

*Recipe best made just before serving*

**500g fresh fettuccine pasta**
**30g butter**
**1 small (80g) onion, chopped**
**2 bacon rashers, chopped**
**1 clove garlic, crushed**
**250g broccoli, finely chopped**
**$\frac{1}{2}$ cup (125ml) chicken stock**
**300ml cream**
**2 tablespoons grated**
**parmesan cheese**

Add pasta to large pan of boiling water, boil, uncovered, until just tender; drain, keep warm.

Heat butter in pan, add onion, bacon and garlic, cook, stirring, until onion is soft. Add broccoli and stock, cook, covered, 5 minutes. Stir in cream and cheese, bring to boil, simmer, uncovered, about 5 minutes or until sauce thickens slightly. Mix sauce through pasta.

□ SERVES 4

**Freeze** *Not suitable*
**Microwave** *Suitable*

## Minted MEATBALLS
### with hummus

*Recipe can be made a day ahead*

400g minced beef
1 cup (70g) stale breadcrumbs
1 clove garlic, crushed
1 teaspoon beef stock powder
1 egg, lightly beaten
2 tablespoons chopped fresh mint
2 tablespoons olive oil

### Hummus

310g can chickpeas
1 tablespoon olive oil
1 clove garlic, crushed
2 tablespoons lemon juice
2 tablespoons chopped fresh mint

Combine mince, breadcrumbs, garlic, stock powder, egg and mint in medium bowl. Roll level tablespoons of mixture into balls.

Heat oil in pan, add meatballs in batches, cook until well browned all over and cooked through.

Serve with hummus.

**Hummus** Blend or process undrained chick peas with oil, garlic and juice until almost smooth; stir in mint.

□ SERVES 4

**Store**  Covered, in refrigerator
**Freeze**  Meatballs suitable
**Microwave**  Not suitable

## FISH with parsley pesto

*We used snapper cutlets for this recipe*
*Recipe best made just before serving*

2 teaspoons olive oil
4 medium (720g) white
   fish cutlets
$1/3$ cup (80ml) lemon juice

### Parsley pesto

3 cups firmly packed fresh
   flat-leaf parsley
2 cloves garlic, crushed
$1/3$ cup (80ml) olive oil
2 tablespoons grated
   parmesan cheese
$1/2$ cup (125ml) water

Heat oil in medium pan, add fish and juice, cook until browned on both sides and just tender. Add 1/3 cup parsley pesto to fish in pan, turn to coat.

Serve with remaining parsley pesto.

**Parsley pesto** Blend or process all the ingredients until smooth.

□ SERVES 4

*Freeze* Parsley pesto suitable
*Microwave* Fish suitable

# TORTILLAS with beans and green salsa

*Recipe can be prepared several hours ahead*

**1 tablespoon olive oil**
**1 medium (150g) onion, sliced**
**450g can refried beans**
**2 cups shredded lettuce**
**1 tablespoon chopped**
**   fresh coriander**
**$^1/_3$ cup (80ml) sour cream**

### Tortillas

**$^1/_2$ cup (75g) plain flour**
**$^3/_4$ cup (110g) cornmeal**
**2 eggs, lightly beaten**
**1$^1/_4$ cups (310ml) water**
**1 tablespoon vegetable oil**

### Green salsa

**2 medium (400g) green**
**   capsicums, chopped**
**1 small (80g) onion, chopped**
**1 small green chilli,**
**   seeded, chopped**
**1 medium (130g) under-ripe**
**   tomato, chopped**
**1 tablespoon chopped**
**   fresh coriander**

Heat oil in medium pan, add onion, cook, stirring, until soft; add beans, cook, stirring, until heated through.

Spread tortillas with bean mixture, top with lettuce, green salsa, coriander and cream; roll up.

**Tortillas** Sift flour and cornmeal into bowl, gradually stir in combined eggs, water and 2 teaspoons of oil; stir until mixture is smooth. Cover, refrigerate 20 minutes.

Heat a little of the remaining oil in small non-stick pan. Pour $^1/_4$ cup (60ml) batter into pan, cook until browned lightly underneath. Turn tortilla to brown other side. Repeat with remaining batter. (If mixture becomes thick on standing, add little extra water.) You will need to make 8 tortillas for this recipe.

**Green salsa** Blend or process all ingredients until combined. Strain to remove excess liquid.

□ SERVES 4

*Storage* Covered, in refrigerator
*Freeze* Not suitable
*Microwave* Bean mixture suitable

Minted meatballs with hummus, *top left*
Fish with parsley pesto, *left*
Tortillas with beans and green salsa, *above*

# Creamy SALMON and dill spaghetti

*Recipe best made just before serving*

500g spaghetti
30g butter
1 tablespoon olive oil
1 medium (150g) onion, sliced
2 cloves garlic, crushed
250g button mushrooms, quartered
$^1/_2$ cup (125ml) cream
1 cup (250ml) sour cream
415g can red salmon, drained, flaked
$^1/_4$ cup (20g) grated parmesan cheese
1 tablespoon chopped fresh dill

Add spaghetti to large pan of boiling water, boil, uncovered, until tender, drain; keep warm.

Heat butter and oil in medium pan, add onion and garlic, cook, stirring, until onion is soft. Add mushrooms, cook, stirring, about 3 minutes or until mushrooms are soft. Stir in creams, simmer, uncovered, about 3 minutes or until sauce thickens slightly. Gently stir in salmon, cheese and dill, stir until heated through.

Serve salmon mixture over spaghetti.

□ SERVES 4

**Freeze** *Not suitable*
**Microwave** *Suitable*

Creamy salmon and dill spaghetti, *left*
Octopus salad with coriander
dressing, *above*

# OCTOPUS salad with coriander dressing

*If kipfler potatoes are unavailable,
substitute old potatoes
Octopus best prepared a day ahead
Coriander dressing and Spicy chips can be
prepared several hours ahead*

**1.5kg baby octopus**
**2 tablespoons mild sweet
    chilli sauce**
**$1/_4$ cup (60ml) hoisin sauce**
**2 tablespoons white vinegar**
**4 cloves garlic, crushed**
**1 tablespoon grated fresh ginger**
**2 teaspoons grated lime rind**
**1 bunch (380g) green
    onions, trimmed**
**$1/_2$ small (200g) daikon**
**2 medium (240g) carrots**
**2 cups (160g) bean sprouts**

### Coriander dressing

**$1/_4$ cup (60ml) lime juice**
**$1/_2$ cup lightly packed
    fresh coriander**
**1 tablespoon grated fresh ginger**
**$1/_3$ cup (80ml) peanut oil**
**$1/_4$ teaspoon sesame oil**
**2 teaspoons brown sugar**

### Spicy chips

**500g kipfler potatoes**
**vegetable oil, for deep-frying**
**Chinese Szechuan seasoning**

Remove and discard heads and beaks
from octopus; cut octopus in
quarters. Combine octopus, sauces,
vinegar, garlic, ginger and rind in
large bowl. Cover; refrigerate
3 hours or overnight. Drain octopus;
discard marinade.

Add octopus and onions, in batches,
to heated oiled griddle pan (or
barbecue); cook until just tender.

Cut daikon and carrots into long
thin strips. Arrange onions on
serving plate, top with combined
daikon, carrot, sprouts and octopus;
drizzle with coriander dressing.
Serve salad with spicy chips.

**Coriander dressing** Process all
ingredients until combined; keep
tightly covered.

**Spicy chips** Thinly slice potatoes
lengthways. Deep-fry potatoes, in
batches, in hot oil, until browned and
crisp. Drain on absorbent paper;
sprinkle with seasoning.

☐ SERVES 4 TO 6

*Storage Octopus, in airtight container,
in refrigerator Dressing, in airtight container,
in refrigerator Chips, in airtight container,
at room temperature*
*Freeze Uncooked marinated octopus
suitable*
*Microwave Not suitable*

## Buttermilk-mashed roast PUMPKIN

*Recipe best made just before serving*

**2kg pumpkin, peeled**
**¹/₄ cup (60ml) olive oil**
**¹/₄ cup (60ml) buttermilk**
**¹/₄ cup (20g) grated parmesan cheese**
**1 teaspoon ground cumin**

Chop pumpkin into 3cm pieces. Place pumpkin in large baking dish, drizzle with oil.

Bake, uncovered, in moderate oven about 1 hour or until soft and browned; cool 5 minutes.

Process or mash pumpkin until just smooth. Push mixture through coarse sieve into large bowl.

Stir in remaining ingredients, beat until well combined.

□ SERVES 6

***Freeze*** *Not suitable*
***Microwave*** *Not suitable*

## Seasoned racks of LAMB with tomato coulis

*Recipe can be prepared several hours ahead*

**6 x 3-cutlet racks of lamb**
**250g packet frozen spinach, thawed**
**100g fetta cheese, crumbled**
**¹/₄ cup (15g) stale breadcrumbs**
**1 tablespoon chopped fresh basil**
**2 teaspoons seeded mustard**
**1 clove garlic, crushed**
**1 tablespoon olive oil**

### Tomato coulis

**1 tablespoon olive oil**
**1 medium (150g) onion, chopped**
**2 cloves garlic, crushed**
**400g can tomatoes, undrained, crushed**
**1 cup (250ml) water**
**2 tablespoons tomato paste**
**1 tablespoon chopped fresh basil**
**2 teaspoons mild sweet chilli sauce**
**¹/₂ teaspoon sugar**
**¹/₂ teaspoon chicken stock powder**

Trim lamb racks, using sharp knife, separate meat from bones at centre of each rack to form small pocket. Cover bone ends with foil.

Squeeze excess liquid from spinach. Combine spinach, cheese, breadcrumbs, basil, mustard and garlic in medium bowl. Using end of teaspoon, press spinach mixture firmly into pockets.

Heat oil in baking dish, add lamb, cook until well browned. Transfer dish to oven.

Bake, uncovered, in moderately hot oven about 30 minutes or until lamb is tender. Serve with tomato coulis.

**Tomato coulis** Heat oil in pan, add onion and garlic, cook, stirring, until onion is soft. Add tomatoes and remaining ingredients, simmer, uncovered, about 2 minutes or until mixture is pulpy. Blend or process mixture until smooth, push through sieve into medium bowl. Return mixture to pan, simmer, uncovered, about 5 minutes or until thickened.

□ SERVES 6

***Storage*** *Covered, in refrigerator*
***Freeze*** *Not suitable*
***Microwave*** *Not suitable*

## Lemon tarragon CHICKEN with roasted leeks

*Recipe can be prepared a day ahead*

**1¹/₂ tablespoons chopped fresh tarragon**
**1¹/₂ tablespoons Dijon mustard**
**2 teaspoons grated lemon rind**
**1 tablespoon lemon juice**
**3 cloves garlic, crushed**
**1.5kg chicken**
**2 teaspoons olive oil**
**6 small (1.2kg) leeks**
**1 tablespoon plain flour**
**¹/₂ cup (125ml) dry white wine**
**1 cup (250ml) chicken stock**
**¹/₂ cup (125ml) cream**
**1 egg yolk**

Combine tarragon, mustard, rind, juice and garlic in small bowl. Wash chicken, pat dry. Loosen skin of chicken by sliding hand between skin and flesh. Rub a third of the tarragon mixture under skin and remaining mixture all over chicken. Place chicken in baking dish, brush with oil.

Bake, uncovered, in moderate oven, about 30 minutes, brushing chicken occasionally with pan juices.

Cut leeks into 10cm lengths. Add leeks to dish.

Bake, uncovered, about 1 hour or until chicken and leeks are tender, brushing chicken occasionally with pan juices. Remove chicken and leeks from dish, cover.

Add flour to pan juices in dish, stir over heat until browned. Remove from heat, gradually stir in wine and stock; simmer, uncovered, 10 minutes.

Stir in combined cream and egg yolk; strain sauce, stir over heat without boiling, until warm. Serve with chicken and leeks.

□ SERVES 4 TO 6

**Storage**  *Covered, in refrigerator*
**Freeze**  *Uncooked chicken, suitable*
**Microwave**  *Not suitable*

# Chicken and herb SKEWERS

*Recipe can be prepared a day ahead*

³/₄ **cup (150g) brown rice**
**350g minced chicken**
**2 green onions, chopped**
¹/₂ **cup (35g) stale breadcrumbs**
**2 tablespoons grated**
 **parmesan cheese**
**1 clove garlic, crushed**
**1 tablespoon chopped**
 **fresh parsley**
**1 teaspoon dried Italian herbs**
**2 tablespoons olive oil**

Soak 8 bamboo skewers in water for 1 hour. Add rice to large pan of boiling water, boil, uncovered, about 35 minutes or until tender; drain.

Process chicken, onions, crumbs, cheese, garlic, parsley and herbs until finely minced. Transfer mixture to large bowl, stir in rice. Shape mixture onto prepared skewers.

Heat oil in large pan, add skewers, in batches, cook, turning frequently, until browned and cooked through.

□ SERVES 4

**Storage**  *Covered, in refrigerator*
**Freeze**  *Uncooked skewers suitable*
**Microwave**  *Not suitable*

Seasoned racks of lamb with tomato coulis, *left*
Chicken and herb skewers, *below*
Buttermilk-mashed roast pumpkin,
Lemon tarragon chicken with roasted leeks, *below from left*

## CHICKEN salad
### with tangy lime dressing

*Recipe can be prepared several hours ahead*

- **1 large cooked chicken**
- **1 large (300g) red onion, sliced**
- **1 large (350g) red capsicum, sliced**
- **330g teardrop tomatoes, halved**
- **150g mixed salad leaves**

Tangy lime dressing

- **2 teaspoons grated lime rind**
- **$1/4$ cup (60ml) lime juice**
- **2 tablespoons peanut oil**
- **2 teaspoons fish sauce**

Remove and discard skin and bones from chicken; cut chicken into large pieces. Combine chicken with remaining ingredients in medium bowl. Just before serving, add tangy lime dressing; mix gently.

**Tangy lime dressing** Combine all ingredients in jar; shake well.

□ SERVES 4

***Storage*** *Covered, in refrigerator*
***Freeze*** *Not suitable*
***Microwave*** *Not suitable*

## Chicken with CHEESY POTATO topping

*Recipe best made close to serving*

- **3 medium (600g) potatoes, grated**
- **1 medium (150g) onion, grated**
- **1 cup (80g) grated parmesan cheese**
- **2 teaspoons chopped fresh thyme**
- **1 teaspoon chicken stock powder**
- **$1/2$ teaspoon cracked black pepper**
- **1 egg yolk**
- **6 single (1kg) chicken breast fillets**
- **cooking oil spray**

Combine potatoes, onion, cheese, thyme, stock powder, pepper and egg yolk in medium bowl. Place chicken breasts on wire rack over oven tray. Press potato mixture on top of chicken; coat potato mixture with cooking oil spray.

Bake, uncovered, in hot oven about 30 minutes or until chicken is tender. Grill until potato topping is browned.

□ SERVES 6

***Freeze*** *Not suitable*
***Microwave*** *Not suitable*

*clockwise from top left*
Asian chicken stir-fry, Chicken salad with tangy lime dressing, Chicken with cheesy potato topping,

# Asian CHICKEN stir-fry

*Recipe must be made just before serving*

- 1 tablespoon peanut oil
- 500g lean minced chicken
- 3 cloves garlic, crushed
- 6 green onions, chopped
- 1/3 cup (80ml) mild sweet chilli sauce
- 1 bunch (340g) baby bok choy, chopped
- 1 tablespoon fish sauce
- 2 tablespoons soy sauce
- 2 tablespoons shredded fresh basil

Heat oil in wok or large pan, add chicken, cook, stirring, until changed in colour. Add garlic, onions and chilli sauce, cook, stirring until mixture is browned. Add remaining ingredients, cook, stirring, until bok choy is just tender.

□ SERVES 4

*Freeze* Not suitable
*Microwave* Suitable

# Thai-style STEAKS with cucumber salad

*Steaks best prepared a day ahead*
*Salad best made a day ahead*

- 6 (1.2kg) beef scotch fillet steaks
- 1/4 cup (60ml) mild sweet chilli sauce
- 2 teaspoons fish sauce
- 2 cloves garlic, crushed
- 1/4 cup (60ml) lime juice
- 2 tablespoons chopped fresh coriander

## Cucumber salad

- 3 small (400g) Lebanese cucumbers
- 1/3 cup (75g) caster sugar
- 2/3 cup (160ml) white vinegar
- 1 small fresh red chilli, seeded, sliced
- 1/4 cup (35g) chopped unsalted roasted peanuts
- 1 tablespoon chopped fresh coriander

Combine steaks, sauces, garlic, juice and coriander, in single layer, in a shallow dish; turn steaks to coat. Cover; refrigerate several hours or overnight.

Drain steaks from marinade; discard marinade.

Add steaks to heated oiled barbecue (or griddle pan or grill); cook until browned on both sides and tender.

Serve steaks with cucumber salad.

**Cucumber salad** Halve cucumbers lengthways, discard seeds; slice flesh thinly. Combine sugar and vinegar in medium pan, stir over heat, without boiling, until sugar is dissolved. Simmer, uncovered, about 5 minutes or until reduced to 1/2 cup (125ml). Combine hot vinegar mixture with cucumber and remaining ingredients in heatproof medium bowl. Cover; refrigerate 3 hours or overnight. Strain salad and discard vinegar before serving

□ SERVES 6

*Storage* Covered, in refrigerator
*Freeze* Not suitable
*Microwave* Not suitable

Thai-style steaks with cucumber salad, *left*

Chocolate
hazlenut
Biscotti

Pistachio
ALMOND BREAD

## Chocolate hazelnut BISCOTTI

*Recipe can be made a week ahead*

3 eggs, lightly beaten
½ cup (100g) firmly packed
   brown sugar
½ cup (110g) caster sugar
1¼ cups (185g) plain flour
¾ cup (110g) self-raising flour
⅓ cup (35g) cocoa powder
1 teaspoon ground ginger
1 teaspoon instant coffee powder
1¼ cups (185g) hazelnuts, toasted
1 teaspoon vanilla essence
2 tablespoons Irish cream liqueur
100g dark chocolate, finely grated
1⅓ cups (200g) dark chocolate
   Melts, melted

Beat eggs and sugars in small bowl with electric mixer until changed in colour. Transfer to large bowl.

Stir in sifted dry ingredients, nuts, essence, liqueur and grated chocolate; mix to a firm dough. Knead dough on floured surface.

Place on greased large oven tray. Press into 14cm x 28cm rectangle.

Bake, uncovered, in moderate oven 1 hour or until firm. Remove from oven, cool on tray 10 minutes.

Cut into 1cm slices with serrated knife. Place slices close together on oven trays.

Bake, uncovered, in moderate oven 15 minutes. Turn slices over, bake a further 15 minutes or until both sides are crisp; cool.

Spread one side of each biscotti with Melts, set at room temperature.

☐ MAKES 28

*Storage* Airtight container
*Freeze* Uniced biscotti suitable
*Microwave* Melts suitable

## Pistachio almond BREAD

*Recipe can be made a week ahead*

3 egg whites
½ cup (110g) caster sugar
1 cup (150g) plain flour
½ cup (80g) whole
   almond kernels
½ cup (75g) whole
   shelled pistachios

Grease an 8cm x 26cm bar pan.

Beat egg whites in small bowl with electric mixer until soft peaks form, gradually add sugar, beat until dissolved between additions. Transfer to large bowl.

Fold in sifted flour, nuts and pistachios. Spread mixture into prepared pan.

Bake, uncovered, in moderately slow oven 35 minutes or until mixture shrinks slightly from sides of pan. Cool.

Wrap in foil, refrigerate overnight.

Using a sharp knife, cut bread into wafer-thin slices. Place slices close together in a single layer on oven trays.

Bake, uncovered, in very slow oven

about 15 minutes or until completely dry and browned lightly; cool.

*Storage* Airtight container
*Freeze* Not suitable
*Microwave* Not suitable

## Peanut BRITTLE

*Recipe can be made 3 days ahead*

2 cups (440g) caster sugar
¼ teaspoon cream of tartar
½ cup (125ml) water
2 tablespoons golden syrup
60g butter, chopped
2 cups (300g) unsalted
   roasted peanuts
½ teaspoon bicarbonate of soda

Combine sugar, cream of tartar and water in heavy-based medium pan, stir over heat, without boiling, until sugar is dissolved, brushing down inside of pan with a pastry brush dipped in water to remove sugar from side of pan. Boil, uncovered, about 8 minutes, or until mixture reaches temperature of 174°C on a candy thermometer. Remove from heat.

Chocolate hazelnut biscotti,
Peanut brittle,
Pistachio almond bread, *left, from left*

Gently stir in golden syrup, butter, peanuts and soda. Pour onto well-greased oven tray or marble slab; cool. When cold break into pieces.

**Storage** *Airtight container, at room temperature*
**Freeze** *Not suitable*
**Microwave** *Not suitable*

## Chocolate BUTTONS

*Recipe can be made a week ahead*

**125g unsalted butter**
**½ cup (80g) icing sugar mixture**
**1 tablespoon cream**
**1 cup (150g) plain flour**
**1 tablespoon cocoa powder**

### Chocolate butter

**100g milk chocolate Melts, melted**
**45g butter, melted**

Beat butter and icing sugar in small bowl with electric mixer until light and fluffy. Beat in cream and sifted flour and cocoa, beat until smooth.

Place mixture in a piping bag fitted with a medium, plain tube. Pipe 1.5cm rounds of mixture onto greased oven trays, spacing about 3cm apart, pipe a small round of mixture on top.

*Chocolate buttons, Almond nougat, from left*

Bake, uncovered, in moderate oven, about 12 minutes or until firm; cool on wire racks.

Sandwich biscuits together with chocolate butter.

**Chocolate butter** Combine chocolate and butter in bowl, cool to room temperature or until mixture reaches spreading consistency.

☐ MAKES ABOUT 25

**Storage** *Airtight container*
**Freeze** *Unfilled biscuits suitable*
**Microwave** *Chocolate butter suitable*

## Almond NOUGAT

*Use an electric mixer on a fixed stand
Recipe can be made 2 days ahead*

**4 sheets edible rice paper**
**1 cup (220g) caster sugar**
**¾ cup (180ml) honey**
**1 tablespoon rose water**
**1 egg white**
**1½ cups (240g) blanched whole almonds, toasted**

Cover base of 23cm square slab pan with 2 sheets of rice paper.

Combine sugar, honey and rose water in heavy-based small pan, stir over heat, without boiling, until sugar is dissolved. Bring to boil, simmer, uncovered, about 4 minutes, or until mixture reaches 140°C on a candy thermometer (or until a teaspoon of mixture dropped into a cup of cold water forms a fine thread which can be snapped with fingers). Remove from heat.

Beat egg white in small bowl with electric mixer until firm peaks form. With motor operating, gradually pour in hot syrup in thin stream, continue beating about 1 minute, or until mixture is thick.

Fold in almonds, spread into prepared pan. Cover with remaining rice paper; cool. Cut when cold.

**Storage** *Airtight container, in refrigerator*
**Freeze** *Not suitable*
**Microwave** *Not suitable*

## Citrus liqueur almond fruit CAKE

*Recipe can be made 3 months ahead*

**250g butter**
**1 tablespoon grated orange rind**
**1 cup (220g) caster sugar**
**5 eggs**
**¼ cup (60ml) marmalade**
**½ cup (125ml) brandy**
**1 cup (150g) self-raising flour**
**1 cup (150g) plain flour**
**1 cup (250g) chopped
  glace apricots**
**1 cup (230g) chopped
  glace pineapple**
**¾ cup (210g) chopped glace figs**
**1 cup (140g) slivered almonds**
**½ cup (60g) ground almonds**
**¾ cup (180ml) Grand Marnier**

Cover base and side of deep 22cm round or deep 19cm square cake pan with 3 layers of baking paper, bringing paper 5cm above edge.

Beat butter, rind and sugar in large bowl with electric mixer until just combined. Add eggs one at a time, beat until just combined between additions. Stir in marmalade, brandy, sifted flours, fruit, and almonds; mix well. Spread mixture into prepared pan.

Bake uncovered in slow oven 3 hours. Brush hot cake with ¼ cup (60ml) of the liqueur. Cover hot cake tightly with foil; cool in pan.

Brush cake all over with 2 tablespoons of the remaining warmed liqueur weekly for 3 weeks.

**Storage** *Airtight container, in refrigerator*
**Freeze** *Suitable up to 12 months*
**Microwave** *Not suitable*

*Citrus liqueur almond fruit cake, below*

39

Combine cream, $^3/_4$ cup (180ml) stock and basil in small pan. Bring to boil, stir in cornflour blended with remaining stock; stir until sauce boils. Stir in cheese.

□ SERVES 6

**Storage** *Covered, in refrigerator*
**Freeze** *Meatballs suitable*
**Microwave** *Not suitable*

## BEEF and lime tortilla baskets

*Beef can be prepared a day ahead  Tortillas can be made a day ahead  Avocado salsa best prepared just before serving*

- 750g piece beef scotch fillet
- 2 teaspoons grated lime rind
- 2 tablespoons lime juice
- 2 tablespoons Tequila
- 1 tablespoon olive oil
- 2 tablespoons chopped
   fresh coriander
- 2 cloves garlic, crushed
- 1 teaspoon bottled chopped chilli
- 6 x 24cm flour tortillas
- 80g butter, melted
- 425g can Mexican-flavoured red
   kidney beans
- $^1/_2$ cup (125ml) sour cream

### Avocado salsa

- 1 large (320g) avocado, chopped
- 2 medium (260g) tomatoes,
   chopped
- 2 green onions, chopped
- 2 tablespoons olive oil

Cut beef into 3 pieces. Combine beef, rind, juice, Tequila, oil, coriander, garlic and chilli in medium bowl. Cover; refrigerate 3 hours or overnight.

Drain beef from marinade; discard marinade. Heat large oiled griddle or non-stick pan, add beef, cook until browned and tender; cool. Slice the beef thinly.

Brush both sides of the tortillas with butter. Invert 6 x 1-cup (250ml) ovenproof dishes onto a large oiled oven tray. Shape tortillas over dishes.

Bake, uncovered, in moderately hot

## Spicy American-style PORK ribs

*Recipe best made just before serving.*

- 1.8kg American-style pork
   spare ribs
- $^1/_4$ cup (50g) firmly packed
   brown sugar
- $^1/_4$ cup (60ml) tomato sauce
- $^1/_4$ cup (60ml) cider vinegar
- $^1/_4$ cup (60ml) honey
- 2 tablespoons Worcestershire sauce
- $^1/_2$ teaspoon chilli powder

Place ribs in single layer on wire racks in baking dishes.

Bake, uncovered, in moderate oven about 45 minutes or until browned lightly.

Brush ribs with some of the combined remaining ingredients; bake 30 minutes or until well browned. Brush occasionally with remaining sauce mixture during cooking. Cut ribs into serving pieces.

□ SERVES 4 TO 6

**Freeze** *Not suitable*
**Microwave** *Not suitable*

## MEATBALLS with basil sauce

*Meatballs can be prepared a day ahead Sauce best made just before serving*

- $^1/_3$ cup (80ml) olive oil
- 1 medium (150g) onion,
   finely chopped
- 4 bacon rashers, chopped
- 1kg minced beef
- 2 tablespoons tomato paste
- 1 cup (70g) stale breadcrumbs
- 2 eggs, lightly beaten
- 300ml cream
- 1 cup (250ml) beef stock
- $^1/_4$ cup chopped fresh basil
- $1^1/_2$ tablespoons cornflour
- $^1/_3$ cup (25g) grated
   parmesan cheese

Heat a quarter of the oil in a medium pan, add onion and bacon; cook until onion is soft. Combine onion mixture with mince, paste, crumbs and eggs in large bowl. Roll tablespoons of mixture into balls.

Heat remaining oil in pan; cook meatballs in batches until browned all over and cooked through.

oven about 10 minutes or until browned; remove tortillas from dishes.

Place undrained beans in pan, stir over heat until hot. Divide beans between tortilla baskets, top with beef, avocado salsa and cream.

**Avocado salsa** Combine all ingredients in bowl.

□ SERVES 6

*Storage* *Beef, covered, in refrigerator Tortillas, in airtight container, at room temperature*
*Freeze* *Uncooked marinated beef suitable*
*Microwave* *Not suitable*

Spicy American-style pork ribs, *left*
Meatballs with basil sauce, *right*
Beef and lime tortilla baskets, *below*

# Pasta and herb QUICHE

*Recipe can be made a day ahead*

200g spaghetti
1 tablespoon olive oil
1 medium (150g) onion, chopped
1 clove garlic, crushed
1 medium (120g) zucchini, grated
1 medium (120g) carrot, grated
5 eggs, lightly beaten
1 cup (125g) grated
   cheddar cheese
$1/2$ teaspoon dried oregano
$1/2$ teaspoon dried basil
410g can tomatoes,
   drained, crushed

Lightly oil 23cm pie dish.

Break spaghetti into 10cm pieces, add to large pan of boiling water, boil, uncovered, until just tender; drain. Heat oil in large pan, add onion, garlic, zucchini and carrot, cook, stirring, until liquid has evaporated. Combine spaghetti, vegetable mixture, eggs, cheese, dried herbs and tomatoes in large bowl. Spoon mixture into prepared dish.

Bake, uncovered, in moderate oven about 45 minutes or until set.

☐ SERVES 4

**Storage** *Covered, in refrigerator*
**Freeze** *Not suitable*
**Microwave** *Pasta and vegetable mixture suitable*

# Penne with ASPARAGUS and broad beans

*Recipe best made close to serving*

500g fresh asparagus
500g penne pasta
1 tablespoon olive oil
3 cloves garlic, crushed
1 large (300g) red onion, chopped
2 medium (240g) zucchini, sliced
500g frozen broad beans,
   thawed, peeled
60g butter, chopped
$3/4$ cup (180ml) lemon juice
$1/3$ cup (80ml) olive oil, extra
$1/3$ cup (50g) pine nuts, toasted
1 tablespoon chopped fresh oregano
$1/4$ cup loosely packed
   flat-leaf parsley

Snap and discard coarse ends from asparagus, cut into 4cm lengths. Boil, steam or microwave asparagus until just tender; drain, rinse under cold water, drain well.

Add pasta to large pan of boiling water. Boil, uncovered, until just tender; drain, keep warm.

Heat oil in medium pan, add garlic, onion and zucchini; cook, stirring, until onion is soft. Stir in asparagus, broad beans, butter, juice, extra oil, pine nuts and herbs; stir until hot. Combine pasta and vegetable mixture in large bowl.

☐ SERVES 6

**Freeze** *Not suitable*
**Microwave** *Suitable*

## Sun-dried tomato pesto GNOCCHI

*Sauce can be made 2 days ahead*

**3 bacon rashers, finely chopped**
**1 small (100g) red onion, chopped**
**$1/2$ cup (125ml) cream**
**$1^1/_3$ cups (330ml) water**
**1 small chicken stock cube**
**750g potato gnocchi**

### Sun-dried tomato pesto

**1 cup firmly packed fresh basil**
**$1/3$ cup (35g) drained sun-dried tomatoes**
**1 clove garlic, crushed**
**1 tablespoon pine nuts, toasted**
**$3/_4$ cup (60g) grated parmesan cheese**
**2 tablespoons olive oil**

Add bacon and onion to dry medium pan; cook, stirring, until bacon is browned. Add cream, water, crumbled stock cube and sun-dried tomato pesto; simmer, uncovered, about 5 minutes, stirring occasionally, or until the mixture is thickened slightly.

Add gnocchi to large pan of boiling water; boil, uncovered, until gnocchi float; drain. Combine gnocchi with sun-dried tomato pesto mixture.

**Sun-dried tomato pesto** Blend or process basil, tomatoes, garlic, nuts and cheese until finely chopped. Add oil in a thin stream while motor is operating; process until combined. Cover surface tightly with plastic wrap.

□ SERVES 4

*Storage Covered, in refrigerator*
*Freeze Sun-dried tomato pesto suitable*
*Microwave Not suitable*

## Fettuccine with FRESH TOMATO sauce

*Sauce can be made 2 days ahead*

**375g tomato and herb fettuccine pasta**
**125g spinach fettuccine pasta**

### Fresh tomato sauce

**6 medium (1.2Kg) ripe tomatoes, chopped**
**1 large (200g) onion, chopped**
**$1^2/_3$ cups (200g) seeded black olives, halved**
**2 tablespoons drained capers, chopped**
**3 small fresh red chillies, seeded, sliced**
**2 teaspoons cracked black pepper**
**1 tablespoon chopped fresh parsley**
**1 tablespoon shredded fresh basil**
**2 tablespoons chopped fresh chives**
**2 cloves garlic, crushed**
**2 tablespoons lemon juice**
**$1/2$ cup (125ml) olive oil**

Add both pastas to large pan of boiling water; boil, uncovered, until just tender; drain.

Combine hot pasta with fresh tomato sauce.

**Fresh tomato sauce** Combine all ingredients in large bowl.

□ SERVES 4 TO 6

*Storage Covered, in refrigerator*
*Freeze Not suitable*
*Microwave Not suitable*

Pasta and herb quiche, *left clockwise from top left,* Penne with asparagus and broad beans, Fettuccine with fresh tomato sauce, Sun-dried tomato pesto gnocchi

# Seasoned loin of VEAL

*Ask your butcher to bone loin of veal*
*Roll can be prepared a day ahead*
*Veal is best cooked close to serving*

2 tablespoons olive oil
1 clove garlic, crushed
$1/_3$ cup (50g) pine nuts
1.5 kg loin of veal, boned
1 cup shredded fresh basil
1 cup (100g) grated
   mozzarella cheese
8 slices prosciutto
1 tablespoon olive oil, extra
1 tablespoon plain flour
$1^1/_4$ cups (310ml) water
1 small beef stock cube, crumbled

Heat oil in small pan, add garlic and nuts, cook, stirring, until browned lightly; cool.

Unroll veal, cut through fleshy part of meat to form a flap, open out flap to form one large piece of veal. Flatten veal with meat mallet, sprinkle evenly with basil and cheese, then nut mixture, cover with prosciutto. Roll up veal firmly to enclose filling, secure at 2cm intervals with string.

Heat extra oil in baking dish, add veal, cook until browned all over. Bake, uncovered, in moderate oven about 1 hour or until tender. Remove from oven, reserve 2 tablespoons of pan juices; cover veal with foil.

Heat reserved pan juices in small pan, add flour, stir over heat until flour is browned lightly. Remove from heat, gradually stir in combined water and stock cube. Return to heat, stir until sauce boils and thickens; strain.

Discard string from veal, cut veal into slices, serve with sauce.

□ SERVES 6

***Storage*** *Veal roll, covered, in refrigerator*
***Freeze*** *Suitable*
***Microwave*** *Not suitable*

# Vegetable TAGLIATELLE

*Recipe is best made close to serving*

500g tagliatelle pasta
1 medium (200g) red capsicum
1 medium (200g) green capsicum
2 medium (240g) carrots
2 tablespoons olive oil
1 medium (150g) onion, chopped
2 cloves garlic, crushed
2 medium (240g) zucchini, sliced
6 small (75g) yellow
   squash, sliced
2 cups shredded radicchio
60g butter
$3/_4$ cup (60g) grated
   parmesan cheese
2 tablespoons chopped
   fresh basil

Add pasta to large pan of boiling water, boil, uncovered, until just tender, drain; keep warm.

Cut capsicums and carrots into thin strips. Heat oil in large pan, add onion and garlic, cook, stirring, until onion is soft. Add capsicums, carrots, zucchini and squash, cook, stirring, until vegetables are just tender. Add radicchio, butter, cheese and basil, stir over heat until butter is melted.

Spoon vegetable mixture over pasta, serve immediately.

□ SERVES 4

***Freeze*** *Not suitable*
***Microwave*** *Suitable*

# Herbed LAMB with red wine sauce

*Recipe can be made a day ahead*

1.25kg lamb strip loin
plain flour
1 egg, lightly beaten
2 tablespoons milk
2 cups (140g) stale breadcrumbs
2 tablespoons chopped
   fresh chives
2 tablespoons chopped
   fresh parsley
1 tablespoon chopped fresh thyme
$1/_3$ cup (80ml) olive oil
60g butter

Vegetable tagliatelle, *above left*
Seasoned loin of veal, *left*
Herbed lamb with red wine sauce, *right*

## Red wine sauce

1 cup (250ml) light red wine
$1/_2$ cup (125ml) water
2 green onions, chopped
$1/_2$ small beef stock cube, crumbled
$1^1/_2$ teaspoons sugar
1 teaspoon Worcestershire sauce
30g butter
3 teaspoons cornflour
1 tablespoon water, extra

Cut lamb into 18 slices, flatten slightly with meat mallet; toss in flour. Dip in combined egg and milk, then coat with combined breadcrumbs and herbs. Cover, refrigerate 30 minutes.

Heat half the oil and half the butter in large pan, add half the lamb, cook over heat about 3 minutes on each side or until cooked as desired; keep warm. Repeat with remaining oil, butter and lamb. Serve with red wine sauce.

**Red wine sauce** Combine wine, water, onions, stock cube, sugar and sauce in medium pan, bring to boil; simmer 10 minutes. Add butter and blended cornflour and extra water, stir over heat until mixture boils and thickens; strain.

□ SERVES 6

***Storage*** *Covered, in refrigerator*
***Freeze*** *Suitable*
***Microwave*** *Red wine sauce suitable*

## Roast LAMB with herbed potatoes

*Recipe best made just before serving*

1 large (200g) onion, chopped
2 cloves garlic, crushed
1 tablespoon chopped fresh chives
1 tablespoon chopped fresh thyme
5 large (1.5kg) old potatoes,
    peeled, sliced
50g butter, chopped
1 cup (250ml) water
2kg leg of lamb
3 cloves garlic, extra

Oil 27cm x 34cm baking dish.

Combine onion, garlic and herbs in small bowl. Place half the potatoes over base of prepared dish, sprinkle with onion mixture, top with remaining potatoes, dot with butter; add water.

Bake, uncovered, in hot oven 1 hour.

Cut 3 small slits in top of lamb, push a clove of extra garlic into each slit. Place lamb on top of potatoes in baking dish.

Bake, uncovered, in moderate oven $1\frac{1}{2}$ hours or until cooked as desired.

Turn lamb halfway through cooking.

Remove lamb to heatproof plate, cover with foil, stand 10 minutes before carving. Keep potatoes warm.

☐ SERVES 6

**Freeze** *Not suitable*
**Microwave** *Not suitable*

Roast lamb with herbed potatoes, above
Fruity lamb cutlets, *above right*
Salmon and alfalfa lettuce parcels, *right*

# SALMON and alfalfa
## lettuce parcels

*Recipe can be made several hours ahead*

- 1 iceberg lettuce
- 440g can red salmon, drained, flaked
- 2 tablespoons mayonnaise
- 2 teaspoons chopped fresh dill
- 1 tablespoon lemon juice
- 1 small stick celery, chopped
- 65g alfalfa sprouts

Separate lettuce leaves (you will need 10 large leaves), boil, steam or microwave leaves about 30 seconds, or until just wilted; drain. Rinse leaves under cold water; drain, pat dry.

Combine salmon, mayonnaise, dill, juice and celery in medium bowl. Place a tenth of the salmon mixture onto base end of lettuce leaf, top with some of the sprouts, fold in sides, carefully roll up to form a parcel. Repeat with remaining salmon mixture, lettuce leaves and alfalfa sprouts. Cover, refrigerate, 1 hour before serving.

□ MAKES 10

**Storage**  *Covered, in refrigerator*
**Freeze**  *Not suitable*
**Microwave**  *Lettuce suitable*

# Fruity LAMB cutlets

*Recipe best prepared just before serving*

- $1/3$ cup fruit chutney
- 1 egg, lightly beaten
- 1 tablespoon plain flour
- 8 lamb cutlets
- 1 cup (100g) packaged breadcrumbs
- oil, for shallow-frying

Combine chutney, egg and flour in small bowl. Brush cutlets with chutney mixture, dip in breadcrumbs.

Shallow-fry cutlets in hot oil until browned and cooked through; drain on absorbent paper.

□ SERVES 4

**Freeze**  *Not suitable*
**Microwave**  *Not suitable*

47

## Cheesy BRIOCHE Tarts

*Tarts best made on day of serving*

**7g compressed yeast**
**$\frac{1}{2}$ teaspoon sugar**
**$\frac{1}{3}$ cup (80ml) warm water**
**2 cups (300g) plain flour**
**2 eggs, lightly beaten**
**90g butter, softened**
**100g brie cheese, sliced**
**$\frac{1}{2}$ cup (60g) grated**
   **gruyere cheese**
**2 eggs, lightly beaten, extra**
**$\frac{1}{2}$ cup (125ml) cream**
**1 tablespoon chopped fresh chives**

Cream yeast with sugar in small bowl, add water. Cover, stand in warm place about 10 minutes or until mixture is frothy.

Sift flour into large bowl, make a well in centre, stir in combined eggs and yeast mixture. Turn dough onto floured surface, knead, about 5 minutes or until dough is smooth and elastic.

Cut butter into small pieces. Add a few pieces to dough, knead until combined. Continue adding and kneading in butter, a few pieces at a time, until all the butter is incorporated (this should take about 5 minutes).

Pick up and throw down dough onto a clean surface, about 5 minutes or until dough is smooth and elastic. Place dough in small lightly oiled bowl; cover, refrigerate about 30 minutes or until firm.

Lightly oil bases and sides of two 20cm round sandwich pans. Roll out half the dough on floured surface until large enough to fit base and side of one of the prepared pans, allowing excess dough to hang over edge of pan. Repeat with remaining dough and pan.

Place half of the combined cheeses over dough in one of the pans, repeat with remaining cheeses and pan. Pour combined extra eggs, cream and chives over cheeses in pans, fold edge of dough over top of egg mixture. Stand pans in a warm place for 20 minutes.

Bake, uncovered, in moderate oven about 30 minutes or until filling is set and dough is browned. Let tarts stand 5 minutes before removing from pans.

☐ MAKES 2

*Freeze* Not suitable
*Microwave* Not suitable

# CHICKEN and cheese turnovers

*You will need 1 large barbecued chicken*
*Recipe can be made a day ahead*

- 1 tablespoon vegetable oil
- 1 medium (350g) leek,
  finely chopped
- 1 large (180g) carrot, thinly sliced
- 1 tablespoon chopped
  fresh rosemary
- 2 cups (300g) chopped
  cooked chicken
- 1 tablespoon seeded mustard
- 1 cup (250ml) sour cream
- $1/2$ cup (60g) frozen peas, thawed
- $1/4$ cup (60ml) milk
- $1/2$ cup (40g) grated
  parmesan cheese
- 6 sheets ready-rolled puff pastry
- 1 egg yolk, lightly beaten

Heat oil in pan, add leek, carrot and rosemary; cook, stirring, until leek is soft. Stir in chicken, mustard, cream, peas, milk and half the cheese; cool.

Cut one 20cm round from each sheet of pastry. Place a sixth of filling onto half of a pastry round, leaving a 1.5cm border; brush edge of pastry with a little egg yolk, fold over pastry to enclose filling. Press edges together with a floured fork to seal, brush pastry with some of the remaining egg yolk, sprinkle with some of the remaining cheese. Repeat with the remaining pastry, chicken mixture, egg yolk and cheese. Place turnovers on oiled oven trays.

Bake, uncovered, in moderately hot oven about 25 minutes or until browned.

□ MAKES 6

***Storage*** *Covered, in refrigerator*
***Freeze*** *Uncooked turnovers suitable*
***Microwave*** *Vegetable mixture suitable*

Cheesy brioche tarts, *above left*
Chicken and cheese turnovers,
Spicy buttermilk drumsticks,
*right, from left*

# Spicy buttermilk DRUMSTICKS

*Recipe can be a day ahead*

- 8 (1.4kg) chicken drumsticks
- 3 cloves garlic, crushed
- 2 teaspoons sambal oelek
- $1/4$ cup (60ml) soy sauce
- 1 cup (250ml) buttermilk
- 1 cup (150g) plain flour
- $1/4$ cup sweet paprika
- 1 tablespoon lemon
  pepper seasoning
- oil, for shallow frying

Remove and discard the skin from drumsticks. Add drumsticks to pan of boiling water, simmer, uncovered, about 10 minutes or until just cooked through; drain well. Combine drumsticks with garlic, sambal oelek and sauce in shallow dish, cover, refrigerate 3 hours.

Drain drumsticks from marinade; discard marinade. Dip drumsticks into buttermilk, toss in combined flour, paprika and seasoning; gently shake away excess flour mixture.

Shallow-fry chicken in hot oil until browned; drain on absorbent paper.

□ SERVES 4

***Storage*** *Covered, in refrigerator*
***Freeze*** *Not suitable*
***Microwave*** *Not suitable*

*49*

# Pasta and fetta SALAD
## with artichokes

*Salad best made close to serving*
*Dressing can be made a day ahead*

300g penne pasta
1 medium (170g) red onion, sliced
1 bunch (500g) English
   spinach, chopped
250g fetta cheese, chopped
390g can artichoke hearts,
   drained, chopped
250g cherry tomatoes, halved
$^2/_3$ cup (100g) seeded black olives

Pasta and fetta salad with artichokes,
below

### Oregano dressing

$^1/_3$ cup (80ml) lemon juice
$^1/_3$ cup (80ml) extra light olive oil
1 clove garlic, crushed
2 teaspoons sugar
$^1/_4$ cup chopped fresh oregano

Add pasta to large pan of boiling water, boil, uncovered, until just tender; drain. Rinse pasta under hot water; drain well.

Combine pasta with remaining ingredients and oregano dressing in large bowl.

**Oregano dressing** Combine all ingredients in jar; shake well.

□ SERVES 6

***Storage*** *Dressing, covered, in refrigerator*
***Freeze*** *Not suitable*
***Microwave*** *Suitable*

# PIZZA dough

*Recipe must be made close to serving*

4 teaspoons (14g) dried yeast
1 teaspoon sugar
$1^1/_2$ cups (375ml) warm water
4 cups (600g) plain flour
2 teaspoons salt
$^1/_3$ cup (80ml) olive oil

Combine yeast, sugar and water in small bowl, cover, stand in warm place about 10 minutes or until frothy.

Sift flour and salt into large bowl, stir in yeast mixture and oil.

Knead dough on floured surface about 5 minutes. Place dough in lightly oiled bowl, cover, stand in warm place until doubled in size.

Knead dough on floured surface until smooth.

# Hot sausage PIZZA

*Recipe best made close to serving*

$^1/_2$ quantity pizza dough (see above)
$^1/_4$ cup (60ml) tomato paste
2 cloves garlic, crushed
2 small fresh red chillies,
   seeded, chopped
2 tablespoons shredded
   fresh basil
250g mozzarella cheese, grated
150g sliced Italian sausage
100g sliced spicy salami, chopped
1 small (150g) red
   capsicum, sliced
80g button mushrooms, sliced
$^1/_4$ cup (40g) seeded sliced
   black olives

Roll dough until large enough to line a lightly oiled 34cm pizza tray.

Spread dough with combined paste, garlic, chillies and basil. Top with half the mozzarella then sausage, salami, capsicum, mushrooms and olives; sprinkle with remaining mozzarella.

Bake, uncovered, in hot oven about 25 minutes.

□ SERVES 4

***Freeze*** *Uncooked pizza suitable*
***Microwave*** *Not suitable*

## Rocket PESTO pizza

*Rocket pesto can be made a day ahead*

$^1/_2$ **quantity pizza dough (see left)**
**250g marinated artichoke hearts,**
  **drained, sliced**
**1 cup (150g) drained sun-**
  **dried tomatoes**
**150g bocconcini cheese, sliced**
$^1/_2$ **cup (40g) grated**
  **parmesan cheese**

<u>Rocket pesto</u>

**1 bunch (120g) rocket, trimmed**
$^1/_3$ **cup (25g) grated**
  **parmesan cheese**
**1 teaspoon cracked black pepper**
**1 clove garlic, crushed**
**2 tablespoons olive oil**

Roll dough until large enough to line a lightly oiled 34cm pizza tray. Spread dough with rocket pesto, top with artichokes, tomatoes and cheeses.

Bake, uncovered, in hot oven about 35 minutes.

**Rocket pesto** Blend or process all ingredients until smooth.

☐ SERVES 4

*Storage* Rocket pesto, in airtight container, in refrigerator
*Freeze* Uncooked pizza suitable
*Microwave* Not suitable

<u>Rocket pesto pizza, Hot sausage pizza, above, from left</u>

# VEAL and snow pea stir-fry

*Recipe best made close to serving*

100g rice vermicelli
6 green onions
1 small (150g) red capsicum
2 sticks celery
1 medium (120g) zucchini
2 tablespoons vegetable oil
750g veal steak, sliced
150g button mushrooms
200g snow peas
425g can baby corn, drained
100g bean sprouts
1 tablespoon cornflour
$^1/_4$ cup (60ml) water
2 tablespoons soy sauce
1 tablespoon oyster sauce
2 tablespoons dry sherry

Place vermicelli in medium bowl, cover with cold water, stand for 15 minutes; drain.

Cut the onions, capsicum, celery and zucchini into long, thin strips.

Heat oil in wok, add veal, in batches, stir-fry for about 2 minutes or until veal is browned all over; remove from wok.

Reheat wok, stir in onions, capsicum and celery; stir-fry 2 minutes. Add zucchini, mushrooms, snow peas, corn and bean sprouts; stir-fry 1 minute, stir in veal and vermicelli.

Blend cornflour with water, sauces and sherry, stir into wok, stir-fry until mixture boils and thickens.

☐ SERVES 4

*Freeze*  Not suitable
*Microwave*  Not suitable

# Mexican-style spicy LASAGNE

*Recipe best made a day ahead*

1 tablespoon olive oil
1 medium (170g) red
 onion, chopped
2 cloves garlic, crushed
35g packet taco seasoning mix
1 tablespoon ground cumin
1 teaspoon sweet paprika
1kg lean minced beef
1 medium (200g) red
 capsicum, chopped
3 x 400g cans tomatoes,
 undrained, crushed
$^1/_2$ cup (125ml) tomato paste
15 sheets instant lasagne pasta
$^1/_2$ cup (40g) grated
 parmesan cheese
$^1/_2$ cup (60g) grated
 cheddar cheese

### Creamy cheese sauce

60g butter
$^1/_3$ cup (50g) plain flour
3 cups (750ml) milk
$^1/_2$ cup (125ml) sour cream
$^1/_2$ cup (60g) grated
 cheddar cheese

Heat oil in large pan, add onion, garlic, seasoning mix, cumin and paprika; cook, stirring, about 5 minutes or until onion is soft. Add mince, cook, stirring, until browned.

Stir in capsicum, tomatoes and paste; simmer, uncovered, about 1 hour, stirring occasionally, or until mixture is thick.

Place 5 lasagne sheets over base of oiled shallow ovenproof 3 litre (12-cup) dish, top with half the mince mixture and a third of creamy cheese sauce. Repeat layers, then top with remaining lasagne sheets and creamy cheese sauce; sprinkle the top with combined cheeses.

Bake, covered, in moderate oven 30 minutes. Bake uncovered about 10 minutes or until lasagne sheets are tender.

**Creamy cheese sauce**  Melt butter in medium pan, remove from heat, stir in flour, stir over heat, about 1 minute or until bubbling. Remove from heat, gradually stir in milk, stir over heat until mixture boils and thickens. Remove from heat, stir in cream and cheese.

☐ SERVES 8

*Storage*  Covered, in refrigerator
*Freeze*  Suitable
*Microwave*  Creamy cheese sauce suitable

Veal and snow pea stir-fry, *left*
Mexican-style spicy lasagne, Szechuan pepper beef with noodles, *opposite, from left*

# Szechuan pepper beef with NOODLES

*Recipe can be prepared a day ahead*

**600g beef rump steak,
thinly sliced**
**1/4 cup (60ml) soy sauce**
**1/3 cup (80ml) hoisin sauce**
**1/4 cup (60ml) water**
**1 1/2 tablespoons Szechuan pepper**
**2 teaspoons sugar**

**2 teaspoons lemon juice**
**1kg fresh rice noodles**
**1 1/2 tablespoons peanut oil**
**8 green onions, finely sliced**
**2 tablespoons sesame seeds**

Combine steak, sauces, water, pepper, sugar and juice in large bowl. Cover, refrigerate 2 hours. Drain steak from marinade; reserve marinade.

Place noodles in large heatproof bowl, pour over boiling water, stir to separate; drain well. Mix 1 teaspoon of the oil through noodles.

Heat remaining oil in large wok, add steak in batches, stir-fry until tender; remove steak. Add onions and reserved marinade to wok; stir until hot. Return steak to wok with noodles and seeds; stir-fry until hot.

□ SERVES 4

***Storage*** *Covered, in refrigerator*
***Freeze*** *Not suitable*

## Chocolate ICE-CREAM
### with strawberry sauce

*Ice-cream can be made several days ahead*
*Sauce can be made a day ahead*

**2¹/₂ cups (375g) milk chocolate Melts, chopped**
**2¹/₂ cups (625ml) custard**
**1³/₄ cups (450ml) thickened cream**

### Strawberry sauce

**250g strawberries**
**1 tablespoon caster sugar**
**1 tablespoon Grand Marnier**

Lightly grease 14cm x 21cm loaf pan, line base and sides with plastic wrap.

Combine Melts and custard in heatproof bowl, stir over pan of simmering water until smooth; cool.

Beat cream in small bowl with electric mixer until soft peaks form, fold into chocolate mixture.

Pour mixture into prepared pan, cover, freeze until firm.

Serve slices of ice-cream with strawberry sauce.

**Strawberry sauce** Blend or process half the strawberries with sugar and liqueur until smooth. Combine with remaining strawberries in medium bowl. Cover; refrigerate 30 minutes.

☐ SERVES 4 TO 6

***Storage*** *Ice-cream, covered, in freezer*
*Sauce covered, in refrigerator*
***Freeze*** *Strawberry sauce suitable*
***Microwave*** *Suitable*

## Triple chocolate
## MOUSSE Dessert

*Recipe can be made a day ahead*

**125g dark chocolate, chopped**
**2 tablespoons thickened cream**
**1 egg, separated**
**1 teaspoon gelatine**
**3 teaspoons water**
**²/₃ cup (160ml) thickened cream, extra**

### Milk chocolate mousse

**125g milk chocolate, chopped**
**2 tablespoons thickened cream**
**1 egg, separated**
**1 teaspoon gelatine**
**3 teaspoons water**
**²/₃ cup (160ml) thickened cream, extra**

### White chocolate mousse

**125g white chocolate, chopped**
**2 tablespoons thickened cream**
**1 egg, separated**
**1 teaspoon gelatine**
**3 teaspoons water**
**²/₃ cup (160ml) thickened cream, extra**

### Chocolate leaves

**60g dark chocolate, melted**

Combine dark chocolate and cream in small heatproof bowl, stir over pan of simmering water until smooth. Transfer to medium bowl; cool to room temperature. Stir in egg yolk.

Combine gelatine and water in a cup, stand in small pan of simmering water, stir until dissolved. Stir gelatine mixture into chocolate mixture.

Beat extra cream in small bowl until soft peaks form, fold into chocolate mixture. Beat egg white in small bowl until soft peaks form, fold into chocolate mixture. Cover, refrigerate, several hours or until set.

Place a scoop of each mousse on serving plates, decorate with chocolate leaves.

**Milk chocolate mousse** Follow instructions for dark chocolate mousse, using chopped milk chocolate in place of dark chocolate.

**White chocolate mousse** Follow instructions for dark chocolate mousse, using chopped white chocolate in place of dark chocolate.

**Chocolate leaves** Spoon chocolate into small piping bag fitted with a small plain tube. Pipe 5cm-long outlines of leaves on baking paper or foil, fill in with lacy lines. Place paper over rolling pin, allow leaves to set.

□ SERVES 6

*Storage* covered, in refrigerator
*Freeze* not suitable
*Microwave* Suitable

# Strawberry wine SORBET

*Sorbet can be made several days ahead*

**$^1/_2$ cup (110g) sugar**
**1 cup (250ml) water**
**250g strawberries**
**$^1/_3$ cup (80ml) sweet white wine**
**$^1/_3$ cup (80ml) lemon juice**
**1 egg white**

Combine sugar and water in small pan, stir over heat, without boiling, until sugar is dissolved. Bring to boil, boil, uncovered, without stirring, 5 minutes; cool to room temperature.

Blend or process berries, sugar syrup, wine and juice until smooth, pour into lamington pan. Cover; freeze until almost set.

Process egg white and berry mixture until smooth, return to pan. Cover; freeze until set.

□ SERVES 4

*Storage* Covered, in freezer
*Microwave* Not suitable

Chocolate ice-cream with strawberry sauce, *above left*
Triple chocolate mousse dessert, *top right*
Strawberry wine sorbet, *right*

## Classic cheese STRUDEL

*Recipe best made just before serving*

$1/2$ cup (100g) ricotta cheese
250g packet cream cheese, chopped
2 teaspoons grated lemon rind
1 tablespoon lemon juice
$1/2$ cup (110g) caster sugar
3 eggs, separated
$1/2$ cup (80g) sultanas
$1/4$ cup (30g) ground almonds
10 sheets fillo pastry
100g butter, melted

Beat ricotta and cream cheese in large bowl with electric mixer until smooth. Beat in rind, juice and sugar, then egg yolks. Fold in sultanas and almonds.

Brush 2 sheets of pastry with some of the butter. With buttered sides up, overlap one long side of one pastry sheet with one long side of the other pastry sheet to form large square. Continue adding layers, with remaining pastry sheets and butter, to form a square stack.

Beat egg whites in small bowl until firm peaks form, fold into cheese mixture.

Spoon cheese mixture along one edge of pastry, leaving 5cm border at each end. Roll up once, fold in ends, then continue rolling up to form a log. Place strudel on greased oven tray, brush with butter.

Bake in moderate oven about 35 minutes or until puffed and browned lightly.

□ SERVES 8

**Freeze** *Not suitable*
**Microwave** *Not suitable*

## Lattice apple PIE

*Recipe can be made a day ahead*

2 cups (300g) self-raising flour
$1/4$ cup (40g) icing sugar mixture
125g cold butter, chopped
$1/2$ cup (125ml) milk
1 egg white, lightly beaten

### Apple filling

10 medium (1.5kg) apples
$1/3$ cup (80ml) water
2 tablespoons brown sugar
$1/2$ teaspoon ground cinnamon

Grease 23cm pie dish.

Process flour, icing sugar and butter until just crumbly. Add milk gradually while motor is operating, process until ingredients just cling together. Knead dough on floured surface until smooth. Cover with plastic wrap, refrigerate 30 minutes.

Roll half the pastry between sheets of baking paper until large enough to line prepared dish. Lift pastry into dish, ease into side, trim edge. Place dish on oven tray. Cover, refrigerate 30 minutes.

Bake pastry case, blind, in moderately hot oven about 20 minutes or until browned lightly; cool.

Roll remaining pastry between sheets of baking paper until 4mm thick. Cut strips, 1.5cm wide x 26cm long, from dough, refrigerate on baking paper-lined tray 10 minutes or until firm. Weave strips to form lattice pattern large enough to cover top of pie. Return to tray; refrigerate 10 minutes or until firm.

Spoon apple filling into pastry case. Lift lattice onto apple filling, trim edge, brush with egg white.

Bake in moderately hot oven about 20 minutes or until browned.

**Apple filling** Peel, core and thinly slice apples. Combine apples and water in large pan, simmer, covered, about 5 minutes or until apples are tender. Drain apples; discard liquid. Transfer apples to large bowl, gently stir in sugar and cinnamon; cool.

□ SERVES 6 TO 8

***Storage*** *Airtight container*
***Freeze*** *Pastry suitable*
***Microwave*** *Apple filling suitable*

Classic cheese strudel, *left*
Lattice apple pie, *below*

## MANGO sorbet

*Recipe can be made several days ahead*

1/2 cup (110g) caster sugar
1 cup (250ml) water
2 medium (800g)
    mangoes, chopped
2 egg whites
1 tablespoon finely chopped
    glace ginger

Combine sugar and water in small pan, stir over heat, without boiling, until sugar is dissolved, brushing down inside of pan with a pastry brush dipped in water to remove sugar crystals. Simmer, uncovered, without stirring, 10 minutes; cool.

Blend or process mangoes until smooth (you will need 2 cups (500ml) of puree). Combine sugar syrup and mangoes, stir until smooth. Pour mixture into lamington pan, cover, freeze until just firm.

Chop mango mixture, place in food processor with egg whites, process until smooth. Stir in ginger. Spoon mixture into loaf pan; cover, freeze until firm.

□ SERVES 4

**Storage** *Covered, in freezer*
**Microwave** *Not suitable*

## Rich CHOCOLATE liqueur cheesecake

*Recipe can be made a day ahead*

2 1/2 cups (250g) plain chocolate
    biscuit crumbs
125g butter, melted
1 teaspoon dry instant coffee
3 teaspoons gelatine
1/2 cup (125ml) water
500g packaged cream
    cheese, chopped
1/2 cup (110g) caster sugar
125g dark chocolate, melted
1 tablespoon creme de cacao
1 tablespoon creme de menthe
300ml cream

Mango sorbet, *left*
Minted apricot jelly, *above right*
Rich chocolate liqueur cheesecake, *right*

Grease 20cm springform tin, line side with baking paper.

Combine crumbs and butter in medium bowl. Press crumb mixture firmly over base of prepared tin; refrigerate 1 hour.

Combine coffee, gelatine and water in a cup, stand in small pan of simmering water, stir until dissolved; cool.

Beat cream cheese and sugar in medium bowl with electric mixer until smooth, add gelatine mixture, chocolate and liqueurs; beat until combined.

Beat cream in small bowl until soft peaks form, fold into chocolate mixture, in 2 batches. Pour chocolate mixture over crumb crust. Cover; refrigerate 3 hours or until set.

□ SERVES 8

**Storage** *Covered, in refrigerator*
**Freeze** *Not suitable*
**Microwave** *Suitable*

# Minted apricot JELLY

*Recipe can be made a day ahead*

**1 tablespoon gelatine**
**2 tablespoons water**
**425g can apricot halves**
**$1^1/_4$ cups (300ml) apricot nectar**
**1 cup (250ml) natural sparkling mineral water**
**1 tablespoon chopped fresh mint**

Combine gelatine and water in a cup, stand in small pan of simmering water, stir until dissolved; cool slightly.

Drain apricots, cut in half. Combine apricots, nectar, mineral water, mint and gelatine mixture in medium bowl.

Refrigerate apricot mixture until the consistency of unbeaten egg white, stirring occasionally to distribute apricots and mint evenly.

Spoon mixture into 4 x $^3/_4$-cup (180ml) glasses, refrigerate several hours or until set.

□ SERVES 4

**Storage** *Covered, in refrigerator*
**Freeze** *Not suitable*
**Microwave** *suitable*

## Passionfruit liqueur SOUFFLES

*You will need about 4 passionfruit for this recipe Recipe must be made just before serving*

**caster sugar**
**2 egg yolks**
**1/3 cup (80ml) passionfruit pulp**
**2 tablespoons Grand Marnier**
**1/2 cup (80g) icing sugar mixture**
**4 egg whites**

Grease 4 x $^3/_4$ cup (180ml) ovenproof dishes. Sprinkle bases and sides evenly with a little caster sugar; shake away excess. Place dishes on oven tray.

Whisk egg yolks, passionfruit, liqueur and 2 tablespoons of the icing sugar in medium bowl until combined.

Beat egg whites in small bowl with electric mixer until soft peaks form; add remaining icing sugar, continue beating until firm peaks form. Fold about a quarter of the egg white mixture into passionfruit mixture, then fold in remaining egg white mixture. Spoon into prepared dishes.

Bake in moderately hot oven about 12 minutes or until souffles are puffed. Serve immediately dusted with a little sifted icing sugar.

SERVES 4

***Freeze*** *Not suitable*
***Microwave*** *Not suitable*

## Frozen layered MOUSSE

*Recipe can be made several days ahead*

**150g white chocolate, melted**
**$^1/_4$ cup (60ml) thickened cream**
**2 eggs, separated**
**$^1/_2$ cup (125ml) thickened cream, extra**

### Strawberry mousse

**250g strawberries**
**150g white chocolate, melted**
**$^1/_4$ cup (60ml) thickened cream**
**2 eggs, separated**
**$^1/_2$ cup (125ml) thickened cream, extra**

### Strawberry sauce

**250g strawberries**
**2 teaspoons grated orange rind**
**1 tablespoon Grand Marnier**
**1$^1/_2$ tablespoons caster sugar**

Line base and side of deep 23cm loose-base flan tin with plastic wrap.

Combine chocolate, cream and egg yolks in medium bowl. Beat extra cream in small bowl until soft peaks form, fold into chocolate mixture.

Beat egg whites in small bowl until soft peaks form, fold into chocolate mixture. Pour chocolate mixture into prepared tin. Cover, freeze 3 hours or until firm.

Pour strawberry mousse over frozen chocolate mousse, cover, freeze 3 hours or until firm. Turn mousse onto serving plate, serve with strawberry sauce.

**Strawberry mousse** Blend or process strawberries until smooth. Combine puree, chocolate, cream and egg yolks in medium bowl. Beat extra cream in small bowl until soft peaks form, fold into strawberry mixture. Beat egg whites in small bowl until soft peaks form, fold into strawberry mixture.

**Strawberry sauce** Blend or process all ingredients until smooth.

□ SERVES 6 TO 8

***Storage*** *Covered, in refrigerator*
***Freeze*** *Sauce suitable*
***Microwave*** *Chocolate suitable*

## MOCHA mousse dessert

*Recipe best made a day ahead*

**125g ladyfinger biscuits**
**2 tablespoons Tia Maria or Kahlua**
**$^1/_4$ cup (60ml) milk**
**300ml thickened cream**
**1$^1/_4$ cups (185g) dark chocolate Melts**
**1 tablespoon Tia Maria or Kahlua, extra**
**2 teaspoons gelatine**
**1 tablespoon water**
**4 egg whites**
**$^3/_4$ cup (165g) caster sugar**

# CHOCOLATE ROLL
## with white chocolate ganache

*Recipe best made a day ahead*

**4 eggs, separated**
**1/2 cup (110g) caster sugar**
**2 tablespoons hot water**
**60g milk chocolate, grated**
**1/2 cup (75g) self-raising flour**

### White chocolate ganache

**2/3 cup (160ml) cream**
**200g white chocolate, grated**

Lightly grease 25cm x 30cm Swiss roll pan, line base with baking paper.

Beat egg yolks and sugar in medium bowl with electric mixer until thick and creamy, stir in water and chocolate. Stir in sifted flour.

Beat egg whites in a small bowl until soft peaks form, fold lightly into chocolate mixture, in 2 batches. Pour mixture into prepared pan.

Bake in moderate oven, about 15 minutes or until puffed and browned lightly. Turn onto wire rack covered with a teatowel, carefully remove lining paper, roll up from a long side, using towel to lift and guide roll. Let stand 3 minutes, carefully unroll; cool.

Spread white chocolate ganache evenly over cake, roll up. Cover, refrigerate until serving.

**White chocolate ganache** Bring cream to boil in small pan, pour into medium heatproof bowl; quickly stir in chocolate, beat until smooth. Cover, refrigerate 3 hours, stirring occasionally or until mixture is cold and thick. Beat mixture until soft peaks form.

□ SERVES 6 TO 8

**Storage** *Covered, in refrigerator*
**Freeze** *Suitable*
**Microwave** *Not suitable*

Lightly brush biscuits with combined liqueur and milk, arrange biscuits around side of wetted 1 litre (4-cup) mould.

Heat cream in small pan, bring to boil, remove from heat, stir in Melts and extra liqueur; stir until smooth. Transfer to large bowl.

Combine gelatine and water in a cup, stand in small pan of simmering water; stir until dissolved. Stir gelatine mixture into chocolate mixture.

Beat egg whites in medium bowl with electric mixer until soft peaks form, gradually add sugar; beating until sugar is dissolved after each addition. Fold egg white mixture into chocolate

mixture, in 2 batches, pour into prepared mould. Cover, refrigerate for 3 hours or overnight. Turn onto plate to serve.

□ SERVES 6 TO 8

**Storage** *Covered, in refrigerator*
**Freeze** *Not suitable*
**Microwave** *Suitable*

Passionfruit liqueur souffles, *left clockwise from top left*, Mocha mousse dessert, Chocolate roll with white chocolate ganache, Frozen layered mousse

# Banana Caramel MERINGUE torte

*Meringue and sauce can be made a day ahead  Assemble close to serving*

**4 egg whites**
**1 cup (220g) caster sugar**
**1/2 teaspoon vanilla essence**
**1 1/2 cups (375ml) thickened cream, whipped**
**3 medium (600g) bananas, sliced**

### Caramel sauce

**3/4 cup (150g) firmly packed brown sugar**
**3/4 cup (180ml) thickened cream**
**60g butter**
**1 tablespoon cornflour**
**2 tablespoons water**

Line 3 oven trays with baking paper, mark 17cm circles on paper.
Beat egg whites in small bowl with electric mixer until soft peaks form. Gradually add sugar, beating until dissolved between each addition; beat in essence. Divide meringue between circles on paper, smooth tops.

Bake in slow oven about 30 minutes or until dry; cool in oven with door ajar.

Place one meringue circle on plate, spread with a third of the cream, top with a third of the bananas, then drizzle with a third of the caramel sauce; repeat layers twice.

**Caramel sauce**  Combine sugar, cream and butter in medium pan, stir over heat until sugar is dissolved. Stir in blended cornflour and water, stir until mixture boils and thickens; cool.

□ SERVES 6

**Storage**  *Covered, in refrigerator*
**Freeze**  *Not suitable*
**Microwave**  *Caramel sauce suitable*

Banana caramel meringue torte, *below*

# PUMPKIN pie

*You will need to cook about 600g pumpkin
for this recipe Recipe can be made
a day ahead*

**1 cup (150g) plain flour**
**¹/₄ cup (35g) self-raising flour**
**2 tablespoons cornflour**
**2 tablespoons icing sugar mixture**
**125g butter, chopped**
**2 tablespoons water, approximately**
**3 eggs**
**¹/₃ cup (65g) firmly packed**
   **brown sugar**
**2 tablespoons maple-**
   **flavoured syrup**
**1¹/₂ cups (600g) cooked**
   **mashed pumpkin**
**³/₄ cup (180ml) cream**
**¹/₂ teaspoon ground cinnamon**
**¹/₂ teaspoon ground nutmeg**
**1 teaspoon ground ginger**
**¹/₄ teaspoon ground cardamom**

Lightly grease 23cm pie plate.

Sift flours and icing sugar into large
bowl, rub in butter, add enough water
to make ingredients cling together.
Press dough into a ball, knead
dough on floured surface until
smooth. Cover with plastic wrap,
refrigerate 30 minutes.

Roll pastry between sheets of
baking paper until large enough
to line prepared plate. Lift pastry into
plate, ease into side, trim and
decorate edge. Place plate on lightly
greased oven tray. Cut leaf shapes
from leftover pastry, place around
plate on tray. Cover, refrigerate for
30 minutes.

Bake pastry case, blind, in
moderately hot oven about 20 minutes
or until browned lightly; cool. Remove
leaves from tray.

Whisk eggs, brown sugar and syrup
together in medium bowl.

Stir in pumpkin, cream and spices;
pour into pastry case.

Bake in moderate oven about
55 minutes or until filling is set (cover
edge of pastry if over-browning).

Decorate pie with leaves.

☐ SERVES 6 TO 8

**Storage** *Covered, in refrigerator*
**Freeze** *Not suitable*
**Microwave** *Pumpkin suitable*

Pumpkin pie, *above*

# Hot apple CAKE with
## quick caramel sauce

*Recipe can be made several days ahead*

**3 medium (450g) apples**
**250g butter, chopped**
**1 teaspoon vanilla essence**
**1 cup (220g) caster sugar**
**2 eggs, lightly beaten**
**1¹/₂ cups (225g) plain flour**
**¹/₄ teaspoon ground nutmeg**
**1 teaspoon ground cinnamon**
**1 teaspoon bicarbonate of soda**
**¹/₂ cup (60g) finely**
**chopped walnuts**

### Quick caramel sauce

**1 cup (200g) firmly packed**
**brown sugar**
**300ml thickened cream**
**1 tablespoon dark rum**

*Frozen puffs with butterscotch sauce,*
*above left*

# Frozen PUFFS with
## butterscotch sauce

*Puffs can be made several days ahead*

**75g butter, chopped**
**1 cup (250ml) water**
**1 cup (150g) plain flour**
**4 eggs**
**1.5 litres vanilla ice-**
**cream, softened**
**250g chocolate-coated honeycomb**

### Butterscotch sauce

**1 cup (200g) firmly packed**
**brown sugar**
**¹/₄ cup (60ml) glucose syrup**
**¹/₄ cup (60ml) water**
**75g butter**
**¹/₃ cup (80ml) cream**

Place butter and water in small pan, stir over heat until butter is melted. Bring to boil, stir in sifted flour, stir until mixture forms a ball and leaves side of pan. Transfer mixture to small bowl of electric mixer; cool 5 minutes.

Beat in eggs, one at a time, beating well after each addition (pastry mixture should be thick and glossy).

Place pastry into piping bag fitted with 1cm plain tube. Pipe 4cm-wide circular mounds of pastry onto lightly greased oven trays, allowing room for spreading between each mound.

Bake in hot oven, 10 minutes, reduce heat to moderate, bake further 20 minutes or until puffs are browned and firm.

Remove from oven, cut in half horizontally, remove soft pastry from centre of puffs. Return halved puffs to moderate oven, on oven tray, bake about 5 minutes or until dry and crisp; cool on wire racks.

Fill centre of puffs with combined ice-cream and chopped honeycomb. Cover, freeze until ice-cream is firm. Serve with warm butterscotch sauce.

**Butterscotch sauce** Combine sugar, syrup, water and butter in small pan, stir over heat until mixture boils. Simmer, about 5 minutes or until "soft-ball" stage is reached (112°C to 116°C on a candy thermometer, or until a teaspoon of mixture moulds easily into a ball when dropped into a glass of cold water). Remove pan from heat, allow bubbles to subside, stir in cream. Return to heat, stir until toffee is dissolved.

□ SERVES 4

***Storage*** *Puffs, in airtight container, in refrigerator Sauce, in airtight container, at room temperature*
***Freeze*** *Unfilled puffs suitable*
***Microwave*** *Not suitable*

Grease 24cm springform tin, line base with baking paper.

Peel and core apples, chop finely. Beat butter, essence and sugar in small bowl with electric mixer until light and fluffy. Add eggs, one at a time, beat until just combined. Transfer mixture to large bowl, stir in sifted dry ingredients, apples and nuts. Spread mixture into prepared tin; place tin on oven tray.

Bake in moderate oven 1 hour. Stand 10 minutes before removing from tin.

**Quick caramel sauce** Combine sugar and cream in small pan, stir over heat, without boiling, until sugar is dissolved. Simmer, stirring, about 5 minutes or until thickened slightly; stir in rum.

□ SERVES 4 TO 6

*Storage* Covered, in refrigerator
*Freeze* Suitable
*Microwave* Quick Caramel Sauce suitable

## Vanilla SLICE with two-tone custard

*Recipe best made a day ahead*

**2 sheets ready-rolled puff pastry**

### Custard

**$3/4$ cup (165g) caster sugar**
**$2/3$ cup (100g) cornflour**
**$1/2$ cup (60g) custard powder**
**1 litre (4 cups) milk**
**60g butter, chopped**
**2 egg yolks**
**2 teaspoons vanilla essence**
**100g dark chocolate, finely chopped**

Line base and sides of 23cm square slab pan with foil, bringing foil 5cm above edges of pan.

Place pastry sheets on ungreased oven trays.

Bake in moderately hot oven about 15 minutes or until pastry sheets are puffed and browned; cool.

Gently flatten pastry sheets with palm of hand, trim to fit prepared pan. Place one sheet in base of pan, drop alternate spoonfuls of hot custards over pastry. Top with remaining pastry sheet, flat-side up, press down firmly. Cover; refrigerate 3 hours or until cold.

**Custard** Combine sugar, cornflour and custard powder in pan, gradually stir in milk, stir over heat until mixture boils and thickens. Remove from heat, stir in butter, egg yolks and essence. Place half of custard in bowl, stir chocolate into remaining custard, stir over heat until smooth.

□ SERVES 8

*Storage* Covered, in refrigerator
*Freeze* Not suitable
*Microwave* Custard suitable

Vanilla slice with two-tone custard, *above*

Hot apple cake with quick caramel sauce, *left*

# Strawberry glazed CHEESECAKES

*Recipe can be made 2 days ahead*

1½ cups (150g) plain sweet
   biscuit crumbs
80g butter, melted
250g strawberries, halved
¼ cup (60ml) strawberry jam

### Filling
250g packet cream cheese
300ml sour cream
¼ cup (55g) caster sugar
3 eggs, lightly beaten
2 teaspoons grated lemon rind
2 teaspoons lemon juice

Grease 4 x 1¼-cup (300ml) ovenproof dishes, line bases with baking paper.

Combine crumbs and butter in small bowl, divide between dishes, press over bases. Pour filling over bases.

Bake uncovered in moderate oven about 25 minutes or until just set. Refrigerate several hours or until firm.

Decorate cheesecakes with strawberries, brush with sieved jam.

**Filling** Beat all ingredients in small bowl with electric mixer until smooth.

□ SERVES 4

**Storage** *Covered, in refrigerator*
**Freeze** *Suitable without strawberries*
**Microwave** *Not suitable*

# Berry MOUSSE sponge

*Recipe can be made 2 days ahead*

280g packet sponge cake mix
2 x 85g packets raspberry-
   flavoured jelly crystals
2 cups (500ml) boiling water
¼ cup (60ml) Grand Marnier
600ml thickened cream
¼ cup (40g) icing sugar mixture
1 teaspoon vanilla essence
½ cup (40g) flaked
   almonds, toasted

### Berry mousse
500g strawberries
3 egg yolks
½ cup (110g) caster sugar
1 tablespoon gelatine
¼ cup (60ml) water
300ml thickened cream

Grease deep 23cm square cake pan, line base with baking paper.

Make up cake mix according to packet directions. Spread into prepared pan.

Bake in moderate oven, about 35 minutes or until cake is firm to touch. Stand 5 minutes before turning onto wire rack to cool. Split cooled cake, horizontally, into 3 layers.

Combine jelly crystals, water and liqueur in large bowl, stir until

dissolved, refrigerate until almost set. Pour jelly mixture into base of clean, deep 23cm square cake pan. Cover with layer of cake, top with half berry mousse. Repeat layers with remaining cake and mousse, ending with cake layer. Cover; refrigerate, 3 hours or until firm.

Dip base of pan into sink of hot water about 15 seconds. Run a knife carefully around edge of cake, turn onto serving plate.

Beat cream, icing sugar and essence in medium bowl until soft peaks form. Decorate cake with cream mixture and almonds.

**Berry mousse** Blend or process berries until smooth. Beat egg yolks and sugar in small bowl with electric mixer until pale and thick, stir in berry puree. Combine gelatine and water in a cup, stand in small pan of simmering water, stir until dissolved; cool to

# Passionfruit SORBET
## with coconut tuilles

*Recipe can be made several hours ahead*

**14 passionfruit, approximately**
**³/₄ cup (165g) caster sugar**
**1 cup (250ml) water**
**4 egg whites**

### Coconut tuilles
**1 egg white**
**¹/₄ cup (55g) caster sugar**
**2 tablespoons plain flour**
**30g butter, melted**
**¹/₂ teaspoon coconut essence**
**1¹/₂ tablespoons**
　　**desiccated coconut**

Remove pulp from passionfruit, strain; reserve 2 tablespoons of seeds and ²/₃-cup (160ml) strained passionfruit.

Combine sugar and water in small pan, stir over heat until sugar is dissolved; simmer, uncovered, without stirring, 5 minutes. Combine sugar syrup with strained passionfruit pulp and reserved seeds in 23cm square slab pan; cover, freeze until firm.

Chop passionfruit mixture, place in medium bowl of electric mixer with egg whites, beat until combined. Return to pan, cover; freeze until firm.

Serve several scoops of passionfruit sorbet with coconut tuilles.

**Coconut tuilles** Line oven tray with baking paper, mark 3 x 12cm circles on paper, 5cm apart. Beat egg white in small bowl until soft peaks form, gradually beat in sugar, beat until sugar is dissolved. Fold in sifted flour, butter and essence. Spread 1 tablespoon of mixture into each circle, sprinkle with ¹/₂ teaspoon coconut. Bake in moderate oven 7 minutes or until browned lightly. Carefully remove tuilles from paper while hot, place over rolling pin, stand until firm. Repeat with remaining mixture. You will need 8 tuilles for this recipe.

□ SERVES 4

**Storage** *Covered, in freezer*
**Freeze** *Tuilles not suitable*
**Microwave** *Not suitable*

room temperature. Stir gelatine mixture into berry mixture. Beat cream in small bowl until soft peaks form, fold into berry mixture.

□ SERVES 8 TO 10

**Storage** *Covered, in refrigerator*
**Freeze** *Not suitable*
**Microwave** *Gelatine suitable*

Berry mousse sponge, *above*
Strawberry glazed cheesecakes, *left*
Passionfruit sorbet with coconut
tuilles, *right*

*h*ot weather, long days, seaside get-togethers. Summer is the season made for lazy lounging and light-hearted food. This lighter style of eating is reflected in the recipes chosen for summer, some for the great outdoors, some for late-night dining summer *it's sensational* with the windows thrown open to the stars.

Succulent seafood, scrumptious salads, and mouth-watering desserts using plump, ripe berries are the real treats of the season. There is something for everyone and nothing's so time-consuming that you're tied to the kitchen when the weather says 'come out and play'.

# summer

## seafood

*'In the cool, cool, cool, of the evening'*

SERVES 6 to 8

## Cocktails at twilight

Tiny FISH CAKES
with chilli dipping sauce  *(page 80)*

TANDOORI chicken skewers
with yogurt dip  *(page 78)*

Cheese and basil SAUSAGE rolls  *(page 79)*

VINE LEAVES with pine nuts
and dried currants  *(page 72)*

EGGPLANT dip  *(page 83)*

Decadent MUD CAKE stars  *(page 99)*

SERVES 15

## Food of the sun

Cheese TURNOVERS  *(page 83)*

EGGPLANT cake with tomato sauce  *(page 92)*

SPINACH and fetta pie  *(page 91)*

Greek SALAD  *(page 73)*

Thyme-roasted CAPSICUMS
and tomatoes  *(page 113)*

Citrus GELATO  *(page 122)*

SERVES 6

sorbets & gelato

## VINE LEAVES with pine nuts and dried currants

*Recipe can be made 3 days ahead*

**300g packet vine leaves in brine**
**1 tablespoon lemon juice**
**³/₄ cup (180ml) water**
**1 tablespoon olive oil**

Nut currant filling

**¹/₄ cup (60ml) olive oil**
**1 medium (150g) onion, finely chopped**
**2 tablespoons pine nuts**
**¹/₂ cup (100g) short-grain rice**
**2 tablespoons dried currants**
**¹/₂ cup (125ml) water**
**2 tablespoons chopped fresh parsley**

Rinse vine leaves under cold running water; drain well, pat dry.

Place vine leaves vein-side up on bench, place rounded teaspoons of nut currant filling on base of each leaf, fold in sides, roll up firmly.

Place rolls, in single layer, in large heavy-based pan, pour juice, water and oil over top. Cover, simmer, 1 hour.

Remove from heat, stand, covered, 1 hour before serving.

**Nut currant filling** Heat oil in small pan, add onion, cook, stirring, until onion is soft. Add nuts, cook, stirring, until browned lightly. Stir in rice and currants.

Add water, simmer, covered, about 10 minutes or until all liquid is absorbed; cool. Stir in parsley.

□ MAKES ABOUT 24

***Storage*** *Covered, in refrigerator*
***Freeze*** *Not suitable*
***Microwave*** *Not suitable*

## ZUCCHINI fritters

*Recipe best made close to serving*

**5 large (750g) zucchini, grated**
**1 medium (150g) onion, grated**
**¹/₂ cup (75g) plain flour**
**3 eggs, lightly beaten**
**1 tablespoon chopped fresh oregano**
**1 tablespoon chopped fresh basil**
**1 tablespoon chopped fresh parsley**
**vegetable oil, for shallow-frying**

Combine zucchini, onion, flour, eggs, oregano, basil and parsley in large bowl; mix well.

# Greek SALAD

*Recipe best made close to serving*

1 medium (200g) red capsicum
200g fetta cheese
4 leaves (320g) silverbeet (spinach)
1 medium (150g) onion, sliced
125g cherry tomatoes
100g seeded black olives

### Herb dressing
2 tablespoons olive oil
2 tablespoons lemon juice
2 teaspoons chopped
    fresh marjoram
2 teaspoons chopped fresh oregano

Cut capsicum into quarters lengthways, remove membranes and seeds. Roast under grill or in very hot oven, skin-side up, until skin blackens and blisters. Cover capsicum pieces in plastic or paper for 5 minutes, peel away skin.

Cut capsicum into small diamond shapes. Cut cheese into 1cm cubes. Tear silverbeet into large pieces.

Combine all ingredients with herb dressing in a medium bowl.

**Herb dressing** Combine all ingredients in jar; shake well.

□ SERVES 4

*Freeze* Not suitable
*Microwave* Not suitable

Shallow-fry, level ¼ cups of mixture, in hot oil until fritters are browned lightly underneath, turn and cook until browned on other side; drain on absorbent paper.

□ MAKES ABOUT 14

*Freeze* Not suitable
*Microwave* Not suitable

Vine leaves with pine nuts and dried currants, Zucchini fritters, *above from left* Greek salad, *right*

### Caper dressing

1/2 cup (125ml) olive oil
2 tablespoons red wine vinegar
1 tablespoon drained
    capers, chopped
1 teaspoon Dijon mustard
1 teaspoon sugar
1/2 teaspoon cracked black pepper

Place asparagus in large heatproof bowl, cover with boiling water; stand 1 minute, drain. Rinse under cold water, drain.

Beat cream cheese, mustard, juice and basil in small bowl with electric mixer until smooth; stir in cucumber.

Slightly overlap 3 slices of smoked salmon on board, spread with a sixth of cream cheese mixture; top with 3 asparagus spears. Roll up from long side, trim edges. Repeat with remaining salmon, cream cheese mixture and asparagus. Place rolls on tray, cover, refrigerate 2 hours. Cut each roll into 4 slices. Serve 3 slices per person, with caper dressing.

**Caper dressing** Combine all ingredients in jar; shake well.

□ SERVES 4

**Storage** *Covered, separately, in refrigerator*
**Freeze** *Not suitable*
**Microwave** *Asparagus suitable*

# Grilled ZUCCHINI and garlic dip

*Recipe can be made 2 days ahead*

7 medium (840g) zucchini
2 tablespoons olive oil
1/3 cup (80ml) plain yogurt
1 tablespoon lime juice
1 clove garlic, crushed
1 teaspoon ground coriander
1/4 cup (60ml) tahini
1 tablespoon chopped fresh mint
1 tablespoon chopped
    fresh coriander

Cut zucchini in half lengthways; brush with oil. Grill zucchini until browned on both sides and very soft; cool.

Process zucchini with remaining ingredients until just combined. Cover, refrigerate at least 1 hour.

□ MAKES ABOUT 2 1/2 CUPS

**Storage** *Covered, in refrigerator*
**Freeze** *Not suitable*
**Microwave** *Not suitable*

# SMOKED SALMON rolls with caper dressing

*Recipe can be prepared a day ahead*

9 spears fresh asparagus, halved
200g packaged cream
    cheese, softened
1 teaspoon Dijon mustard
1 1/2 tablespoons lemon juice
2 tablespoons chopped fresh basil
1 medium (170g) Lebanese
    cucumber, seeded, chopped
18 slices (375g) smoked salmon

Grilled zucchini and garlic dip, *above*
Smoked salmon rolls with caper
dressing, *right*

# ROCKET and macadamia salad

*Dressing can be made 3 days ahead*
*Salad can be prepared several hours ahead*

**500g asparagus, chopped**
**2 bunches (250g) rocket**
**1/2 cup (75g) macadamias, toasted, coarsely chopped**
**1 cup (80g) parmesan cheese flakes**

### Dressing

**1/3 cup (80ml) macadamia oil**
**1/4 cup (60ml) orange juice**
**2 tablespoons white vinegar**
**1 teaspoon cracked black pepper**
**1 tablespoon peanut butter**
**1 clove garlic, crushed**

Boil, steam or microwave asparagus until just tender; drain. Rinse under cold water; drain well. Combine asparagus with remaining ingredients in large bowl; drizzle with dressing.

**Dressing** Combine all ingredients in jar; shake well.

☐ SERVES 8

**Storage** *Dressing, in airtight container, in refrigerator Salad, covered, in refrigerator*
**Freeze** *Not suitable*
**Microwave** *Asparagus suitable*

# RATATOUILLE rolls with basil cream

*Basil cream best made just before serving*
*Filling can be prepared a day ahead*
*Assemble rolls close to serving*

**3 large (1.5kg) eggplants**
**2 teaspoons salt**
**2/3 cup (160ml) olive oil**
**1 large (200g) onion, chopped**
**4 cloves garlic, crushed**
**1 large (350g) red capsicum, chopped**
**1 large (350g) green capsicum, chopped**
**4 medium (480g) zucchini, chopped**
**400g can tomatoes, undrained, crushed**
**1/2 cup (40g) grated parmesan cheese**

## Basil cream

**1 cup (250ml) vegetable stock**
**2 cups (500ml) cream**
**1 tablespoon cornflour**
**2 tablespoons shredded fresh basil**

Cut eggplants lengthways into 7mm thick slices, discard small end slices – you will need 24 slices for this recipe.

Sprinkle slices with salt, stand 30 minutes. Rinse slices under cold running water, drain; pat dry.

Reserve 1 tablespoon oil, brush eggplant slices all over with remaining oil. Add slices, in batches, to heated oiled large pan, cook on both sides until browned and tender; remove from pan, keep warm.

Heat reserved oil in same pan, add onion and garlic, cook, stirring, until onion is soft. Add capsicums and zucchini, cook, stirring, until capsicums begin to soften. Add tomatoes, simmer, uncovered about 7 minutes or until thick, stirring occasionally.

Divide hot tomato mixture among eggplant slices, roll up to enclose filling; place on oiled oven trays. Top rolls with cheese, cook under hot grill until browned. Serve rolls with basil cream.

**Basil cream** Reserve 1 tablespoon stock. Add remaining stock and cream to pan, simmer, uncovered, 12 minutes or until thickened slightly. Stir in blended reserved stock and cornflour, stir over heat until sauce boils and thickens; stir in basil.

☐ SERVES 8

**Storage** *Filling, covered, in refrigerator*
**Freeze** *Not suitable*
**Microwave** *Not suitable*

Rocket and macadamia salad,
Ratatouille rolls with basil cream,
*below, from top*

## Tomato TARTS with balsamic dressing

*Pastry cases and dressing can
be made a day ahead*

**2 sheets ready-rolled puff pastry**
**1 egg yolk, lightly beaten**
**1 tablespoon olive oil**
**1 medium (150g) onion, chopped**
**2 cloves garlic, crushed**
**$^1/_2$ cup shredded fresh basil**
**1 tablespoon chopped
fresh oregano**
**250g cherry tomatoes**
**300g can Tomato Supreme**
**2 tablespoons balsamic vinegar**
**$^1/_2$ cup (125ml) olive oil, extra**
**50g mixed salad leaves**

Cut one sheet of pastry into quarters
to form bases; place onto lightly oiled
oven trays. Make a 12.5cm square
paper pattern. Inside this, cut an
8.5cm square, leaving a 2cm frame.

Using paper pattern, cut 4 frame
shapes from remaining sheet of
pastry. Brush edges of bases lightly
with water, press pastry frames onto
bases, forming shallow pastry cases.
Place remaining pastry squares, which
form lids, onto another oiled oven
tray. Cover, refrigerate several hours
or overnight.

Brush tops of frames and lids evenly
with egg yolk, prick bases of pastry
cases with fork.

Bake, separately, in very hot oven
about 6 minutes or until pastry is
browned and risen.

Heat oil in pan, add onion and
garlic, cook, stirring, until onion is
soft; add herbs and cherry tomatoes,
cook, stirring occasionally, until
tomatoes soften slightly. Add Tomato
Supreme, cook, stirring, until heated
through.

Combine vinegar and extra oil in a
jar; shake well.

Just before serving, spoon tomato
mixture into pastry cases, top with
pastry lids.

Serve tarts with salad leaves and
balsamic dressing.

□ MAKES 4

***Storage*** *Pastry cases, in airtight
container, at room temperature  Dressing,
in airtight container, in refrigerator*
***Microwave*** *Filling suitable*
***Freeze*** *Uncooked pastry cases suitable*

# Prawn and coriander GAZPACHO

*Recipe can be made a day ahead*

2 small (260g) Lebanese cucumbers
salt
8 large (2kg) very ripe tomatoes,
    peeled, seeded
665ml can vegetable juice
$1/_4$ cup (60ml) red wine vinegar
2 tablespoons olive oil
1 tablespoon chopped
    fresh coriander
1 tablespoon chopped fresh basil
few drops Tabasco sauce
200g cooked shelled prawns

Garlic croutons

$1/_2$ French bread stick, thinly sliced
1 clove garlic, crushed
2 tablespoons olive oil
ground black pepper

Cut cucumbers in half lengthways, discard seeds, sprinkle cucumbers with salt, stand 30 minutes. Rinse cucumbers under cold running water, drain, pat dry; slice thinly.

Blend or process tomatoes, juice, vinegar and oil in batches until smooth; transfer to large serving bowl. Stir in cucumber and remaining ingredients. Serve with garlic croutons.

**Garlic croutons** Brush bread slices on both sides with combined garlic, oil and pepper. Grill bread on both sides until browned lightly.

□ SERVES 6

**Storage** *Soup, covered, in refrigerator Garlic croutons, in airtight container, at room temperature*
**Freeze** *Not suitable*
**Microwave** *Not suitable*

Tomato tarts with balsamic dressing, *left*
Prawn and coriander gazpacho, *below*

77

## TANDOORI chicken skewers with yogurt dip

*Recipe can be prepared a day ahead*

**800g chicken thigh fillets**
**$1/4$ cup (60ml) tandoori paste**
**$1/2$ cup (125ml) plain yogurt**
**pinch ground saffron**
**2 tablespoons chopped**
   **fresh coriander**

### Yogurt dip

**1 cup (250ml) plain yogurt**
**2 tablespoons chopped**
   **fresh coriander**
**1 tablespoon chopped fresh chives**
**$1/4$ teaspoon grated lime rind**

Soak 40 small bamboo skewers in water for 1 hour.

Cut chicken into thin strips; thread onto prepared skewers. Place skewers in shallow dish. Combine remaining ingredients in medium bowl. Brush chicken all over with tandoori mixture; cover, refrigerate 3 hours or overnight.

Grill skewers in batches until tender. Serve skewers with yogurt dip.

**Yogurt dip** Combine all ingredients in small bowl.

□ MAKES ABOUT 40

***Storage*** *Covered, in refrigerator*
***Freeze*** *Marinated chicken suitable*
***Microwave*** *Not suitable*

## Cheese and basil SAUSAGE rolls

*Recipe can be made 2 days ahead*

**500g minced beef**
**250g sausage mince**
**$1/3$ cup (35g) grated**
 **mozzarella cheese**
**$1/3$ cup (25g) grated**
 **parmesan cheese**
**$1/3$ cup chopped fresh basil**
**$1/3$ cup (50g) pimiento-stuffed**
 **green olives, sliced**
**$1/4$ cup (60ml) tomato paste**
**1 cup (70g) stale breadcrumbs**
**4 sheets ready-rolled puff pastry**
**1 egg, lightly beaten**

Combine minces with cheeses, basil, olives, paste and breadcrumbs in large bowl. Cut each pastry sheet into 3 rectangles. Place $1/3$ cup mince mixture in a line along centre of each rectangle. Brush edges of rectangles with a little egg, roll over to enclose.

Score top of each roll with a sharp knife, brush rolls with some of the egg. Cut each roll diagonally into 4 pieces. Place rolls, seam side down, on oven trays.

Bake, uncovered, in hot oven about 20 minutes or until browned.

☐ MAKES 48

***Storage*** *Covered, in refrigerator*
***Freeze*** *Uncooked rolls, suitable*
***Microwave*** *Not suitable*

## Garlic CHICKEN wings with herb sauce

*Recipe can be prepared a day ahead*

**1.5kg chicken wings**
**2 cloves garlic, crushed**
**2 tablespoons vegetable oil**
**2 tablespoons lemon juice**
**1 tablespoon apricot jam**
**1 teaspoon sweet paprika**

### Herb sauce

**$3/4$ cup (180ml) plain yogurt**
**2 tablespoons chopped**
 **fresh parsley**
**2 teaspoons chopped fresh chives**

Combine chicken with remaining ingredients in large bowl, stir well to coat chicken. Cover, refrigerate 3 hours or overnight. Remove chicken from marinade, reserve marinade. Place chicken on wire rack in baking dish.

Bake, uncovered, in moderate oven about 50 minutes or until well browned and tender, brushing occasionally with reserved marinade.

Serve chicken with herb sauce.

**Herb sauce** Combine all ingredients in small bowl.

☐ SERVES 4

***Storage*** *Airtight container, in refrigerator*
***Freeze*** *Marinated chicken suitable*
***Microwave*** *Not suitable*

Tandoori chicken skewers with yogurt dip, *above left*
Cheese and basil sausage rolls, *left*
Garlic chicken wings with herb sauce, *above*

### Fetta and basil MUSHROOMS

*Recipe best made close to serving*

4 green onions, chopped
3 cloves garlic, crushed
300g ham, finely chopped
250g fetta cheese, crumbled
1 cup (250ml) mild tomato salsa
¹/₃ cup chopped fresh basil
8 large (480g) flat mushrooms
2 tablespoons olive oil
2 tablespoons flaked
   parmesan cheese

Combine onions, garlic, ham, fetta, salsa and basil in medium bowl.

Remove stems from mushrooms, brush mushrooms all over with oil; place in Swiss roll pan. Divide fetta mixture among mushrooms.

Bake, uncovered, in moderately hot oven about 15 minutes or until filling is hot. Serve mushrooms topped with parmesan cheese.

□ SERVES 4

*Freeze* Not suitable
*Microwave* Suitable

### Tiny FISH CAKES with chilli dipping sauce

*We used redfish fillets  Recipe can be made several hours ahead*

500g white fish fillets, chopped
500g uncooked prawns, shelled
6 green onions, chopped
2 medium (240g) carrots, grated
2 cloves garlic, crushed
2 teaspoons grated fresh ginger
2 teaspoons grated lime rind

1 tablespoon lime juice
1 tablespoon fish sauce
¹/₂ cup (50g) packaged
   breadcrumbs
2 teaspoons mild sweet chilli sauce
2 tablespoons chopped
   fresh coriander
2 eggs
vegetable oil, for deep-frying

#### Chilli dipping sauce

¹/₃ cup (80ml) white vinegar
2 tablespoons caster sugar
1 teaspoon cornflour
¹/₄ cup (60ml) water
1 teaspoon oyster sauce
1 fresh red chilli, finely chopped

Blend or process all ingredients, except oil, until combined. Shape rounded teaspoons of mixture into ovals.

Deep-fry fish cakes in hot oil until cooked through; drain on absorbent paper. Serve with chilli dipping sauce.

**Chilli dipping sauce**  Combine vinegar and sugar in small pan; stir over heat until sugar is dissolved. Add blended cornflour and water, sauce and chilli. Stir over heat until sauce boils and thickens.

□ MAKES ABOUT 50

*Storage*  Covered, in refrigerator
*Freeze*  Not suitable
*Microwave*  Not suitable

## Roasted tomato, fetta and eggplant TARTS

*This recipe can be prepared several hours ahead*

**2 medium (600g) eggplants**
**3 large (270g) egg tomatoes**
**salt**
**2¹/₂ tablespoons olive oil**
**1 teaspoon sugar**
**1 tablespoon balsamic vinegar**
**1 tablespoon chopped fresh sage**
**2 sheets ready-rolled puff pastry**
**65g fetta cheese, crumbled**

Cut eggplants and tomatoes into slices 1cm thick. Sprinkle eggplant with salt, stand 30 minutes. Rinse eggplant under cold running water; drain, pat dry.

Heat 2 tablespoons oil in pan, add eggplant in batches, cook until browned lightly; drain on absorbent paper.

Heat remaining oil in pan, add tomatoes and sugar, cook, uncovered, about 2 minutes or until tomatoes are just soft. Stir in vinegar and sage, cook, uncovered, 1 minute.

Cut both pastry sheets in half. Place pastry on oiled oven trays, about 3cm apart. Turn edges of pastry in 1.5cm; pinch corners together.

Divide eggplant and tomato among pastry pieces, top with cheese.

Bake, uncovered, in very hot oven about 15 minutes or until pastry is puffed and browned.

□ MAKES 4

**Storage** *Covered, in refrigerator*
**Freeze** *Not suitable*
**Microwave** *Not suitable*

Fetta and basil mushrooms, *above left*
Tiny fish cakes with chilli dipping sauce, *left*
Roasted tomato, fetta and eggplant tarts, *above*

# EGGPLANT dip

*Recipe best made a day ahead*

1 large (500g) eggplant
1 medium (150g) onion,
    finely chopped
$^3/_4$ cup (75g) packaged
    breadcrumbs
2 tablespoons plain yogurt
3 cloves garlic, crushed
$^1/_2$ cup (125ml) olive oil
$^1/_2$ cup chopped fresh parsley
1 tablespoon cider vinegar
1$^1/_2$ tablespoons lemon juice

Place whole eggplant on lightly oiled oven tray. Bake, uncovered, in hot oven about 1 hour, or until eggplant is soft.

Remove eggplant from oven, cool 10 minutes.

Discard skin from eggplant, chop roughly. Combine eggplant with remaining ingredients, in food processor, process until smooth.

Place eggplant dip in medium bowl; cover, refrigerate overnight.

□ MAKES ABOUT 2 CUPS

**Storage**  *Covered, in refrigerator*
**Freeze**  *Not suitable*
**Microwave**  *Not suitable*

# Cheese TURNOVERS

*Turnovers can be made 2 days ahead*

1 cup (150g) self-raising flour
1 cup (150g) plain flour
$^1/_2$ cup (125ml) olive oil
$^1/_2$ cup (125ml) warm water
1 egg yolk

### Cheese filling
100g fetta cheese, grated
$^1/_2$ cup (100g) ricotta cheese
1 egg, lightly beaten
1 tablespoon packaged
    breadcrumbs
$^1/_4$ teaspoon ground nutmeg

Sift flours into large bowl, add oil and water, mix to a soft dough. Cover, refrigerate 2 hours.

Cut dough in half, roll out half on floured surface until 2mm thick; cut into 8cm rounds. Place slightly rounded teaspoons of cheese filling onto centre of each round, brush edges with a little water, fold rounds in half; press edges to seal. Repeat with remaining dough and cheese filling.

Place turnovers on lightly oiled oven trays, brush with egg yolk.

Bake, uncovered, in moderately hot oven about 20 minutes or until browned lightly; cool on trays. Serve warm or cold.

**Cheese filling**  Combine all ingredients in bowl.

□ MAKES ABOUT 16

**Storage**  *Airtight container, in refrigerator*
**Freeze**  *Uncooked turnovers suitable*
**Microwave**  *Not suitable*

# Baked lemon and tomato SARDINES

*Recipe best made just before serving*

8 (400g) fresh sardines
2 medium (260g) tomatoes, sliced
$^1/_4$ cup (60ml) olive oil
2 tablespoons lemon juice
2 cloves garlic, crushed
2 teaspoons grated lemon rind
2 tablespoons chopped
    fresh parsley
1 tablespoon chopped
    fresh oregano

Cut off sardine heads and remove entrails. Place one sardine on its side, cut along underside of belly, cutting through to backbone; rinse sardine under cold running water. Without piercing skin, carefully snip through backbone at tail end to separate bone from tail end. Pull out backbone, starting from tail end and pulling towards head. Remove small bones; press flat. Repeat with remaining sardines.

Place tomato slices, in single layer, over base of lamington pan.

Place sardines over tomatoes, pour combined oil, juice, garlic and rind over top; sprinkle with herbs.

Bake, uncovered, in moderately hot oven about 7 minutes or until sardines are cooked through.

□ SERVES 4

**Freeze**  *Not suitable*
**Microwave**  *Not suitable*

Eggplant dip, Cheese turnovers,
*far left, from top*
Baked lemon and tomato sardines, *left*

# PORK with caramelised pineapple

*Recipe best prepared a day ahead*

**1 tablespoon grated fresh ginger**
**$^1/_2$ cup (125ml) pineapple juice**
**$^1/_2$ cup (125ml) green ginger wine**
**$^1/_3$ cup (80ml) honey**
**2 tablespoons vegetable oil**
**8 (1kg) pork midloin butterfly steaks**
**$^1/_2$ medium (600g) pineapple, halved, sliced**

Combine ginger, juice, wine, honey and oil in jug, whisk until combined.

Trim excess fat from pork, place in shallow dish, pour over ginger mixture. Cover, refrigerate 3 hours or overnight.

Drain pork from marinade, reserve marinade. Add pork and pineapple to heated oiled griddle pan (or barbecue or grill); cook until browned on both sides and just tender, brushing occasionally with reserved marinade.

□ SERVES 4 TO 6

**Storage** *Covered, in refrigerator*
**Freeze** *Marinated pork suitable*
**Microwave** *Not suitable*

# Spicy RED CABBAGE salad

*Recipe can be prepared several hours ahead*

**$^1/_2$ small (600g) red cabbage, finely shredded**
**4 medium (480g) carrots, grated**
**$^1/_2$ cup fresh flat-leaf parsley, coarsely chopped**
**$^1/_2$ cup (80g) pine nuts, toasted**
**$^1/_2$ cup (75g) dried currants**

### Spicy dressing

**$^1/_3$ cup (80ml) lemon juice**
**$^1/_2$ cup (125ml) olive oil**
**1 teaspoon ground cumin**
**1 teaspoon ground coriander**
**1 teaspoon bottled chopped chillies**
**1 tablespoon tomato paste**

Combine cabbage, carrots, parsley, nuts and currants in large bowl. Just before serving, add spicy dressing; mix well.

**Spicy dressing** Combine all ingredients in jar; shake well.

□ SERVES 6

*Storage  Covered, in refrigerator*
*Freeze  Not suitable*

## SEAFOOD salad with lime coriander dressing

*We used Ling for this recipe*
*Potato slices can be cooked a day ahead*
*Seafood can be browned and dressing*
*made several hours ahead  Recipe best*
*assembled close to serving*

**2 large (600g) old potatoes**
**vegetable oil, for deep-frying**
**1kg medium uncooked prawns**
**700g white fish fillets**
**4 small (450g) squid tubes**
**1kg baby octopus**
**200g mixed salad leaves**

#### Lime coriander dressing

**¹/₂ cup (125ml) vegetable oil**
**¹/₃ cup (80ml) lime juice**
**1 tablespoon chopped
  fresh coriander**
**2 cloves garlic, crushed**
**1 teaspoon sugar**

Cut potatoes into very thin slices, pat dry on absorbent paper. Deep-fry potatoes, in batches, in hot oil until browned and crisp. Drain well, cool on wire racks.

Shell and devein prawns, leaving tails intact. Cut fish into large pieces. Cut calamari tubes open, cut shallow diagonal slashes on inside surface; cut in half. Remove and discard heads and beaks from octopus; cut octopus in half.

Add seafood, in batches, to heated oiled griddle pan (or barbecue); cook until browned on both sides. Spread seafood on 2 shallow oven trays.

Just before serving, bake, uncovered, in very hot oven about 5 minutes or until just cooked. Serve seafood and potatoes with salad leaves; drizzle with lime coriander dressing.

**Lime coriander dressing**  Combine all ingredients in jar; shake well.

□ SERVES 8

*Storage  Potatoes, in airtight container, at room temperature  Seafood, covered, in refrigerator*
*Dressing, covered in refrigerator*
*Freeze  Not suitable*
*Microwave  Not suitable*

## Roasted TOMATO salad

*Recipe can be made a day ahead*

**12 large (1kg) egg tomatoes**
**2 tablespoons olive oil**
**2 tablespoons mild sweet
  chilli sauce**
**2 cloves garlic, crushed**
**1 teaspoon salt**
**1 teaspoon cracked black pepper**

#### Dressing

**1 tablespoon balsamic vinegar**
**¹/₃ cup (80ml) olive oil**
**1 teaspoon chopped fresh thyme**
**1 clove garlic, crushed**

Halve tomatoes lengthways. Place tomatoes, cut side up, on wire rack in large baking dish.

Brush cut side of tomatoes with combined oil, sauce and garlic; sprinkle with combined salt and pepper.

Bake, uncovered, in moderate oven about 1¹/₂ hours or until browned lightly and softened; cool.

Drizzle tomatoes with dressing just before serving.

**Dressing**  Combine all ingredients in jar; shake well.

□ SERVES 8

*Storage  Covered, in refrigerator*
*Freeze  Not suitable*
*Microwave  Not suitable*

Pork with caramelised pineapple, Spicy red cabbage salad, *left*
Roasted tomato salad, Seafood salad with lime coriander dressing, *above, from top*

# Crisp PRAWN salad with basil dressing

*Basil dressing and croutons can be made 2 days ahead*

1kg cooked medium prawns
2 small cos lettuce
6 bacon rashers, thinly sliced
1/2 loaf unsliced white bread
80g butter
1/3 cup (25g) flaked
    parmesan cheese

### Basil dressing

1 clove garlic, crushed
2 egg yolks
2 tablespoons lemon juice
1 teaspoon hot English mustard
1 cup firmly packed fresh basil
6 canned anchovy fillets, drained
1 cup (250ml) olive oil
1/2 cup (125ml) buttermilk

Shell and devein prawns, leaving tails intact. Tear large lettuce leaves in half, leave small leaves whole. Add bacon to heated small pan; cook, stirring, until crisp; drain.

Remove crusts from bread, cut bread lengthways into slices 2cm thick. Cut shapes from bread (we used a tree-shaped cutter). Melt butter in clean pan, add bread shapes, cook until browned lightly on both sides; drain croutons on absorbent paper.

Combine prawns, lettuce and bacon in serving bowl; drizzle with basil dressing. Top with croutons and cheese.

**Basil dressing** Blend or process garlic, egg yolks, juice and mustard until combined. Add basil and anchovies, blend until smooth. Add oil in thin stream while motor is operating; blend until thick. Add buttermilk, blend until combined.

☐ SERVES 4 TO 6

*Storage  Basil dressing, covered, in refrigerator  Croutons, in airtight container, at room temperature*
**Freeze**  *Not suitable*
**Microwave**  *Not suitable*

Crisp prawn salad with basil dressing, *below*

# STEAKS with capsicum salsa

*Salsa can be made several hours ahead*

4 (800g) beef rump steaks
1 small (150g) red capsicum,
    finely chopped
1 small (150g) green capsicum,
    finely chopped
1 medium (170g) red onion,
    finely chopped
1 large (250g) tomato, seeded,
    finely chopped
1 tablespoon chopped
    fresh coriander
2 tablespoons lemon juice
2 tablespoons olive oil
2 cloves garlic, crushed
1 teaspoon ground cumin

Trim fat from steaks. Add steaks to heated oiled griddle pan (or barbecue or grill); cook until browned on both sides and tender.

Combine remaining ingredients in medium bowl. Serve steaks with salsa.

☐ SERVES 4

*Storage  Salsa, covered, in refrigerator*
**Freeze**  *Not suitable*
**Microwave**  *Not suitable*

# Thai-flavoured RISOTTO

*Recipe must be made just before serving*

1 tablespoon peanut oil
250g asparagus, chopped
500g beef rump steak, thinly sliced
1 large (200g) onion, chopped
2 tablespoons Thai red curry paste
2 cups (400g) arborio rice
1.5 litres (6 cups) hot beef stock
2 tablespoons coconut milk powder
1/3 cup chopped fresh coriander

Heat oil in large pan, add asparagus, cook, stirring, until just tender; remove from pan. Add steak, in batches to same pan, cook, stirring, until well browned; remove from pan. Add onion to same pan, cook, stirring, until onion is soft. Add curry paste and

rice, cook, stirring, until fragrant.

Stir ½ cup (125ml) combined stock and coconut milk powder into rice mixture, cook, stirring, over low heat until liquid is absorbed. Continue adding stock mixture gradually, stirring until absorbed before next addition. Total cooking time should be about 25 minutes or until rice is just tender and mixture is creamy.

Return steak and asparagus to pan with coriander; stir until hot.

□ SERVES 6

*Freeze  Not suitable*
*Microwave  Not suitable*

# Satay beef and noodle
## STIR-FRY

*If frozen vegetables contain a flavour sachet, do not use sachet for this recipe  Recipe must be made just before serving*

**500g Hokkien noodles**
**1 tablespoon peanut oil**
**800g beef skirt steak, thinly sliced**
**2 cloves garlic, crushed**
**8 green onions, sliced**
**³/₄ cup (180ml) beef stock**
**¹/₃ cup (85g) crunchy**
**peanut butter**
**¹/₄ cup (60ml) mild sweet**
**chilli sauce**
**2 teaspoons lemon juice**
**400g packet frozen stir-fry**
**vegetables, thawed**

Place noodles in heatproof bowl, cover with boiling water, stir to separate; drain.

Heat half the oil in wok or large pan, add steak in batches, stir-fry until browned; remove from wok.

Heat remaining oil in wok, add garlic and onions, stir-fry until soft. Add stock, peanut butter, sauce and juice; simmer, uncovered, 1 minute. Return steak to wok with vegetables and noodles, cook, stirring, until hot.

□ SERVES 6

*Freeze  Not suitable*
*Microwave  Not suitable*

*clockwise from top left*, Thai-flavoured risotto, Satay beef and noodle stir-fry, Steaks with capsicum salsa

# CHICKEN and herb
## mayonnaise bagels

*Chicken can be prepared several hours ahead   Recipe best assembled close to serving*

**4 chicken breast fillets**
**1 egg, lightly beaten**
**2 tablespoons milk**
**1 cup (100g) packaged breadcrumbs**
**$^1/_3$ cup (80ml) vegetable oil**
**$^1/_3$ cup (80ml) mayonnaise**
**1 teaspoon seeded mustard**
**1 tablespoon chopped fresh chives**
**$^1/_4$ teaspoon ground black pepper**
**4 bagels**
**4 lettuce leaves**
**16 cherry tomatoes, halved**

Dip chicken in combined egg and milk, toss in breadcrumbs, press breadcrumbs on firmly. Cover, refrigerate 30 minutes.

Heat oil in large pan, add chicken, cook, about 5 minutes each side or until chicken is cooked through; drain.

Combine mayonnaise, mustard, chives and pepper in small bowl.

Split bagels in half, place lettuce, chicken, mayonnaise mixture and tomatoes over bases; replace tops.

□ SERVES 4

*Storage  Chicken, covered, in refrigerator
Freeze  Not suitable
Microwave  Not suitable*

# Cheesy spinach
## PASTA pie

*Recipe can be made a day ahead*

**200g macaroni pasta**
**2 tablespoons olive oil**
**1 medium (150g) onion, chopped**
**200g mushrooms, finely chopped**
**$^1/_2$ teaspoon dried chilli flakes**
**250g packet frozen spinach,
    thawed, drained**
**310g can chickpeas,
    rinsed, drained**
**$1^1/_2$ cups (300g) ricotta
    cheese, sieved**
**200g fetta cheese, crumbled**
**1 cup (250ml) milk**
**4 eggs, lightly beaten**
**1 tablespoon chopped fresh basil**
**1 tablespoon chopped fresh thyme**
**1 cup (125g) grated cheddar cheese**

## Sesame CHICKEN and
### mandarin salad

*Salad can be prepared a day ahead*

**500g chicken thigh fillets**
**1 tablespoon peanut oil**
**100g snow peas**
**100g yellow squash, sliced**
**100g button mushrooms, sliced**
**1 small (150g) red**
 **capsicum, sliced**
**2¹/₂ cups (100g) mung bean sprouts**
**310g can mandarin**
 **segments, drained**
**230g can water chestnuts, drained**
**2 tablespoons sesame**
 **seeds, toasted**
**1 mignonette lettuce**

### Sesame dressing

**1 tablespoon sesame oil**
**2 teaspoons peanut oil**
**2 tablespoons lemon juice**
**1 teaspoon sugar**
**1 clove garlic, crushed**

Cut chicken into strips. Heat oil in large pan, add chicken, stir over heat, about 7 minutes or until chicken is cooked through; drain, cool.

Boil, steam or microwave snow peas and squash until just tender; rinse under cold water, drain, cool.

Combine chicken, snow peas, squash, mushrooms, capsicum, sprouts, mandarins, chestnuts and seeds in large bowl. Stir in sesame dressing. Serve over lettuce leaves.

**Sesame dressing** Combine all ingredients in jar; shake well.

□ SERVES 4

*Storage Covered, in refrigerator*
*Freeze Not suitable*
*Microwave Snow peas and squash suitable*

Sesame chicken and mandarin salad,
*below*

Lightly oil a 1.5 litre (6-cup) ovenproof dish.

Add pasta to large pan of boiling water, boil, uncovered, until tender; drain, cool.

Heat oil in medium pan, add onion, mushrooms and chilli, cook, stirring, until onion is soft. Add spinach, cook, stirring, until liquid is evaporated. Transfer mixture to large bowl, stir in pasta, chickpeas, ricotta and fetta, milk, eggs and herbs; mix well. Pour mixture into prepared dish, sprinkle with cheddar. Bake, uncovered, in moderate oven about 1 hour or until set.

□ SERVES 6 TO 8

*Storage Covered, in refrigerator*
*Freeze Not suitable*
*Microwave Onion mixture and pasta suitable*

Chicken and herb mayonnaise bagels, *left*
Cheesy spinach pasta pie, *above*

# Baked TORTELLINI with pesto

*Recipe can be made a day ahead*

2 medium (500g) red capsicums
2 small (500g) eggplants, sliced
$1/4$ cup (60ml) olive oil
750g veal tortellini pasta
2 x 500ml jars tomato pasta sauce
2 tablespoons chopped
   fresh oregano

### Pesto

1 cup firmly packed fresh basil
2 cloves garlic, crushed
1 cup (80g) grated
   parmesan cheese
1 cup (150g) roasted
   unsalted cashews
$3/4$ cup (180ml) olive oil
$1/3$ cup (80ml) water

### Cheese topping

1 cup (200g) ricotta cheese
200g fetta cheese, crumbled
2 cloves garlic, crushed
2 tablespoons chopped
   fresh oregano

Quarter capsicums, remove seeds and membranes. Roast under grill or in very hot oven, skin side up, until skin blisters and blackens. Cover capsicum pieces in plastic or paper 5 minutes, peel away skin, cut capsicums into thin strips. Brush eggplant slices on both sides with oil; grill until browned on both sides.

Add tortellini to large pan of boiling water, simmer, uncovered, until just tender; drain.

Combine tortellini, pasta sauce and oregano in large bowl. Spoon tortellini mixture over base of oiled 3 litre (12-cup) ovenproof dish. Top tortellini mixture with pesto then eggplant; spread with cheese topping. Arrange capsicum strips in lattice pattern over cheese topping.

Bake, uncovered, in moderate oven about 45 minutes or until browned.

**Pesto** Blend or process basil, garlic, cheese and cashews until combined. Add oil in thin stream while motor is operating; blend until combined. Add water gradually, blend until smooth and creamy.

**Cheese topping** Combine all ingredients in medium bowl.

□ SERVES 8 TO 10

***Storage*** *Covered, in refrigerator*
***Freeze*** *Suitable*
***Microwave*** *Not suitable*

# Sweet and sour STIR-FRY with noodles

*Recipe best made just before serving*

1 medium (350g) golden
   nugget pumpkin
250g asparagus
1 medium (120g) carrot
100g sugar snap peas
300g Hokkien noodles
2 teaspoons peanut oil
375g packet firm tofu,
   drained, cubed
2 cloves garlic, crushed
2 teaspoons grated fresh ginger
2 sticks celery, thinly sliced
1 medium (1.2kg) pineapple,
   chopped
$1/3$ cup (80ml) tomato sauce
1 tablespoon brown malt vinegar
1 tablespoon brown sugar
3 teaspoons cornflour
$2/3$ cup (160ml) water

Cut pumpkin in half, remove seeds, cut each half into 6 wedges. Cut asparagus into 3cm pieces and carrot into long thin strips. Boil, steam or microwave pumpkin, asparagus, carrot and peas separately until just tender; drain. Rinse under cold water; drain well.

Placed noodles in heatproof bowl, cover with boiling water, stir to separate; drain.

Add oil to heated wok or large pan, add tofu in batches, stir-fry until browned lightly; drain on absorbent paper. Add garlic, ginger and celery to wok, stir-fry 2 minutes. Add vegetables, pineapple, noodles, sauce, vinegar, sugar and blended cornflour and water; cook, stirring, until sauce boils and thickens slightly; stir in tofu.

□ SERVES 4

*Freeze  Not suitable*
*Microwave  Pumpkin, asparagus, carrots and snow peas suitable*

# SPINACH and fetta pie

*Spinach filling can be made day a ahead*

**500g broccoli, chopped**
**3 cups (450g) plain flour**
**10g packet instant dry yeast**
**$^1/_2$ teaspoon sugar**
**$^1/_2$ teaspoon salt**
**$^1/_4$ teaspoon chilli powder**
**$^1/_3$ cup (25g) grated**
**parmesan cheese**
**$^1/_4$ cup (60ml) olive oil**

**$1^1/_4$ cups (310ml) warm water, approximately**
**$^1/_2$ cup (100g) ricotta cheese**
**100g fetta cheese, crumbled**
**1 tablespoon grated parmesan cheese, extra**

### Spinach filling

**1 tablespoon olive oil**
**1 medium (150g) onion, finely chopped**
**2 cloves garlic, crushed**
**1 tablespoon chopped fresh thyme**
**2 bunches (1kg) English spinach, roughly chopped**

Lightly oil 31cm pizza pan. Add broccoli to large pan of boiling water, boil 1 minute, drain, rinse under cold water; drain well.

Sift flour into large bowl, stir in yeast, sugar, salt, chilli and parmesan. Make well in centre, stir in oil and enough water to mix to firm dough. Knead on floured surface, 10 minutes or until smooth and elastic. Transfer dough to large oiled bowl. Cover; stand in warm place about 1 hour or until doubled in size.

Turn dough onto floured surface, knead until smooth. Halve dough, roll half until large enough to line prepared pan. Spread spinach filling over dough, leaving 3cm border, top with broccoli, ricotta and fetta. Roll remaining dough until large enough to cover pie, seal edges with fork.

Bake, uncovered, in moderately hot oven for 30 minutes, sprinkle with extra parmesan, bake 10 minutes or until browned.

**Spinach filling**  Heat oil in pan, add onion, garlic and thyme, cook, stirring, until onion is soft. Add spinach, cook, stirring, until spinach is wilted and most of the liquid is evaporated.

□ SERVES 4 TO 6

*Storage  Covered, in refrigerator*
*Freeze  Not suitable*
*Microwave  Filling suitable*

Baked tortellini with pesto, *left*
Spinach and fetta pie, Sweet and sour stir-fry with noodles, *above, from left*

# Chilli LAMB kebabs

*Recipe can be prepared a day ahead*

**1kg lamb fillets**
**$^1/_2$ cup (125ml) olive oil**
**1 small fresh red chilli,**
   **seeded, chopped**
**2 tablespoons chopped**
   **fresh thyme**
**4 cloves garlic, crushed**
**2 tablespoons grated lemon rind**
**$^1/_3$ cup (80ml) lemon juice**
**1 teaspoon cracked black pepper**

Soak 18 bamboo skewers in water for
1 hour.

Cut lamb in 3cm pieces. Combine
with remaining ingredients in large
bowl. Cover, refrigerate 3 hours or
overnight.

Thread lamb onto prepared
skewers. Grill or barbecue kebabs until
lamb is browned and tender.

□ SERVES 6

**Storage**  *Covered, in refrigerator*
**Freeze**  *Marinated lamb suitable*
**Microwave**  *Not suitable*

# EGGPLANT cake with
# tomato sauce

*Recipe can be made a day ahead*

**2 tablespoons packaged**
   **breadcrumbs**
**2 large (1kg) eggplants**
**salt**
**1 tablespoon olive oil**
**440g can new potatoes,**
   **drained, sliced**

### Mince layer

**2 teaspoons olive oil**
**500g minced beef**
**1 clove garlic, crushed**
**$^1/_2$ teaspoon ground cumin**
**2 tablespoons plain flour**
**410g can tomatoes,**
   **undrained, crushed**
**1 tablespoon tomato paste**
**1 teaspoon sugar**
**1 egg white, lightly beaten**

### Tomato sauce

**1 tablespoon olive oil**
**1 medium (350g) leek, chopped**
**1 clove garlic, crushed**
**2 large (500g) tomatoes,**
 **seeded, chopped**
**$1/4$ cup (60ml) dry red wine**
**$1/4$ cup (60ml) tomato sauce**
**2 tablespoons shredded fresh basil**

Lightly oil deep 22cm round cake pan; sprinkle with crumbs.

Cut eggplants into slices 5mm thick, sprinkle with salt, let stand for 30 minutes.

Rinse eggplants under cold running water, drain, pat dry.

Brush both sides of eggplants with oil, grill until browned lightly on both sides; drain on absorbent paper.

Line base and side of prepared pan with two-thirds of the eggplants. Spoon in half the mince layer, top with potatoes, remaining mince layer, then remaining eggplants.

Bake, covered, in moderate oven about 1 hour or until firm. Stand 5 minutes before turning out.

Serve hot or cold with tomato sauce.

**Mince layer** Heat oil in large pan, add mince, garlic and cumin, cook, stirring, until mince is well browned. Remove from heat, stir in flour, tomatoes, paste and sugar, stir over heat until mixture boils and thickens; cool. Stir in egg white.

**Tomato sauce** Heat oil in large pan, add leek and garlic, cook, stirring, until leek is soft. Add tomatoes and wine, simmer, uncovered, until reduced by a third. Add sauce and basil, stir until heated through.

□ SERVES 6

***Storage*** *Covered, in refrigerator*
***Freeze*** *Not suitable*
***Microwave*** *Tomato sauce suitable*

# PASTA with tomato, olives and artichokes

*Sauce can be prepared a day ahead*

**2 tablespoons olive oil**
**1 medium (150g) onion,**
 **finely chopped**
**2 cloves garlic, crushed**
**$1/4$ cup (60ml) dry white wine**
**2 x 425g cans tomatoes,**
 **undrained, crushed**
**2 tablespoons tomato paste**
**$1/2$ teaspoon sugar**
**2 small fresh red chillies,**
 **seeded, chopped**
**$1/2$ cup (80g) seeded black olives**
**390g can artichoke hearts,**
 **drained, quartered**
**2 tablespoons chopped**
 **fresh parsley**
**375g spiral pasta**

Heat oil in medium pan, add onion and garlic, cook, stirring, until soft. Add wine, tomatoes, paste, sugar and chillies. Simmer, uncovered, about 20 minutes or until sauce is thickened slightly. Add olives, artichokes and parsley, cook, stirring, until hot.

Meanwhile, add pasta to large pan of boiling water, boil, uncovered, until just tender; drain.

Combine pasta and half the sauce in large bowl. Serve pasta mixture topped with remaining sauce.

□ SERVES 4

***Storage*** *Sauce, covered, in refrigerator*
***Freeze*** *Not suitable*
***Microwave*** *Pasta suitable*

Chilli lamb kebabs, *top left*
Eggplant cake with tomato sauce, *left*

Pasta with tomato, olives and artichokes, *above*

## Rosemary potato WEDGES

*Recipe best made just before serving*

**6 medium (1.2kg) unpeeled potatoes**
**4 unpeeled cloves garlic**
**2 tablespoons rosemary sprigs**
**$1/4$ cup (60ml) olive oil**

Cut each potato into 8 wedges.

Combine potatoes with remaining ingredients in large baking dish.

Bake, uncovered, in moderately hot oven about 1 hour or until tender. Turn potatoes twice during cooking. Serve immediately.

☐ SERVES 4 TO 6

**Freeze** *Not suitable*
**Microwave** *Not suitable*

Rosemary potato wedges, *left*
Garlic and rosemary chicken, Roasted tomatoes and green onions, *below*

## Garlic and rosemary CHICKEN

*Recipe best made just before serving*

**1 bulb (70g) garlic**
**1.5kg chicken**
**$^1/_4$ cup (60ml) olive oil**
**$^1/_2$ cup fresh rosemary sprigs**

Break garlic bulb into cloves; do not peel. Bruise garlic, place 3 cloves in cavity of chicken.

Place 2 tablespoons of oil in baking dish, add chicken to dish; brush remaining oil over chicken. Peel a clove of remaining garlic, cut in half; rub over chicken. Place remaining garlic and rosemary around chicken.

Bake, uncovered, in moderate oven about 1$^1/_2$ hours or until chicken is tender and golden brown.

☐ SERVES 4

**Freeze** *Not suitable*
**Microwave** *Not suitable*

## Roasted TOMATOES and green onions

*Recipe can be prepared several hours ahead*

**8 large (720g) egg tomatoes**
**3 green onions, peeled**
**2 sprigs fresh oregano**
**2 tablespoons olive oil**
**1 tablespoon balsamic vinegar**
**1 tablespoon brown sugar**

Cut tomatoes in half lengthways. Place tomatoes, cut-side-up, in baking dish with onions and oregano. Drizzle with combined oil and vinegar, sprinkle with sugar.

Bake, uncovered, in moderate oven about 1$^1/_4$ hours or until tomatoes and onions are soft.

☐ SERVES 4

**Storage** *Covered, in refrigerator*
**Freeze** *Not suitable*
**Microwave** *Not suitable*

## Chicken and vegetable BURRITOS

*Flour tortillas are available
from bread section of supermarkets
Recipe best made just before serving*

**1 tablespoon vegetable oil**
**300g chicken thigh fillets,
    thinly sliced**
**2 medium (300g) onions, sliced**
**2 teaspoons ground cumin**
**2 teaspoons ground coriander**
**1 teaspoon sweet paprika**
**400g can tomatoes,
    undrained, crushed**
**2 small (140g) carrots, chopped**
**250g broccoli, chopped**
**2 tablespoons sour cream**
**4 flour tortillas**
**$^1/_2$ cup (60g) grated
    cheddar cheese**

Heat oil in large pan, add chicken in batches, cook, stirring, until browned lightly; drain on absorbent paper. Add onions to same pan, cook, stirring, until onions are soft. Add spices, cook, stirring until fragrant. Stir in tomatoes and carrots, cook, stirring, until liquid is reduced by a third.

Return chicken to pan with broccoli, cook, stirring, until broccoli is just tender and sauce is thickened; stir in cream. Divide mixture among tortillas, roll up. Serve topped with cheese.

☐ SERVES 4

**Freeze** *Not suitable*
**Microwave** *Not suitable*

Chicken and vegetable burritos, *below*

# present perfect
*a gift for all seasons*

## Tomato caper TAPENADE

*Recipe can be made 3 days ahead*

¾ cup (80g) drained sun-dried
   tomatoes, chopped
¼ cup (60ml) olive oil
¼ cup (45g) drained capers
2 cloves garlic, crushed
1 teaspoon grated lemon rind
1 tablespoon lemon juice
1 teaspoon chopped fresh thyme

Process all ingredients until finely minced. Pack tightly into hot sterilised jars. Seal immediately.

MAKES ABOUT 1 CUP (250ML)

**Storage**  *Refrigerator for 2 weeks*
**Freeze**  *Not suitable*

## Seed CRACKERS

*Recipe can be made a week ahead*

1 cup (150g) plain flour
30g butter
1 tablespoon poppy seeds
1 tablespoon sesame seeds
1 egg, lightly beaten
1 tablespoon water
2 teaspoons milk
1 tablespoon coarse sea salt

Sift flour into medium bowl, rub in butter, stir in seeds.

Add egg and enough water to make ingredients cling together. Knead on floured surface, until smooth.

Divide dough into quarters, roll each portion to 1mm thick. Place on lightly oiled oven trays, brush with milk, sprinkle with salt.

Bake, uncovered, in moderate oven 10 minutes or until well browned. Cool on wire rack.

**Storage**  *Airtight container*
**Freeze**  *Suitable*
**Microwave**  *Not suitable*

## Chilli and lemon grass flavoured OLIVES

*Recipe best made a week ahead*

1 lime
600g drained pickled black olives
1½ teaspoons cumin seeds
¼ cup chopped fresh lemon grass
1 (about 25g) pickling onion,
   finely chopped
2 small fresh red chillies,
   finely chopped
3 cups (750ml) hot olive oil,
   approximately

Using a vegetable peeler, peel rind from lime; cut rind into fine strips. Combine rind, olives, seeds, lemon grass, onion and chillies in bowl.

Place olive mixture into hot sterilised 1-litre (4-cup) jar; pour in enough oil (taking care as it will bubble) to leave 1cm space between olives and top of jar; seal while hot.

**Storage**  *Refrigerator, for 6 months*
**Freeze**  *Not suitable*
**Microwave**  *Not suitable*

Savoury cheese rounds,
Chilli and lemon grass flavoured olives,
*below, from left*

## Savoury CHEESE rounds

*Recipe can be made 2 days ahead*

250g packet cream cheese
3 cups (375g) grated
   cheddar cheese
½ cup gherkin relish
100g ham, chopped
2 green onions, chopped
½ cup (40g) flaked
   almonds, toasted

Process cheeses and relish until smooth, add ham and onions, process until combined. Shape mixture into 3 balls, flatten slightly to form rounds, cover, refrigerate until firm.

Coat rounds with almonds. Refrigerate, covered, until required.

**Storage**  *Covered, in refrigerator*
**Freeze**  *Not suitable*

*above, clockwise from left*
Tomato caper tapenade,
Seed crackers,
Chilli and lemon grass flavoured olives,

## Decadent MUD CAKE stars

*Recipe can be made 2 days ahead*

    350g butter, melted
    3 cups (660g) caster sugar
    6 eggs
    ¾ cup (75g) cocoa powder
    ¾ cup (110g) plain flour
    ¾ cup (110g) self-raising flour
    paper stars
    cocoa powder, extra
    icing sugar mixture

Grease a 26cm x 32cm Swiss roll pan. Cover base with 2 layers of baking paper, extend paper 3cm above sides.

Whisk butter and sugar in large bowl until combined. Whisk in eggs, one at a time, whisking between additions. Whisk in sifted cocoa and flours. Pour mixture into prepared pan.

Bake uncovered in moderate oven 30 minutes. Cover with foil, bake 1 hour; leave covered, cool.

Invert cake onto board, cut out 5cm

stars. Place paper stars in centre of cakes, dust half with sifted extra cocoa and half with sifted icing sugar; remove paper stars carefully.

MAKES ABOUT 30

*Storage*  *Airtight container, in refrigerator*
*Freeze*  *Suitable*
*Microwave*  *Not suitable*

## Little gift CAKES

*Recipe can be made a month ahead*

    5 cups (1kg) mixed dried fruit
    ¼ cup (35g) slivered
        almonds, toasted
    2 tablespoons sweet sherry
    1¼ cups (250g) firmly packed
        brown sugar
    250g butter, chopped
    ½ cup (125ml) milk
    3 eggs, lightly beaten
    3 cups (450g) plain flour
    ½ teaspoon bicarbonate of soda
    2 teaspoons mixed spice
    ¾ cup (180ml) apricot jam,
        warmed, strained
    1 kg packaged fondant (soft icing)
    icing sugar mixture
    red powdered food colouring
    ribbons and raffia

Grease deep 19cm square cake pan, cover base and sides with 3 layers baking paper, extend paper 5cm above edge of pan.

Combine fruit, nuts, sherry and sugar in large bowl.

Combine butter and milk in small pan, stir over heat, without boiling, until butter is melted. Add butter

mixture, eggs and sifted flour, soda and spice to fruit mixture; mix well. Spread mixture into prepared pan.

Bake uncovered, in very slow oven 5 hours. Cover hot cake tightly with foil, invert cake onto board; cool upside down in pan.

Cut cake into 9 even pieces, split each piece in half horizontally to give 18 cakes. Brush sides and tops of cakes with ½ cup (125ml) of jam.

Knead fondant until smooth on surface dusted with sifted icing sugar.

Tint fondant by kneading in food colouring mixed with a little hot water. Cover fondant with plastic wrap until ready to use.

Divide fondant into 18 pieces. Using hands dusted with icing sugar, roll out each piece between sheets of baking paper until large enough to cover top and sides of cake. Lift fondant onto cake then lightly mould fondant onto cake; trim edges neatly. Repeat with remaining fondant and cakes. Scraps can be cut to make decorative shapes. Secure shapes to cakes with a little of remaining jam.

Decorate cakes with ribbons and raffia.

☐ MAKES 18

*Storage*  *Airtight container, at room temperature*
*Freeze*  *Uniced cakes suitable*
*Microwave*  *Butter mixture suitable*

Decadent mud cake stars,
Little gift cakes, *below, from left*

# PORK and pineapple stir-fry

*Recipe best made just before serving*

**500g pork fillet, sliced**

**1 tablespoon vegetable oil**

**440g can pineapple pieces, drained**

**125g broccoli, chopped**

**125g mushrooms, sliced**

**1 small (150g) red capsicum, sliced**

**1 small (150g) yellow capsicum, sliced**

**1 small (150g) green capsicum, sliced**

**125g snow peas**

**1 cup (80g) mung bean sprouts**

### Marinade

**2 tablespoons soy sauce**

**2 tablespoons honey**

**1 clove garlic, crushed**

**1 teaspoon grated fresh ginger**

**2 tablespoons dry sherry**

Combine pork and marinade in large bowl; cover, refrigerate 3 hours or overnight.

Heat oil in wok or large pan, add undrained pork mixture, in batches, stir-fry about 3 minutes or until pork is cooked through.

Add pineapple, stir-fry about 1 minute. Add combined remaining vegetables, stir-fry about 4 minutes or until vegetables are just tender and heated through.

**Marinade** Combine all ingredients in large bowl.

☐ SERVES 4

*Storage Marinated pork, covered, in refrigerator*
***Freeze** Not suitable*
***Microwave** Suitable*

Pork and pineapple stir-fry, *above*

# Minted LAMB curry

*Ask the butcher to bone lamb for you*
*Recipe can be made a day ahead*

**1.5kg lean leg of lamb, boned**
**cooking-oil spray**
**2 large (400g) onions, sliced**
**4 cloves garlic, crushed**
**3 small fresh red chillies,**
    **seeded, chopped**
**1 teaspoon garam masala**
**1 teaspoon ground coriander**
**1 teaspoon ground turmeric**
**$^1/_2$ cup chopped fresh mint**
**$^1/_4$ cup (60ml) tomato paste**
**5 medium (650g) tomatoes,**
    **chopped**
**2 cups (500ml) beef stock**

Cut lamb into 2cm cubes. Spray base large non-stick pan with cooking-oil spray. Heat pan, add lamb in batches; cook, stirring, until browned.

Add onions and garlic to pan; cook, stirring, until soft. Add chillies and spices; cook, stirring, until fragrant.

Return lamb to pan with mint, paste, tomatoes and stock; simmer, covered, about 1 hour or until lamb is tender.

□ SERVES 4

***Storage*** *Covered, in refrigerator*
***Freeze*** *Suitable*
***Microwave*** *Not suitable*

# STEAK Diane

*Recipe best made just before serving*

**1 tablespoon olive oil**
**4 (750g) beef Scotch fillet steaks**
**30g butter**
**2 cloves garlic, crushed**
**300ml cream**
**3 teaspoons Worcestershire sauce**
**3 teaspoons brandy**

Heat oil in large pan, add steaks, cook, about 3 minutes each side or until cooked as desired, remove from pan; cover to keep warm.

Add butter and garlic to pan, stir over heat 30 seconds. Add cream, sauce and brandy; simmer, uncovered, about 2 minutes or until thickened slightly. Pour sauce over steaks.

□ SERVES 4

***Freeze*** *Not suitable*
***Microwave*** *Not suitable*

Minted lamb curry, *top*
Steak diane, *above*

# Italian VEAL roll

*Ask the butcher to bone veal for you*
*Recipe can be made 2 days ahead*

**1 tablespoon olive oil**
**1 medium (150g) onion,**
  **finely chopped**
**1 clove garlic, crushed**
**250g pork and veal mince**
**$1/2$ cup (40g) grated**
  **parmesan cheese**
**$1/4$ cup chopped fresh basil**
**$3/4$ cup (45g) stale breadcrumbs**
**12 slices spicy salami**
**$1/4$ cup (35g) drained sun-**
  **dried tomatoes**
**1kg veal shoulder, boned**

Heat oil in large pan, add onion and garlic, cook, stirring, until onion is soft; cool. Combine onion mixture mince, cheese, basil and crumbs in medium bowl.

Arrange salami slices on a large sheet of greaseproof paper to form 17cm x 21cm rectangle, overlapping edges of salami. Spread mince mixture evenly over salami.

Place tomatoes along centre of mince mixture, roll up salami using paper as a guide.

Trim excess fat from veal, pound veal with meat mallet until even thickness. Place salami roll on veal, roll up veal to enclose salami; secure with string at 3cm intervals. Place veal in baking dish.

Bake, uncovered, in moderate oven about $1^1/4$ hours or until cooked through; cool.

Cover, refrigerate several hours or overnight before serving.

□ SERVES 4

**Storage** *Covered, in refrigerator*
**Freeze** *Not suitable*
**Microwave** *Not suitable*

# Kumara and capsicum PIE

*Recipe can be made a day ahead*

**2 medium (400g) red capsicums**
**1 large (200g) onion, chopped**
**1 clove garlic, crushed**
**1kg old potatoes, chopped**
**1kg kumara, chopped**
**2 tablespoons olive oil**
**2 teaspoons chicken stock powder**
**$1/3$ cup (25g) finely grated**
  **parmesan cheese**
**$1/3$ cup chopped fresh basil**
**1 egg, lightly beaten**
**1 cup (70g) stale breadcrumbs**
**$2/3$ cup (100g) seeded black**
  **olives, chopped**
**$1^1/3$ cups chopped fresh**
  **flat-leaf parsley**
**200g fetta cheese, crumbled**
**1 tablespoon grated parmesan**
  **cheese, extra**

Lightly oil 24cm springform tin, line base and side with baking paper.

Quarter capsicums, remove seeds and membranes. Roast under grill or in very hot oven, skin side up, until skin blisters and blackens. Cover capsicum pieces in plastic or paper 5 minutes, peel away skin, chop capsicums.

Add onion and garlic to heated small non-stick pan, cook, stirring, until onion is soft.

Boil, steam or microwave potatoes and kumara until tender; drain. Mash potatoes and kumara with oil, stock powder and parmesan until smooth; stir in basil, egg and crumbs.

Spread half the potato mixture over base of prepared tin, top with capsicums, onion mixture, olives, parsley and fetta. Spread remaining potato mixture over fetta layer, sprinkle with extra parmesan.

Bake, uncovered, in moderately hot oven about 50 minutes or until browned and firm. Stand 15 minutes before serving.

□ SERVES 8

**Storage** *Covered, in refrigerator*
**Freeze** *Not suitable*
**Microwave** *Potatoes and kumara suitable*

Kumara and capsicum pie, *below*

Italian veal roll, *left*

# Spiced FISH with yogurt cucumber sauce

*Yogurt cucumber sauce can be made several hours ahead  Spiced fish is best made just before serving*

**4 (about 600g) white fish fillets**
**¹/₃ cup (50g) plain flour**
**2 tablespoons ground cumin**
**1 tablespoon ground coriander**
**2 teaspoons chilli powder**
**1 teaspoon garlic powder**
**vegetable oil, for shallow-frying**

### Yogurt cucumber sauce

**1 small (130g) Lebanese cucumber, seeded, thinly sliced**
**1 cup (250ml) plain yogurt**
**1 clove garlic, crushed**

Toss fish in combined flour, cumin, coriander, chilli and garlic; shake away excess flour mixture.

Shallow-fry fish in hot oil until browned lightly and cooked through; drain on absorbent paper. Serve with yogurt cucumber sauce.

**Yogurt cucumber sauce**  Combine all ingredients in small bowl.

□ SERVES 4

*Storage  Yogurt cucumber sauce, covered, in refrigerator*
*Freeze  Not suitable*
*Microwave  Not suitable*

Spiced fish with yogurt cucumber sauce, *above right,clockwise from top left,* Bok choy rice salad, Indonesian gado gado, Prawn, lime and noodle salad

# Indonesian GADO gado

*Recipe can be prepared 3 hours ahead*

**¹/₄ cup (60ml) peanut oil**
**375g packet firm tofu, drained, sliced**
**¹/₄ medium (200g) Chinese cabbage, finely shredded**
**1 large (500g) kumara**
**150g snow peas**
**1¹/₄ cups (120g) mung bean sprouts**
**4 hard-boiled eggs, quartered**
**1 medium (160g) green cucumber, thinly sliced**
**¹/₄ cup loosely packed coriander leaves**

### Peanut sauce

**³/₄ cup (110g) unsalted roasted peanuts**
**1¹/₄ cups (300ml) coconut milk**
**2 green onions, chopped**
**¹/₄ cup (65g) peanut butter**
**2 tablespoons fish sauce**
**1 teaspoon sambal oelek**
**2 teaspoons sugar**

Heat 2 tablespoons oil in medium pan, add tofu; cook until browned on both sides; drain on absorbent paper.

Heat remaining oil in clean pan, add cabbage; cook, stirring, until just wilted; cool.

Slice kumara into long, thin strips. Boil, steam or microwave snow peas and kumara separately until just tender; drain, rinse under cold water; drain well.

Just before serving, place kumara on serving plate, drizzle with a little of the peanut sauce. Repeat layering with remaining vegetables, eggs, tofu and peanut sauce. Serve topped with coriander leaves.

**Peanut sauce**  Blend or process peanuts until roughly chopped. Add remaining ingredients, blend  until combined.

□ SERVES 6

*Storage  Covered, in refrigerator*
*Freeze  Not suitable*
*Microwave  Vegetables suitable*

# Bok choy rice SALAD

*You will need to cook about
1 cup (200g) rice for this recipe  Recipe
can be prepared 3 hours ahead*

**2 bunches (800g) baby bok choy**
**1 medium (200g) yellow
capsicum, chopped**
**1 medium (200g) red
capsicum, chopped**
**200g snow peas, halved**
**1¼ cups (120g) mung bean sprouts**
**3 cups cooked long-grain rice**
**2 green onions, sliced**
**2 medium (240g) carrots, sliced**
**½ cup (75g) unsalted
roasted peanuts**

### Dressing

**½ cup (125ml) vegetable oil**
**2 tablespoons lemon juice**
**¼ cup (60ml) mild sweet
chilli sauce**
**2 tablespoons soy sauce**
**2 teaspoons sesame oil**
**2 teaspoons grated fresh ginger**
**2 cloves garlic, crushed**

Cut bok choy leaves from stems. Add stems to large pan of boiling water, simmer, uncovered, 1 minute. Add leaves to pan, drain immediately; rinse under cold water, drain well.

Just before serving, combine bok choy, remaining ingredients and dressing in bowl.

**Dressing**  Combine all ingredients in jar; shake well.

□ SERVES 6

***Storage***  *Covered, in refrigerator*
***Freeze***  *Not suitable*
***Microwave***  *Bok choy suitable*

# Prawn, lime and NOODLE salad

*Recipe best made close to serving*

**200g thin rice stick noodles**
**800g medium cooked prawns**
**200g snow peas, thinly sliced**
**250g teardrop tomatoes, halved**
**8 green onions, thinly sliced**

**1 large (350g) red capsicum,
thinly sliced**
**½ cup loosely packed fresh coriander**

### Dressing

**1 tablespoon finely chopped fresh
lemon grass**
**¼ cup (60ml) mild sweet
chilli sauce**
**¼ cup (60ml) lime juice**
**¼ cup (60ml) vinegar**

Place noodles in heatproof bowl, cover with boiling water, stand 10 minutes or until softened; drain.

Shell and devein prawns, leaving tails intact.

Boil, steam or microwave snow peas until just tender.

Combine noodles, prawns, snow peas, tomatoes, onions, capsicum, coriander and dressing in large serving bowl; combine gently.

**Dressing**  Combine all ingredients in jar; shake well.

□ SERVES 4

***Freeze***  *Not suitable*
***Microwave***  *Suitable*

# Chilli lemon OCTOPUS

*Recipe best prepared a day ahead*

**2kg baby octopus**
**1 tablespoon grated lemon rind**
**³/₄ cup (180ml) lemon juice**
**¹/₄ cup (60ml) olive oil**
**2 tablespoons hot chilli sauce**
**4 cloves garlic, crushed**

Remove and discard heads and beaks from octopus, cut octopus in half. Combine octopus, rind, juice, oil, sauce and garlic in large bowl. Cover, refrigerate 3 hours or overnight.

Drain octopus from marinade; discard marinade.

Add octopus to heated oiled griddle pan (or barbecue or grill); cook over high heat until just tender.

☐ SERVES 4 TO 6

**Storage** *Covered, in refrigerator*
**Freeze** *Marinated octopus suitable*
**Microwave** *Not suitable*

Chilli lemon octopus, *above*

# FISH with mustard buttermilk dressing

*We used snapper cutlets  Buttermilk dressing can be made a day ahead*

**1 tablespoon Dijon mustard**
**1 small clove garlic, crushed**
**1 tablespoon lemon juice**
**¹/₃ cup (80ml) sour cream**
**¹/₃ cup (80ml) buttermilk**
**1 green onion, chopped**
**¹/₄ teaspoon sugar**
**8 medium (720g) white fish cutlets**

# SALMON and dill
## tortellini salad

*Recipe can be prepared several hours ahead*

**375g ricotta tortellini pasta**
**415g can salmon, drained, flaked**
**1 tablespoon drained capers**
**2 sticks celery, sliced**
**1 small (130g) Lebanese**
    **cucumber, sliced thinly**

### Dill dressing

**$1/_2$ cup (125ml) plain yogurt**
**2 teaspoons seeded mustard**
**$1/_4$ cup (60ml) Italian salad dressing**
**2 teaspoons chopped fresh dill**
**2 tablespoons water**
**1 teaspoon sugar**

Add tortellini to large pan of boiling water, simmer, uncovered until just tender; drain. Rinse under cold water; drain well, cool.

Combine tortellini, salmon and remaining ingredients in large bowl. Just before serving, drizzle with dill dressing.

**Dill dressing** Whisk all ingredients together in small bowl.

□ SERVES 6

***Storage*** *Covered, in refrigerator*
***Freeze*** *Not suitable*
***Microwave*** *Tortellini suitable*

Salmon and dill tortellini salad,
Fish with mustard buttermilk dressing,
*below, from top*

Whisk mustard, garlic, juice and cream in small bowl until combined. Add buttermilk, onion and sugar; whisk well. Add fish to heated oiled griddle pan (or barbecue or grill); cook until cooked through. Serve with buttermilk dressing.

□ SERVES 4

***Storage*** *Buttermilk dressing, covered, in refrigerator*
***Freeze*** *Not suitable*
***Microwave*** *Not suitable*

# Vegetable-filled CAPSICUMS

*Recipe can be prepared a day ahead*

4 medium (800g) red capsicums
2 tablespoons olive oil
2 medium (700g) leeks, chopped
1¹/₂ tablespoons chopped
    fresh rosemary
4 cloves garlic, crushed
6 small (500g) zucchini, chopped
300g button mushrooms, halved
2 x 400g cans artichoke hearts,
    drained, quartered
1 cup (120g) seeded black olives
¹/₂ cup (125ml) pesto
²/₃ cup (50g) flaked
    parmesan cheese

Halve capsicums, remove seeds and membranes; place halves in large baking dish.

Heat oil in pan, add leeks, rosemary and garlic; cook, stirring, until leeks are soft. Add zucchini, mushrooms, artichokes and olives; cook, stirring, until zucchini begins to soften.

Divide zucchini mixture among capsicums.

Bake, covered, in moderately hot oven about 45 minutes or until capsicums and filling are tender. Serve topped with pesto and cheese.

☐ MAKES 8

**Storage** *Covered, in refrigerator*
**Freeze** *Not suitable*
**Microwave** *Suitable*

Vegetable-filled capsicums, *below*
Mango chicken salad with lime
dressing, *above right*
Bok choy, pork and noodle stir-fry, *right*

# Mango chicken SALAD with lime dressing

*Recipe can be prepared several hours ahead*

2 medium (850g) mangoes
2 medium (240g) carrots
2 medium (240g) zucchini
1 medium (200g) red
    capsicum, sliced
1 medium (200g) yellow
    capsicum, sliced
1¹/₂ cups (160g) mung bean sprouts
4 green onions, sliced
¹/₄ cup chopped fresh coriander
4 cups (600g) roughly chopped
    cooked chicken
1 cup (150g) unsalted
    roasted cashews

### Lime dressing

2 tablespoons mild sweet
    chilli sauce
¹/₄ cup chopped fresh coriander
2 cloves garlic, crushed
2 fresh red chillies,
    seeded, chopped
¹/₄ cup (60ml) lime juice
1 egg yolk
1 cup (250ml) vegetable oil

Cut cheeks from mango as close to seed as possible. Using tip of sharp knife, make about 4 cuts through flesh, without cutting through skin. Make another 4 cuts in the opposite direction. Turn mango cheek inside out by pressing skin gently in the centre. Cut away mango flesh from skin. The remaining strip of mango can be cut from seed, if desired. Repeat with remaining mango.

Peel strips lengthways from the carrots and zucchini with a vegetable peeler.

Just before serving, combine mangoes, vegetable strips and remaining ingredients in large bowl; drizzle with lime dressing.

**Lime dressing** Blend or process all ingredients until creamy.

☐ SERVES 6 TO 8

**Storage** *Covered, in refrigerator*
**Freeze** *Not suitable*

## Bok choy, pork and noodle STIR-FRY

*Recipe best made just before serving*

**500g Hokkien noodles**
**1 tablespoon vegetable oil**
**$^1/_2$ teaspoon sesame oil**
**400g pork fillet, thinly sliced**
**1 tablespoon vegetable oil, extra**
**2 medium (300g) onions, sliced**
**1 clove garlic, crushed**
**1 medium (200g) red**
    **capsicum, sliced**
**230g can bamboo shoots, undrained**
**1 bunch (400g) baby**
    **bok choy, chopped**
**$^1/_4$ cup (60ml) oyster sauce**
**$^1/_4$ cup (60ml) water**

Place noodles in medium heatproof bowl, cover with boiling water, stir to separate; drain.

Heat oils in wok or large pan, stir-fry pork, in batches, until browned and tender; remove from wok. Heat extra oil in wok, add onions and garlic; stir-fry until onions are soft. Add capsicum, bamboo shoots and bok choy, stir-fry until bok choy is just wilted. Return pork to wok with noodles, sauce and water, cook, stirring, until heated through.

□ SERVES 4

***Freeze*** *Not suitable*
***Microwave*** *Noodles suitable*

## Coriander pork and veal PATTIES

*You will need to cook about $^2/_3$ cup (130g) rice  Recipe can be prepared a day ahead*

- **500g minced pork and veal**
- **2 cups cooked white rice**
- **$^1/_4$ cup (60ml) coconut milk**
- **1 small (80g) onion, grated**
- **1 tablespoon Thai red curry paste**
- **2 tablespoons chopped fresh coriander**

Combine all ingredients in large bowl. Shape mixture into 12 patties. Add patties, in batches, to heated oiled griddle pan (or barbecue or grill); cook until browned on both sides. Place patties on oven tray.

Bake, uncovered, in moderately hot oven about 10 minutes or until cooked through.

□ SERVES 4

*Storage  Covered, in refrigerator*
*Freeze  Uncooked patties suitable*
*Microwave  Rice suitable*

## SEAFOOD rice stir-fry

*You will need to cook about 2 cups (400g) rice  Recipe can be prepared a day ahead*

- **6 cups cooked long-grain rice**
- **6 Chinese dried mushrooms**
- **500g uncooked medium prawns**
- **500g white fish fillets**
- **2 tablespoons peanut oil**
- **1 medium (150g) onion, thinly sliced**
- **1 teaspoon sesame oil**
- **1 clove garlic, crushed**
- **1 tablespoon grated fresh ginger**
- **1 medium (200g) red capsicum, chopped**
- **1 medium (120g) carrot, thinly sliced**
- **2 sticks celery, sliced**
- **100g snow peas**
- **$^3/_4$ cup (80g) mung bean sprouts**
- **6 green onions, sliced**
- **$^1/_4$ cup (60ml) oyster sauce**
- **$^1/_4$ cup (60ml) hoisin sauce**
- **1 tablespoon fish sauce**

Spread cooked rice on tray, cover with absorbent paper; refrigerate overnight.

Place mushrooms in small heatproof bowl, cover with boiling water, stand 20 minutes. Drain mushrooms, discard stems, slice caps thinly.

Shell and devein prawns, leaving tails intact. Cut fish into 2cm cubes.

Heat half the peanut oil in large wok or pan, add onion, stir-fry until onion is soft. Add sesame oil, garlic, ginger and prawns, stir-fry until just tender; remove from wok.

Heat remaining oil in wok, add fish, stir-fry until cooked through; remove from wok. Add capsicum, carrot, celery and peas to wok, stir-fry until vegetables are just tender.

Return prawn mixture to wok with mushrooms, fish, rice, sprouts, green onions and sauces; cook, stirring, until hot. Serve immediately.

□ SERVES 6

*Storage  Covered, in refrigerator*
*Freeze  Not suitable*
*Microwave  Rice suitable*

# POTATO, bacon and dill salad

*If kipfler potatoes are unavailable,
substitute baby new potatoes*
*Recipe can be prepared several hours ahead*

**1kg kipfler potatoes**
**3 bacon rashers, chopped**
**2 small (200g) red onions, sliced**
**2 tablespoons drained baby capers**
**2 tablespoons chopped fresh dill**
**1/4 cup chopped fresh
    flat-leaf parsley**

### Dressing

**1/3 cup (80ml) lemon juice**
**1/3 cup (80ml) olive oil**
**2 cloves garlic, crushed**
**1/2 teaspoon balsamic vinegar**
**1/2 teaspoon sugar**
**1/2 teaspoon cracked black pepper**

Add unpeeled potatoes to large pan of
boiling water, simmer, uncovered,
until just tender, drain, cool. Cut
potatoes into 3cm lengths.

Add bacon to heated dry pan, cook,
stirring, until crisp; drain on absorbent
paper. Combine potatoes, bacon,
onions, capers, herbs and dressing;
toss gently.

**Dressing** Combine all ingredients in
jar; shake well.

□ SERVES 6

**Storage**  *Covered in refrigerator*
**Freeze**  *Not suitable*
**Microwave**  *Suitable*

# Sticky plum SPARE RIBS

*Recipe best prepared a day ahead*

**1.5kg American-style
    pork spare ribs**
**3/4 cup (180ml) plum jam**
**1/4 cup (60ml) mild sweet
    chilli sauce**
**1 tablespoon grated fresh ginger**
**2 tablespoons soy sauce**
**2 tablespoons dry sherry**
**4 star anise**
**1/2 teaspoon Szechuan
    pepper, crushed**

Add ribs to large pan of boiling water;
simmer, uncovered, about 10 minutes or
until just cooked through, drain; pat dry.

Transfer ribs to large shallow dish;
cool. Meanwhile, combine remaining
ingredients in small pan, stir over heat
until jam melts; stand 30 minutes,
discard star anise. Brush ribs all over
with jam mixture; cover, refrigerate
3 hours or overnight.

Add drained ribs to heated oiled
griddle pan (or barbecue or grill)
curved side up; cook until browned.
Turn, brush ribs with any remaining
jam mixture; cook until tender.

□ SERVES 4

**Storage**  *Covered, in refrigerator*
**Freeze**  *Not suitable*
**Microwave**  *Jam mixture suitable*

Coriander pork and veal patties,
Seafood rice stir-fry, *above left, from left*
Sticky plum spare ribs,
Potato, bacon and dill salad,
*right*

## Spicy roast CHICKEN

*Recipe can be prepared a day ahead*

**1.5kg chicken**
**1 cup (250ml) coconut milk**
**2 teaspoons Thai green curry paste**
**1 tablespoon grated fresh ginger**
**2 tablespoons lime juice**
**1 teaspoon fish sauce**
**1 small fresh red chilli,
    seeded, sliced**
**2 tablespoons chopped
    fresh coriander**

Place chicken on wire rack in baking dish. Combine coconut milk, paste, ginger, juice, sauce, chilli and coriander in small bowl.

Spoon a third of the coconut mixture into cavity of chicken, then spoon remaining mixture over chicken; cover, refrigerate at least 1 hour.

Bake, uncovered, in moderate oven $1^{1}/_{2}$ hours; brush occasionally with pan juices during cooking.

☐ SERVES 4

***Storage*** *Covered, in refrigerator*
***Freeze*** *Not suitable*
***Microwave*** *Not suitable*

## Marinated LAMB CHOPS with basil aioli

*Recipe can be prepared a day ahead*

**8 lamb chump chops**
**$^{1}/_{4}$ cup (60ml) dry red wine**
**2 tablespoons mild sweet
    chilli sauce**
**1 tablespoon white wine vinegar**
**1 tablespoon vegetable oil**
**1 tablespoon brown sugar**
**2 cloves garlic, crushed**
**2 teaspoons chopped fresh thyme**

### Basil aioli

**1 egg yolk**
**2 teaspoons balsamic vinegar**
**1 teaspoon French mustard**
**$^{1}/_{3}$ cup shredded fresh basil**
**1 clove garlic, crushed**
**$^{1}/_{2}$ cup (125ml) olive oil**
**1 tablespoon hot water,
    approximately**

Trim excess fat from chops. Place chops in shallow dish, pour over combined wine, sauce, vinegar, oil, sugar, garlic, and thyme. Cover, refrigerate several hours or overnight.

Drain chops over bowl; reserve marinade. Add chops to heated oiled griddle pan (or barbecue or grill) and cook until tender, turning once and brushing occasionally with reserved marinade. Serve chops with basil aioli.
**Basil aioli** Process egg yolk, vinegar, mustard, basil and garlic until smooth. Add oil in a thin stream while motor is operating; process until thick. Add enough water to give desired consistency.

☐ SERVES 4

***Storage*** *Covered, in refrigerator*
***Freeze*** *Marinated chops suitable*
***Microwave*** *Not suitable*

## Szechuan barbecued LAMB

*Ask the butcher to butterfly the lamb for you  Recipe best prepared a day ahead*

**2kg leg of lamb, butterflied**
**2 cloves garlic, crushed**
**2 teaspoons sesame oil**
**1 teaspoon five spice powder**
**1 teaspoon Szechuan pepper**
**1 tablespoon grated fresh ginger**
**$^{1}/_{3}$ cup (80ml) soy sauce**
**$^{1}/_{4}$ cup (60ml) dry sherry**
**2 tablespoons chopped
    fresh coriander**
**2 tablespoons honey**

Place lamb in shallow dish. Pour over combined remaining ingredients; turn lamb to coat. Cover, refrigerate 3 hours or overnight.

Drain lamb over bowl; reserve marinade. Cook lamb in heated, covered barbecue (or in moderately hot oven), brushing with marinade during cooking, about 45 minutes or until tender.

☐ SERVES 6

***Storage*** *Covered, in refrigerator*
***Freeze*** *Marinated lamb suitable*
***Microwave*** *Not suitable*

Spicy roast chicken, *above left*
Thyme-roasted capsicums and tomatoes, above *right*
Marinated lamb chops with basil aioli, Szechuan barbecued lamb, *right, from left*

# Thyme-roasted CAPSICUMS and tomatoes

*Recipe best made just before serving*

- **2 medium (400g) red capsicums**
- **2 medium (400g) green capsicums**
- **2 medium (400g) yellow capsicums**
- **4 small (520g) tomatoes, halved**
- **1 clove garlic, thinly sliced**
- **1 teaspoon sugar**
- **1 teaspoon cracked black pepper**
- **1 tablespoon chopped fresh thyme**
- **2 tablespoons olive oil**
- **1 tablespoon balsamic vinegar**

Cut capsicums into strips 3cm thick. Combine capsicums, tomatoes and garlic in large baking dish; sprinkle with combined sugar, pepper and thyme; drizzle with oil.

Bake, uncovered, in hot oven about 45 minutes or until vegetables are tender. Drizzle with vinegar just before serving.

☐ SERVES 6

**Freeze** *Not suitable*
**Microwave** *Not suitable*

Beef parmigiana, Pork chops with apple cream, *above left, from top*
Marinated chicken and vegetable salad, *right*

# Beef PARMIGIANA

*Recipe best made just before serving*

**2 tablespoons olive oil**
**1 medium (300g) eggplant,**
   **thinly sliced**
**4 (750g) beef Scotch fillet steaks**
**1 cup (250ml) tomato puree**
**$1/2$ cup (125ml) beef stock**
**$1/4$ cup (60ml) dry red wine**
**1 clove garlic, crushed**
**2 tablespoons shredded fresh basil**
**80g mozzarella cheese,**
   **thinly sliced**

Heat oil in pan, add eggplant in batches, cook until browned on both sides; drain on absorbent paper.

Add steaks to pan, cook until browned on both sides. Top steaks with eggplant slices in pan, add combined puree, stock, wine and garlic; simmer, uncovered, 5 minutes. Sprinkle eggplant with basil, top with cheese slices, simmer, covered, about 5 minutes or until cheese is melted.

☐ SERVES 4

**Freeze** *Not suitable*
**Microwave** *Not suitable*

## Pork CHOPS with apple cream

*Recipe best made just before serving*

**30g butter**
**2 tablespoons vegetable oil**
**1 clove garlic, crushed**
**1 teaspoon chopped fresh thyme**
**1 medium (150g) onion, sliced**
**150g button mushrooms, sliced**
**1 large (200g) red apple, sliced**
**4 pork loin chops**
**2 cups sparkling apple juice**
**2 teaspoons chopped fresh sage**
**1/2 cup (125ml) cream**
**3 teaspoons cornflour**
**2 tablespoons water**

Heat butter and half the oil in large pan, add garlic, thyme, onion, mushrooms and apple, cook, stirring, until onion is soft; remove from pan.

Add remaining oil to pan, add chops, cook on both sides until browned. Return apple mixture to pan with juice, simmer, covered, until pork is tender.

Stir in sage, cream and blended cornflour and water; stir until mixture boils and thickens slightly.

□ SERVES 4

*Freeze* Not suitable
*Microwave* Not suitable

## Marinated CHICKEN and vegetable salad

*Recipe can be prepared a day ahead*

**600g chicken breast fillets**
**8 small (560g) egg tomatoes**
**5 small (300g) finger eggplants**
**4 small (360g) zucchini**

### Marinade

**1/2 cup (125ml) lemon juice**
**2 cloves garlic, crushed**
**2 teaspoons olive oil**
**1 tablespoon chopped fresh thyme**
**1 tablespoon chopped fresh mint**
**2 teaspoons sugar**

### Mint dressing

**2 tablespoons white wine vinegar**
**1 teaspoon olive oil**
**1 teaspoon sugar**
**1 tablespoon chopped fresh mint**

Cut chicken into strips 4cm wide. Combine chicken and half the marinade in large bowl. Cover, refrigerate 3 hours or overnight.

Cut tomatoes lengthways in quarters. Cut eggplants and zucchini in half lengthways. Brush tomatoes, eggplants and zucchini with remaining marinade, cook vegetables under hot grill until tender.

Drain chicken from marinade; discard marinade. Heat large non-stick pan, add chicken in batches, cook, stirring, until browned and tender.

Return chicken to pan with tomatoes, eggplants and zucchini, cook, stirring, until hot. Serve drizzled with mint dressing.

**Marinade** Combine all ingredients in small bowl.

**Mint dressing** Combine all ingredients in jar; shake well.

□ SERVES 4

*Storage* Covered, in refrigerator
*Freeze* Not suitable
*Microwave* Not suitable

## Pear SORBET

*Recipe can be made 3 days ahead*

**825g can pears in natural juice**
**1 tablespoon lemon juice**
**1 teaspoon honey**
**1 teaspoon grated lemon rind**
**2 egg whites**

Drain pears, reserve $^{1}/_{2}$ cup (125ml) juice. Blend or process pears, reserved juice, lemon juice and honey until smooth; strain through fine sieve.

Stir in rind. Pour mixture into lamington pan, cover, freeze until almost set.

Blend or process pear mixture and egg whites until smooth, pour mixture into loaf pan; cover, freeze 3 hours or until firm.

□ SERVES 4

**Storage** *Covered, in freezer*

Pear sorbet, *above*

## Baked coconut CUSTARDS

*Recipe best made a day ahead*

**$^{1}/_{3}$ cup (80ml) golden syrup**
**$^{1}/_{4}$ cup (55g) caster sugar**
**$^{1}/_{4}$ cup (60ml) golden syrup, extra**
**280g can coconut milk**
**$^{1}/_{2}$ cup (125ml) skim milk**
**4 eggs, lightly beaten**

Divide golden syrup among 4 x 1-cup (250ml) greased ovenproof dishes.

Combine sugar and extra golden syrup in small pan, stir over heat until sugar is almost dissolved, cool slightly. Gradually stir in remaining ingredients; strain into jug.

Place prepared dishes in baking dish, pour mixture into dishes. Pour enough boiling water into baking dish to come halfway up sides of dishes.

Bake, covered, in moderately slow oven 25 minutes. Remove foil, bake another 30 minutes or until just set. Refrigerate 3 hours or overnight before serving.

□ SERVES 4

**Storage** *Covered, in refrigerator*
**Freeze** *Not suitable*
**Microwave** *Not suitable*

## Peach and macadamia GALETTE

*Recipe best made close to serving*

**2 cups (300g) self-raising flour**
**$^{1}/_{2}$ cup (80g) icing sugar mixture**
**125g cold butter, chopped**
**$^{1}/_{2}$ cup (125ml) milk**
**1 cup (125g) ground almonds**
**$^{3}/_{4}$ cup (110g) macadamias,**
**    finely chopped**
**1 tablespoon plain flour**
**8 medium (1.6kg) peaches,**
**    peeled, sliced**
**$^{1}/_{4}$ cup (50g) firmly packed**
**    brown sugar**
**1 egg white, lightly beaten**

Process flour, sugar and butter until just crumbly. Add milk gradually while motor is operating, process until ingredients are just combined – dough will be soft. Knead dough on floured surface until smooth; refrigerate 30 minutes. Roll dough on floured surface until 35cm round, place dough on greased large oven tray. Sprinkle dough with combined nuts and flour, leaving 5cm border. Overlap peaches on nut mixture, sprinkle with brown sugar; fold edge of dough over peaches. Brush dough with egg white.

Bake in moderately hot oven about 35 minutes or until browned.

□ SERVES 8

**Freeze** *Dough suitable*
**Microwave** *Not suitable*

Baked coconut custards, *right*
Peach and macadamia galette, *below*

## Creamy lime SOUFFLES

*Recipe can be made a day ahead*

**3 teaspoons gelatine**
**2 tablespoons water**
**3 eggs, separated**
**$^1/_2$ cup (110g) caster sugar**
**1 cup (250ml) hot milk**
**$^2/_3$ cup (160ml) lime juice**
**$^1/_2$ cup (125ml) cream, whipped**
**$^1/_4$ cup (20g) desiccated coconut, toasted**

Place a collar of greased foil around 4 x $^3/_4$-cup (180ml) dishes; secure.

Combine gelatine and water in a cup, stand in small pan of simmering water, stir until dissolved.

Beat egg yolks and sugar in small bowl until creamy. Whisk egg mixture into hot milk, stir over low heat, without boiling, until thickened slightly; stir in gelatine mixture and juice, cover, chill until partially set.

Whisk cream into lime mixture. Beat egg whites in small bowl until soft peaks form; fold into mixture.

Spoon into prepared dishes; refrigerate until set. Remove foil; press on coconut just before serving.

□ SERVES 4

**Storage** *Covered, in refrigerator*
**Freeze** *Not suitable*
**Microwave** *Gelatine mixture*

## Mango coconut ICE-CREAM

*Recipe can be made 3 days ahead*

**2 medium (860g) mangoes, chopped**
**1$^1/_2$ tablespoons Malibu**
**150g coconut macaroons, quartered**
**2 litres vanilla ice-cream, softened**

Blend or process mangoes and liqueur until smooth; transfer to jug. Stir macaroons into ice-cream, spoon into deep cake pan. Swirl mango puree through ice-cream; cover, freeze 5 hours or until firm.

□ SERVES 4 TO 6

**Storage** *Covered, in freezer*

# Lemon lime
## ICE-CREAM

*Recipe can be made 2 weeks ahead*

**1 teaspoon grated lime rind**
**$1/_3$ cup (80ml) lime juice**
**3 eggs, lightly beaten**
**$1/_2$ cup (110g) caster sugar**
**300ml cream**
**green food colouring**

### Lemon ice-cream

**2 teaspoons grated lemon rind**
**$1/_3$ cup (80ml) lemon juice**
**3 eggs, lightly beaten**
**$1/_4$ cup (55g) caster sugar**
**300ml cream**
**yellow food colouring**

Cover base and 2 long sides of 14cm x 21cm loaf pan with foil, bringing foil 5cm above sides.

Combine rind and juice in small pan, bring to boil, simmer, uncovered, until liquid is reduced by half; cool.

Combine eggs and sugar in top half of double saucepan, or in heatproof bowl over simmering water, whisk until thick and creamy, cover; cool.

Beat cream in small bowl until soft peaks form.

Stir rind mixture into egg mixture, fold in cream, tint with food colouring if desired. Pour mixture into prepared pan; cover, freeze until firm.

Pour lemon ice-cream over lime ice-cream, cover, freeze 3 hours or until firm. Turn ice-cream out of pan, remove foil, cut into slices before serving.

**Lemon ice-cream**  Make as for lime ice-cream.

□ SERVES 6 TO 8

***Storage***  *Covered, in freezer*
***Microwave***  *Not suitable*

Creamy lime souffles, *above left*
Mango coconut ice-cream, *below left*
Lemon lime ice-cream, *below*

**Raspberry mousse** Blend or process raspberries, sugar and liqueur until smooth, push mixture through sieve into large bowl.

Sprinkle gelatine over water in cup, stand cup in small pan of simmering water, stir until gelatine is dissolved; cool to room temperature. Stir gelatine mixture into raspberry mixture. Beat cream in small bowl until soft peaks form, fold into raspberry mixture in 2 batches, cover, refrigerate until set.

**Raspberry lime sauce** Blend or process all ingredients until smooth.

☐ SERVES 6

**Freeze** *Sauce suitable*
**Microwave** *Gelatine suitable*

Raspberry mousse meringues with raspberry lime sauce, *left*
Passionfruit and strawberry charlotte, *right*
Fresh berry compote, *below*

# Raspberry mousse MERINGUES with raspberry lime sauce

*Recipe can be prepared a day ahead*
*Assemble close to serving*

**5 egg whites**
**1¼ cups (275g) caster sugar**

### Raspberry mousse

**400g raspberries**
**⅓ cup (75g) caster sugar**
**2 tablespoons Cointreau**
**1 tablespoon gelatine**
**¼ cup (60ml) water**
**300ml cream**

### Raspberry lime sauce

**200g raspberries**
**¼ cup (40g) pure icing sugar**
**¼ cup (60ml) water**
**1 tablespoon lime juice**

Cover 2 oven trays with baking paper, mark 6 x 9cm-diameter circles on paper.

Beat egg whites in small bowl with electric mixer until soft peaks form, gradually add sugar, beating until dissolved between additions.

Spoon meringue into large piping bag fitted with a large fluted tube.

Pipe meringue over circles to form bases, add 5cm-high sides to form cases.

Bake meringues in very slow oven about 1 hour or until meringues are firm to touch, alternating position of trays halfway through cooking; cool in oven with door ajar.

Gently whisk raspberry mousse mixture, spoon into piping bag fitted with a large fluted tube.

Pipe raspberry mousse into meringue cases. Serve meringues topped with raspberry lime sauce.

until sugar is dissolved. Boil sugar syrup, uncovered, 2 minutes, stir in essence; cool.

Dip each biscuit in syrup, line base and side of prepared mould with biscuits, trimming biscuits to fit. Pour filling into mould, cover, refrigerate 3 hours or until firm.

**Filling** Whisk egg yolks and sugar in medium bowl until smooth. Combine cream and milk in medium pan, stir over heat until mixture boils; remove from heat. Gradually whisk hot cream mixture into egg yolk mixture, return to pan, stir over heat, without boiling about 10 minutes or until custard thickens slightly. Stir in passionfruit, return to bowl, cover, cool to room temperature.

Sprinkle gelatine over water in cup, stand cup in pan of simmering water, stir until gelatine is dissolved. Stir gelatine mixture into custard, refrigerate until partially set. Beat extra cream until soft peaks form, fold into custard mixture in 2 batches, stir in berries.

☐ SERVES 6 TO 8

*Freeze* Not suitable
*Microwave* Cream mixture and gelatine suitable

# Passionfruit and strawberry CHARLOTTE

*You will need about 6 passionfruit*
*Recipe can be made a day ahead*

**1 cup (250ml) water**
**$^1/_2$ cup (110g) caster sugar**
**$^1/_2$ teaspoon vanilla essence**
**16 sponge finger biscuits**

### Filling

**4 egg yolks**
**$^1/_2$ cup (110g) caster sugar**
**$^1/_2$ cup (125ml) cream**
**$^1/_2$ cup (125ml) milk**
**$^1/_2$ cup passionfruit pulp**
**3$^1/_2$ teaspoons gelatine**
**2 tablespoons water**
**300ml cream, extra**
**8 strawberries, quartered**

Line a 1.75 litre (7-cup) charlotte mould with plastic wrap.

Combine water and sugar in small pan, stir over heat, without boiling,

# Fresh BERRY compote

*Recipe can be prepared a day ahead*

**250g strawberries**
**250g blackberries**
**250g raspberries**
**2 tablespoons caster sugar**
**$^1/_4$ cup (60ml) Grand Marnier**
**1 teaspoon grated orange rind**
**1$^1/_2$ cups (375ml) sparkling apple juice**

Combine berries, sugar, liqueur and rind in large bowl; cover, refrigerate 3 hours, stirring occasionally.

Divide berries among 4 serving glasses, pour apple juice over berries just before serving.

☐ SERVES 4

*Freeze* Not suitable

### Citrus GELATO

*Recipe best made a day ahead*

**1 cup (220g) caster sugar**
**1 cup (250ml) dry white wine**
**1 cup (250ml) water**
**$1/2$ cup (125ml) orange juice**
**$1/4$ cup (60ml) lime juice**
**$1/4$ cup (60ml) lemon juice**
**2 egg whites**

Combine sugar, wine and water in medium pan, stir over low heat, without boiling, until sugar is dissolved. Bring to boil, simmer, uncovered, 10 minutes or until reduced to $1^1/2$ cups (375ml); cool.

Stir strained juices into syrup. Pour mixture into lamington pan, cover, freeze about 3 hours or until firm.

Chop frozen mixture, process with egg whites until smooth. Return to pan. Cover, freeze until firm.

Chop frozen mixture, process again, freeze 3 hours or until firm.

□ SERVES 4

***Storage*** *Covered, in freezer*
***Microwave*** *Suitable*

### Passionfruit ICE-CREAM with raspberry sauce

*You will need about 4 passionfruit*
*Recipe can be made 3 days ahead*

**3 egg yolks**
**$1/3$ cup (75g) caster sugar**
**$2/3$ cup (160ml) milk**
**$1/3$ cup (80ml) passionfruit pulp**
**$3/4$ cup (180ml) cream**

#### Raspberry sauce

**1 cup frozen raspberries, thawed**
**2 tablespoons pure icing sugar**

Citrus gelato, *left*

Line 8cm x 26cm bar pan with foil, bringing foil 5cm above sides.
Beat egg yolks and sugar in small bowl with electric mixer until thick and creamy. Bring milk to boil in medium pan, remove from heat. Gradually stir in egg-yolk mixture, stir over heat, without boiling, until mixture thickens slightly. Transfer to small bowl of electric mixer, beat until cool. Transfer mixture to large bowl, fold in passionfruit and cream. Pour into prepared pan, cover, freeze several hours or until firm. Serve ice-cream sliced with raspberry sauce.

**Raspberry sauce** Blend or process all ingredients until smooth.

□ SERVES 4

***Storage*** *Covered, in freezer*
***Microwave*** *Not suitable*

## Lemon passionfruit meringue CAKE

*You will need about 2 passionfruit*
*Recipe is best made a day ahead*

**100g packet pavlova shells**
**1 cup (70g) desiccated coconut**
**100g butter, melted**
**1 teaspoon vanilla essence**
**$1/2$ cup (125ml) thickened cream**
**2 tablespoons passionfruit pulp**

#### Filling

**3 teaspoons gelatine**
**2 tablespoons water**
**$1^1/2$ cups (375ml) custard**
**2 teaspoons grated lemon rind**
**2 tablespoons lemon juice**
**300ml cream**
**3 egg whites**
**2 tablespoons caster sugar**

Cover base and side 22cm springform tin with foil, coat lightly with cooking oil spray.

Process pavlova shells until finely crushed. Combine crushed shells, coconut, butter and essence in bowl. Press mixture evenly over base of prepared tin, refrigerate until firm.

Pour filling into tin, cover, refrigerate until set. Beat cream in small bowl until firm peaks form. Place cake on plate, decorate with cream and passionfruit.

**Filling** Combine gelatine and water in a cup, stand in a small pan of simmering water, stir until dissolved; cool 5 minutes.

Combine custard, rind, juice and gelatine mixture in large bowl. Beat cream in small bowl until soft peaks form, fold into custard mixture. Beat egg whites in clean small bowl until soft peaks form, gradually add sugar, beat until sugar is dissolved; fold into custard mixture.

□ SERVES 6 TO 8

**Freeze** *Not suitable*
**Microwave** *Gelatine suitable*

Passionfruit ice-cream with raspberry sauce, *above*
Lemon passionfruit meringue cake, *right*

# Chocolate FLANS with almond toffee

*Flans can be made 2 days ahead*
*Decorate with toffee just before serving*

**3 sheets ready-rolled**
**shortcrust pastry**

### Chocolate filling

**250g packet cream cheese, softened**
**$1/3$ cup (55g) icing sugar mixture**
**150g dark chocolate, melted**
**$1^1/2$ teaspoons gelatine**
**1 tablespoon water**
**300ml cream**

### Almond toffee

**1 cup (220g) caster sugar**
**$1/3$ cup water**
**$1/2$ cup flaked almonds, toasted**

Lightly grease 6 x deep 10cm flan tins.
Cut two 14cm circles from each sheet
of pastry, line tins with pastry.

Bake pastry cases, blind, in
moderately hot oven 20 minutes, or
until pastry is well browned; cool.

Remove pastry cases from tins
carefully, divide chocolate filling
among cases, refrigerate several hours,
or until firm.

Decorate with almond toffee..

**Chocolate filling** Beat cream cheese
and icing sugar in medium bowl with
electric mixer until light and fluffy,
beat in cooled chocolate.

Combine gelatine and water in a
cup, stand cup in a small pan of
simmering water, stir until dissolved.
Stir gelatine mixture into the
chocolate mixture. Beat cream in
small bowl until soft peaks form, fold
into chocolate mixture.

**Almond toffee** Combine sugar and
water in small heavy-based pan, stir
over heat until sugar is dissolved.
Bring to boil; boil, without stirring,
about 8 minutes or until toffee is well
browned. Gently stir in almonds, pour
onto lightly greased oven tray, cool.

□ MAKES 6

***Storage*** *Covered, in airtight container*
***Freeze*** *Not suitable*
***Microwave*** *Not suitable*

Chocolate flans with almond toffee,
*above*

124

# Chocolate BAVAROIS
## with vanilla and coffee creams

*Recipe best made a day ahead*

**4 egg yolks**
**$1/2$ cup (110g) caster sugar**
**$1^1/_2$ cups (375ml) milk**
**3 teaspoons gelatine**
**2 tablespoons water**
**300ml cream**
**2 tablespoons water, extra**
**120g dark chocolate, melted**

### Vanilla and coffee creams

**8 egg yolks**
**$1/2$ cup (110g) caster sugar**
**3 cups (750ml) milk**
**1 teaspoon vanilla essence**
**1 tablespoon cornflour**
**1 tablespoon cold water**
**1 teaspoon dry instant coffee**
**2 teaspoons hot water**

Beat egg yolks and sugar in small bowl with electric mixer until thick and creamy. Heat milk in small pan until almost boiling. With motor operating, gradually beat hot milk into egg mixture. Return mixture to pan, stir over heat, without boiling, until custard thickens slightly; strain into a large bowl, cover.

Combine gelatine and water in a cup, stand cup in a pan of simmering water, stir until dissolved. Stir gelatine mixture into custard, cover, refrigerate 15 minutes, or until thickened slightly.

Beat cream in small bowl until soft peaks form, fold into custard. Stir in extra water then cooled chocolate. Pour mixture into 4 x 1-cup (250ml) lightly greased moulds, refrigerate until set.

Turn onto serving plates, serve with vanilla and coffee creams.

**Vanilla and coffee creams** Beat egg yolks and sugar in small bowl with electric mixer until thick and creamy. Heat milk and essence in a medium pan until almost boiling. With motor operating, gradually beat hot milk mixture into egg mixture. Return mixture to pan, stir over heat, without boiling, until mixture thickens slightly. Stir in blended cornflour and cold water, stir over heat until mixture boils and thickens. Divide creams among two bowls, stir combined coffee and hot water into one bowl. Cover both bowls, cool to room temperature.

□ SERVES 4

*Storage* Covered, in refrigerator
*Freeze* Not suitable
*Microwave* Not suitable

Chocolate bavarois with vanilla and coffee creams, *left*

# Berries with summer FRUIT and raspberry sauce

*Sauce can be made a day ahead*
*Assemble recipe close to serving*

**425g can peach slices in syrup**
**250g strawberries, halved**
**200g blueberries**
**2 mangoes, sliced**

### Raspberry sauce

**250g fresh or frozen raspberries**
**1 tablespoon pure icing sugar**

Drain peaches, reserve 2 tablespoons of syrup for sauce.

Combine peaches, berries and mangoes in large bowl. Just before serving, pour sauce over fruit.

**Raspberry sauce** Blend or process raspberries, icing sugar and reserved syrup until smooth; strain.

□ SERVES 6

***Storage*** *Covered, in refrigerator*
***Freeze*** *Not suitable*

# Choc-almond BOMBE with mocha sauce

*Bombe and leaves can be made 3 days ahead  Mocha sauce can be made a day ahead and reheated to pouring consistency*

**3 eggs**
**1/2 cup (110g) caster sugar**
**2 tablespoons Kahlua**
**300ml rich cream (48% milk fat)**
**300ml cream, whipped**
**80g dark chocolate, chopped**
**100g toffee-coated almonds, finely chopped**

### Mocha sauce

**1 cup (250ml) cream**
**200g dark chocolate, finely chopped**
**2 teaspoons dry instant coffee**
**1/4 cup (60ml) Kahlua**

### Chocolate leaves

**30g milk chocolate Melts, melted**

Line 1.75-litres (7-cup) pudding steamer with plastic wrap. Combine eggs, sugar and liqueur in small heatproof bowl, whisk over pan of simmering water about 8 minutes or until very thick and tripled in volume; cool 5 minutes.

Combine creams in large bowl, fold in chocolate and nuts. Fold egg mixture into cream mixture in 2 batches, pour into prepared steamer; cover, freeze overnight or until firm.

Turn bombe onto serving plate, drizzle with some of the mocha sauce, decorate with chocolate leaves. Serve with remaining sauce.

**Mocha sauce** Bring cream to boil in small pan. Add chocolate, stir until smooth. Stir in coffee and liqueur; cool to room temperature.

**Chocolate leaves** Draw 10 leaves (about 8cm long) on baking paper; cut out leaves. Place leaves on board, spread thinly with Melts. Lift leaves from board onto tray; allow to set. Carefully peel away paper.

□ SERVES 6

***Storage*** *Bombe, covered, in freezer  Mocha sauce, covered, in refrigerator  Chocolate leaves, in airtight container, in cool place*
***Microwave*** *Mocha sauce and Melts suitable*

# Mocha MOUSSE slice

*Recipe can be made 3 days ahead*

**2 x 125g packets small sponge finger biscuits**
**1 tablespoon dry instant coffee**
**3/4 cup (180ml) boiling water**
**200g white chocolate, chopped**
**1/2 cup (125ml) cream**

### Mocha mousse

**200g dark chocolate, chopped**
**60g butter**
**$^1/_4$ cup (60ml) cream**
**2 egg yolks**
**3 teaspoons Kahlua**
**$^3/_4$ cup (180ml) cream, extra**

Line base and sides of 23cm square slab pan with foil.

Cover base of prepared pan with layer of sponge finger biscuits. Brush biscuits with half the combined coffee and water.

Melt chocolate in medium heatproof bowl over pan of simmering water; cool slightly. Stir in cream. Pour half the white chocolate mixture over prepared biscuits, cover, refrigerate 10 minutes.

Repeat with the remaining biscuits, coffee mixture and white chocolate mixture. Spread mocha mousse over biscuits; cover, refrigerate 3 hours or until firm.

**Mocha mousse** Melt chocolate and butter in medium heatproof bowl over pan of simmering water, cool slightly. Stir in cream, egg yolks and liqueur.

Beat extra cream in small bowl until firm peaks form; fold into chocolate mixture in 2 batches.

☐ SERVES 6 TO 8

**Storage** *Covered, in refrigerator*
**Freeze** *Not suitable*
**Microwave** *Suitable*

Berries with summer fruit and raspberry sauce, *left*
Choc-almond bombe with mocha sauce, *top*
Mocha mousse slice, *above*

127

## MANGO mousse meringues

*Recipe best made on day of serving*

**2 teaspoons gelatine**
**1 tablespoon water**
**400g peach and mango
    fromage frais**
**8 (100g) pavlova shells**
**2 medium (850g) mangoes, sliced**
**125g strawberries, halved**
**50g raspberries**
**50g blueberries**

Combine gelatine and water in a cup, stand in small pan of simmering water, stir until dissolved; cool. Combine gelatine mixture and fromage frais in medium bowl. Cover, refrigerate 3 hours or until firm.

Mango mousse meringues, *above*

Top half the pavlova shells with half the fromage frais mixture and half the mango. Repeat layering with remaining pavlova shells, fromage frais mixture and mango. Serve with berries.

☐ SERVES 4

***Freeze*** *Not suitable*
***Microwave*** *Gelatine suitable*

## Poached PEACHES with custard

*Recipe can be made a day ahead*

**3 cups (750ml) water**
**1 cup (250ml) orange juice**
**1¹/₂ cups (330g) caster sugar**
**4 medium (800g) firm peaches**

### Custard

**3 egg yolks**
**¹/₃ cup (75g) caster sugar**
**1 cup (250ml) hot milk**

Combine water, juice and sugar in pan, stir over heat until sugar is dissolved. Add peaches, simmer, uncovered, 15 minutes or until tender. Transfer peaches and syrup to bowl; cool. Cover, refrigerate 3 hours or until cold.

Remove peaches from syrup; peel. Strain 1¹/₂ cups (375ml) syrup into small pan, discard remaining syrup. Boil syrup, uncovered, until reduced to 1 cup (250ml); cool. Serve poached peaches with syrup and custard.

**Custard**  Whisk egg yolks and sugar in small pan, whisk in milk. Stir over low heat, without boiling, until mixture thickens slightly. Cover, cool.

☐ SERVES 4

***Storage*** *Covered, in refrigerator*
***Freeze*** *Not suitable*
***Microwave*** *Not suitable*

## Lemon and blueberry TART

*Recipe can be made a day ahead*

**2 sheets ready-rolled shortcrust
    pastry, thawed**
**75g fresh blueberries**

### Filling

**2 eggs, separated**
**250g packet cream cheese,
    chopped**
**¹/₂ cup (60g) ground almonds**
**¹/₄ cup (55g) caster sugar**
**1 teaspoon grated lemon rind**
**2 tablespoons lemon juice**
**²/₃ cup (160ml) cream**

Grease 24cm flan tin. Cut one pastry sheet in half, join halves to remaining pastry sheet to make large enough to line prepared tin. Lift pastry into tin, ease into side, trim edge. Place tin on oven tray.

Bake pastry, blind, in moderately hot oven about 20 minutes or until browned lightly; cool.

Place berries in pastry case. Spread filling over berries. Bake in moderate oven about 45 minutes or until firm; cool. Refrigerate 3 hours or until cold.

**Filling** Process egg yolks, cheese, almonds, sugar, rind, juice and cream until smooth. Transfer mixture to large bowl. Beat egg whites in small bowl until soft peaks form; fold into cheese mixture.

□ SERVES 8

**Storage** *Covered, in refrigerator*
**Freeze** *Not suitable*
**Microwave** *Not suitable*

Poached peaches with custard, *right*
Lemon and blueberry tart, *below*

subtle changes from green

to russet on nature's palette signal

the refreshing cool of the new season, and as the sun

casts its shadowplay on all it touches, the outdoors

becomes a place of subtle beauty—an irresistible

invitation to picnic and enjoy

*mellow fruitfulness*

the last balmy days of the year.

Exquisite orchard fruits in many clever guises are

the main attraction and, if anything can be said to compare

with biting into a crisp apple picked fresh from the tree,

it can only be the rich flavours of a home-baked tart

or delicately poached quinces—autumnal ambrosia.

## Picnic in the park

SERVES 4 to 6

## *Vegetarian luncheon*

Vegetarian NUTBURGERS  *(page 139)*

LINGUINE with zucchini sauce  *(page 174)*

Vegetable CANNELLONI  *(page 174)*

Mixed SALAD

Hot RHUBARB butternut pie  *(page 178)*

SERVES 6

## *Family get-together*

Chunky VEGETABLE soup  *(page 136)*

Devilled CHICKEN
with caramelised onions  *(page 167)*

Lemon Thyme POTATO wedges  *(page 167)*

MUSHROOMS in spicy batter  *(page 154)*

Mixed SALAD

Poached PEARS with cinnamon cream  *(page 180)*

SERVES 6

### TAHINI dip

*Recipe can be made a day ahead*

**3 cloves garlic, chopped**
**¹/₂ cup (125ml) tahini**
**¹/₄ cup (60ml) vegetable stock**
**¹/₂ cup (125ml) lemon juice**
**1 tablespoon olive oil**

Blend or process garlic, tahini and
stock until smooth. Gradually add
combined juice and oil in a thin stream
while motor is operating.

Blend until light and smooth.

☐ Serves 6 to 8

***Storage*** *Covered, in refrigerator*
***Freeze*** *Not suitable*

Clockwise from left, Tahini dip, Bread
crisps, Red lentil dip, Tabouli yogurt dip

### Red LENTIL dip

*Recipe can be made a day ahead*

**³/₄ cup (150g) red lentils**
**2 cups (500ml) water**
**1 medium (150g) onion, chopped**
**2 cloves garlic, halved**
**1 medium (200g) potato**
**2 tablespoons olive oil**
**¹/₂ teaspoon ground cumin**
**1 teaspoon ground coriander**
**2 tablespoons lemon juice**
**¹/₄ teaspoon sweet paprika**

Combine lentils, water, onion and
garlic in medium pan; simmer,
uncovered, about 20 minutes or until
lentils are very soft. Boil, steam, or
microwave potato until soft.

Process lentil mixture and potato
until smooth.

Add remaining ingredients; process
until smooth. Serve warm or cold.

☐ SERVES 6 TO 8

***Storage*** *Covered, in refrigerator*
***Freeze*** *Not suitable*
***Microwave*** *Suitable*

### TABOULI yogurt dip

*Recipe can be made a day ahead*

**200g plain yogurt**
**1 cup (200g) firmly**
**packed tabouleh**

Combine yogurt and tabouleh in
medium bowl. Cover, refrigerate at
least 3 hours before serving.

☐ SERVES 6 TO 8

***Storage*** *Covered, in refrigerator*
***Freeze*** *Not suitable*

# Bread CRISPS

*Recipe can be made a day ahead*

**4 large pitta**
**2 tablespoons olive oil**

Brush both sides of bread with oil. Place onto oven trays.

Bake, uncovered, in moderately hot oven about 6 minutes or until browned and crisp. Cool slightly, break into pieces.

□ SERVES 6 TO 8

**Storage** *In airtight container*
**Freeze** *Not suitable*
**Microwave** *Not suitable*

# Turkey and pasta AVOCADOS

*Filling can be prepared 3 hours ahead*

**1 cup cooked elbow macaroni pasta**
**³/₄ cup chopped cooked turkey**
**¹/₄ cup (60ml) sour cream**
**1 tablespoon chopped fresh basil**
**1 tablespoon chopped fresh tarragon**
**¹/₄ cup (60ml) cranberry sauce**
**¹/₂ medium (100g) red capsicum, chopped**
**2 avocados**

Combine pasta, turkey, cream, herbs, sauce and capsicum in medium bowl.

Just before serving, halve avocados, discard seeds, spoon filling into avocado halves.

□ SERVES 4

**Storage** *Covered, in refrigerator*
**Freeze** *Not suitable*
**Microwave** *Pasta suitable*

Turkey and pasta avocados, *below*

## Chunky VEGETABLE soup

*Recipe can be made a day ahead*

2 tablespoons olive oil
20g butter
2 medium (300g) onions, chopped
2 medium (240g) carrots, chopped
2 sticks celery, chopped
1 medium (200g) potato, chopped
2 medium (240g) zucchini, sliced
$^1/_2$ small (500g) cabbage, shredded
1 litre (4 cups) vegetable stock
425g can tomatoes,
    undrained crushed

## GREEN PEA soup

*Recipe can be made a day ahead*

1 tablespoon olive oil
1 small (80g) onion,
    chopped
2 cloves garlic, crushed
2 teaspoons ground cumin
4 cups (500g) frozen peas
1 litre (4 cups) vegetable stock
200g low-fat yogurt

Heat oil in pan, add onion and garlic, cook, stirring, until onion is soft. Add cumin, cook, stirring, until fragrant.

Add peas and stock, simmer, covered, about 15 minutes or until peas are soft.

Blend or process pea mixture until smooth. Return to same pan, stir over heat until hot. Remove from heat, stand 1 minute, whisk in three-quarters of the yogurt. Serve topped with remaining yogurt.

□ SERVES 4 TO 6

**Storage** *Covered, in refrigerator*
**Freeze** *Suitable, without yogurt*
**Microwave** *Suitable*

Heat oil and butter in large pan, add onions, cook, stirring, until onions are soft. Add carrots, celery and potato, cook, stirring, 5 minutes.

Stir in zucchini, cabbage, stock and tomatoes. Simmer, covered, about 1¹/₂ hours or until soup is thickened.

□ SERVES 4 TO 6

**Storage** *Covered, in refrigerator*
**Freeze** *Suitable*
**Microwave** *Suitable*

Green pea soup, *left*
Chunky vegetable soup, *below*
Thai-style chicken noodle soup, *right*

## Thai-style chicken noodle SOUP

*Recipe best made close to serving*

2 tablespoons vegetable oil
2 medium (300g) onions, chopped
2 cloves garlic, crushed
2 stems fresh lemon grass, finely chopped
¹/₂ teaspoon sambal oelek
2 teaspoons ground turmeric
2 teaspoons ground ginger
1 litre (4 cups) chicken stock
2 tablespoons lime juice
2 cups (500ml) coconut milk
2 cups (300g) chopped cooked chicken
1¹/₂ cups (120g) shredded cabbage
¹/₂ medium (100g) red capsicum, thinly sliced
4 green onions, chopped
350g fine egg noodles
1 cup (100g) mung bean sprouts

Heat oil in medium pan, add onions, garlic and lemon grass, cook, stirring, until onions are soft. Stir in sambal oelek, turmeric and ginger, cook, stirring, until fragrant. Add stock and juice, simmer, covered, for 10 minutes.

Stir in coconut milk, chicken, cabbage, capsicum, green onions and noodles, simmer, uncovered, about 5 minutes or until noodles are tender, stirring occasionally. Stir in bean sprouts.

□ SERVES 4 TO 6

**Freeze** *Not suitable*
**Microwave** *Suitable*

137

# BEEF and chickpea soup

*Recipe can be made 2 days ahead*

1 tablespoon vegetable oil
1 medium (150g) onion, chopped
2 cloves garlic, crushed
400g minced beef
1 medium (200g) red
   capsicum, chopped
400g can tomatoes,
   undrained, crushed
2 tablespoons tomato paste
310g can chickpeas,
   rinsed, drained
310g can red kidney beans,
   rinsed, drained
2 cups (500ml) beef stock
$1/4$ teaspoon chilli powder
1 teaspoon dried mixed herbs
$1/2$ teaspoon sugar

Heat oil in large pan, add onion and garlic, cook, stirring, until onion is soft. Add mince, stir over heat until browned. Add capsicum, tomatoes, paste, chickpeas, beans, stock, chilli powder, herbs and sugar, simmer, covered, 30 minutes.

Blend or process mixture, in batches, until well combined. Return soup to pan, stir over heat until hot.

□ SERVES 4

**Storage** *Covered, in refrigerator*
**Freeze** *Suitable*
**Microwave** *Suitable*

Beef and chickpea soup, Mushroom and beef flans, *above right, from left*
Vegetarian nutburgers, *right*

# Mushroom and beef FLANS

*Recipe can be made a day ahead*

2 cups (300g) plain flour
150g butter
1 egg yolk
1 teaspoon lemon juice
1 tablespoon water, approximately
2 eggs, lightly beaten
$2/3$ cup (160ml) cream
2 tablespoons milk

### Filling

1 tablespoon vegetable oil
1 medium (150g) onion, chopped
1 clove garlic, crushed
150g minced beef
100g mushrooms, chopped
1 teaspoon chopped fresh basil
$1/4$ teaspoon dried oregano leaves
2 small (260g) tomatoes,
   peeled, chopped

Oil 8 x 10cm flan tins. Sift flour into large bowl, rub in butter, stir in yolk, juice and enough water to make ingredients cling together. Press dough into ball, knead on lightly floured surface until smooth, cover, refrigerate 30 minutes.

Divide pastry into eighths, roll each portion on lightly floured surface until large enough to line prepared tins. Ease pastry into tins; trim edges. Place tins on oven trays. Bake blind in moderately hot oven about 20 minutes or until pastry is browned lightly. Cool.

Divide filling among pastry cases, pour combined eggs, cream and milk over top.

Bake, uncovered, in moderate oven about 30 minutes, or until browned.

**Filling** Heat oil in pan, add onion and garlic, cook, stirring, until onion is soft. Add mince and mushrooms, stir over heat until mince is well browned. Stir in herbs and tomatoes, simmer, uncovered, until liquid is evaporated. Cool.

□ MAKES 8

**Storage** *Covered, in refrigerator*
**Freeze** *Suitable*
**Microwave** *Not suitable*

## Vegetarian
# NUTBURGERS

*Recipe can be made 3 days ahead*

**1 cup (150g) toasted
    unsalted cashews**
**1 cup (150g) toasted hazelnuts**
**1 cup (160g) blanched
    almond kernels**
**130g can creamed corn**
**1 cup (90g) rolled oats**
**1 medium (120g) carrot,
    finely chopped**
**1 medium (150g) onion,
    finely chopped**
**1 egg, lightly beaten**
**pinch dried mixed herbs**
**plain flour**
**vegetable oil, for shallow-frying**

Process cashews, nuts, corn, oats, carrot, onion, egg and herbs until mixture holds together.

Divide mixture into 12 portions, roll each portion into a ball, flatten slightly into burger shapes. Cover; refrigerate for 30 minutes.

Carefully toss burgers in flour, shake away excess flour.

Shallow-fry burgers in hot oil, turning, until well browned on both sides and hot; drain on absorbent paper.

□ MAKES 12

***Storage*** *Covered, in refrigerator*
***Freeze*** *Suitable*
***Microwave*** *Not suitable*

## Bacon TUNA bites

*You will need to cook about 4 medium (800g) potatoes Recipe can be made a day ahead*

4 bacon rashers, chopped
2 cups mashed, cooked potato
425g can tuna, drained
1 medium (150g) onion,
  finely chopped
3 medium (240g) leaves spinach
  (silverbeet), shredded
1 egg, lightly beaten
plain flour
2 tablespoons vegetable oil

Place bacon in small pan, cook over heat for about 5 minutes or until crisp and well browned; drain. Combine bacon, potato, tuna, onion, spinach and egg in medium bowl. Divide mixture into 18 balls, toss in flour, shake away excess flour.

Heat oil in a pan, cook bites for about 8 minutes or until well browned all over and hot.

□ MAKES 18

**Storage** *Covered, in refrigerator*
**Freeze** *Not suitable*
**Microwave** *Not suitable*

## Endive and prawn PENNE

*Recipe best made close to serving*

300g penne pasta
400g cooked medium prawns
60g butter
1 clove garlic, crushed
$1/2$ cup (125ml) dry white wine
300ml cream
$1/2$ cup drained sun-dried
  tomatoes, chopped
$1/2$ bunch curly endive,
  roughly chopped

Add pasta to large pan of boiling water, boil, uncovered, until just tender; drain well.

Shell and devein prawns, leaving tails intact. Heat butter in pan, add garlic, cook, stirring, until fragrant.

Add wine, simmer uncovered, until reduced by half. Add cream, bring to boil, stir in tomatoes and endive, stir over heat until endive is wilted. Add pasta and prawns, stir until heated through.

□ SERVES 4

**Freeze** *Not suitable*
**Microwave** *Pasta suitable*

## Curried CHICKEN soup

*Soup can be made 2 days ahead*

1 tablespoon vegetable oil
3 (330g) chicken thigh fillets
1 tablespoon vegetable oil, extra
1 tablespoon curry powder
3 bacon rashers, chopped
2 cloves garlic, crushed
1 medium (350g) leek, chopped
1 medium (150g) onion, chopped
1 medium (200g) potato, chopped
1.25 litres (5 cups) water
2 teaspoons chicken stock powder
1 tablespoon cornflour
1 tablespoon water, extra
$3/4$ bunch (225g) curly endive,
  shredded

Heat oil in pan, add chicken, cook until browned all over and partially cooked; drain on absorbent paper. Cut chicken into thick strips.

Heat extra oil in large pan, add curry powder, bacon, garlic, leek and onion, cook, stirring, until leek is soft. Add potato and pepper, cook, stirring, 1 minute. Stir in water, stock powder and chicken, simmer, uncovered, about 20 minutes or until potato is tender.

Stir in cornflour blended with extra water, stir over heat until boiling.

Just before serving, stir in endive.

□ SERVES 4

**Storage** *Covered, in refrigerator*
**Freeze** *Not suitable*
**Microwave** *Suitable*

Bacon tuna bites, *above left*
Endive and prawn penne, Curried chicken soup, *right, from top*

# SEAFOOD soup with basil mayonnaise

*Recipe best made close to serving*

**650g mussels**
**2 tablespoons olive oil**
**2 medium (700g) leeks,**
**thickly sliced**
**1 clove garlic, crushed**
**2 bay leaves**
**2 sticks celery, chopped**
**1.25 litres (5 cups) fish stock**
**2 x 425g cans tomatoes,**
**undrained, crushed**
**1/2 cup (125ml) dry white wine**
**2 tablespoons tomato paste**
**2 teaspoons sugar**
**500g firm white fish fillets,**
**thickly sliced**
**2 tablespoons chopped**
**fresh parsley**

## Basil mayonnaise

**3/4 cup (180ml) mayonnaise**
**1/4 cup firmly packed fresh basil**

Scrub mussels, remove beards. Heat oil in large pan, add leeks and garlic; cook, stirring, until leeks are soft. Add bay leaves, celery, stock, tomatoes, wine, paste and sugar to pan; simmer, covered, 15 minutes.

Add seafood, simmer, uncovered, about 5 minutes or until seafood is just cooked through. Stir in parsley, serve with basil mayonnaise.

**Basil mayonnaise** Blend or process mayonnaise and basil until combined.

☐ SERVES 4 TO 6

*Freeze* Not suitable
*Microwave* Suitable

Seafood soup with basil mayonnaise, above

# CHICKEN and red pesto fettuccine

*Red pesto can be made 3 days ahead*
*Recipe best made close to serving*

**2 tablespoons olive oil**
**2 (350g) chicken breast**
**fillets, sliced**
**2 cloves garlic, crushed**
**1/2 cup (125ml) port**
**1/2 cup (65g) chopped, drained**
**sun-dried tomatoes**
**1/3 cup (40g) seeded black**
**olives, sliced**
**1/2 cup roughly chopped fresh basil**
**300ml cream**
**1/3 cup (25g) grated**
**parmesan cheese**
**400g fettuccine pasta**
**80g bocconcini cheese, sliced**

## Red pesto

**1/2 cup roughly chopped fresh basil**
**2 tablespoons pine nuts, toasted**
**3/4 cup (60g) grated**
**parmesan cheese**
**1 clove garlic, crushed**
**2 tablespoons chopped**
**sun-dried tomatoes**
**2 tablespoons chopped**
**sun-dried capsicums**
**1/4 cup (60ml) olive oil**

Heat oil in pan, add chicken in batches; cook, stirring, until chicken is browned lightly. Add garlic, port, tomatoes, olives and basil; bring to boil. Stir in 1/2 cup (125ml) red pesto, cream and parmesan cheese; simmer, uncovered, until sauce is thickened slightly.

Meanwhile, add pasta to large pan of boiling water; boil, uncovered, until just tender; drain. Combine pasta, sauce and bocconcini in large bowl. Serve topped with remaining red pesto.

**Red pesto** Process all ingredients, except oil, until finely chopped. Gradually add oil in a thin stream while motor is operating; process until combined.

☐ SERVES 4

*Storage* Covered, in refrigerator
*Freeze* Red pesto suitable
*Microwave* Pasta suitable

# Risoni and LAMB soup

*Recipe can be made a day ahead*

$1/2$ cup (110g) risoni pasta
1 large (350g) red capsicum
cooking oil spray
350g lean lamb fillets,
   thinly sliced
$1/2$ cup (125ml) water
1 small (200g) leek, sliced
2 cloves garlic, crushed
1 teaspoon chopped fresh
   rosemary
1 tablespoon tomato paste
$1^1/2$ cups (375ml) vegetable stock
1.5 litres (6 cups) water, extra
1 small (90g) zucchini,
   halved, sliced
4 leaves (320g) spinach
   (silverbeet), shredded

Add risoni to pan of boiling water, boil, uncovered, until just tender; drain. Quarter capsicum, remove seeds and membranes. Roast under grill or in very hot oven, skin side up, until skin blisters and blackens. Cover capsicum pieces in plastic or paper for 5 minutes, peel away skin, cut capsicum into strips 1cm thick.

Coat large non-stick pan with cooking oil spray, add lamb in batches; cook until browned, remove. Add water, leek, garlic and rosemary to pan; cook, stirring, until almost all the water has evaporated. Add paste, stock and extra water; boil, uncovered, 10 minutes; reduce heat, simmer, covered, 10 minutes.

Return lamb to pan, add zucchini; simmer, covered, until tender. Add silverbeet, risoni and capsicum, stir over heat until hot.

□ SERVES 6

*Storage* Covered, in refrigerator
*Freeze* Not suitable
*Microwave* Risoni suitable

Chicken and red pesto fettuccine *top left*
Risoni and lamb soup, *left*

143

# Baked FETTA

*Recipe best made just before serving*

**250g piece fetta cheese**
**$^1/_4$ cup (60ml) olive oil**
**$^1/_4$ teaspoon sweet paprika**
**1 tablespoon chopped
   fresh oregano**
**4 (20g) seeded black olives, sliced**

Place fetta on piece of foil large enough to enclose cheese, drizzle with oil, sprinkle with remaining ingredients. Gather foil around fetta, fold over to seal, place on oven tray.

Bake in moderately hot oven about 20 minutes or until fetta is soft.

Serve warm as an entree with crusty bread, or with salad as a light lunch.

□ SERVES 6 TO 8

***Freeze*** *Not suitable*
***Microwave*** *Not suitable*

Bean nachos, *right*
Baked fetta, *below*

# Bacon, cheese and chive SOUFFLE

*Recipe must be made just before serving*

**2 tablespoons packaged
   breadcrumbs**
**4 bacon rashers, chopped**
**185g butter**
**$^1/_2$ cup (75g) plain flour**
**1$^1/_2$ cups (375ml) evaporated milk**
**1$^1/_2$ cups (180g) grated
   cheddar cheese**
**$^1/_4$ cup chopped fresh chives**
**6 eggs, separated**

Oil 1.5 litre (6-cup) souffle dish, sprinkle with breadcrumbs, shake away excess crumbs.

Cook bacon, in medium pan, about 5 minutes or until well browned and crisp; drain. Heat butter in clean pan, stir in flour, stir over heat for 1 minute. Remove pan from heat, gradually stir in milk, stir over heat until mixture boils and thickens, stir in cheese, bacon and chives.

Transfer mixture to a large bowl, stir in egg yolks. Beat egg whites in a medium bowl until firm peaks form, fold into cheese mixture in 2 batches. Pour mixture into prepared dish, place on oven tray.

Bake, uncovered, in moderately hot oven about 45 minutes, or until well browned and firm to touch. Serve immediately.

□ SERVES 6

***Freeze*** *Not suitable*
***Microwave*** *Not suitable*

Bacon, cheese and chive souffle, *above*

## Bean NACHOS

*Recipe best made just before serving*

450g can refried beans
$^1/_4$ cup (60ml) sour cream
2 green onions, chopped
$1^1/_2$ tablespoons chopped
   fresh coriander
few drops tabasco sauce
200g packet corn chips
1 large (250g) tomato, chopped
1 large (320g) avocado, chopped
1 cup (125g) grated
   cheddar cheese
$^1/_4$ cup (60ml) sour cream, extra
2 tablespoons chopped fresh
   coriander, extra

Combine beans, cream, onions, coriander and sauce in small bowl.

Arrange corn chips on serving plate, top with bean mixture, tomato, avocado, cheese, extra cream and extra coriander.

□ SERVES 4 TO 6

**Freeze** Not suitable

Add pasta to large pan of boiling water, boil, uncovered, until just tender; drain.

Boil, steam or microwave broccoli and zucchini until just tender; drain.

Melt butter in medium pan, stir in cream, cheese and sugar, stir, without boiling, until sauce is heated through. Remove from heat, stir in vegetables, juice and parsley. Combine sauce and pasta in large bowl.

□ SERVES 4

**Freeze** *Not suitable*
**Microwave** *Pasta and vegetables suitable*

Blackened fish, *left*

## Blackened FISH

*Recipe is best cooked outdoors or under a strong exhaust fan indoors We used blue-eye cod cutlets for this recipe Recipe best made just before serving*

**1 tablespoon ground sweet paprika**
**1 teaspoon chilli powder**
**1 teaspoon dried thyme leaves**
**1 teaspoon dried oregano leaves**
**1 teaspoon onion flakes**
**1 teaspoon garlic powder**
**4 white fish cutlets**
**50g butter, melted**

### Butter sauce

**100g butter, melted**
**1 tablespoon lemon juice**
**1 green onion, chopped**
**¹/₄ teaspoon cayenne pepper**

Combine dry ingredients in medium bowl. Brush fish all over with butter, coat in spice mixture; press on firmly.

Heat barbecue plate (or griddle pan) until very hot. Place fish on barbecue plate, cook 3 minutes each side, or until spices are blackened and fish is cooked through.

Serve fish with butter sauce.

**Butter sauce** Combine all ingredients in small bowl.

□ SERVES 4

**Freeze** *Not suitable*
**Microwave** *Butter sauce suitable*

## FETTUCCINE with lemon cream sauce

*Recipe best made close to serving*

**400g fettuccine pasta**
**200g broccoli, chopped**
**2 medium (240g) zucchini, chopped**
**50g butter**
**300ml cream**
**³/₄ cup (60g) grated parmesan cheese**
**1 teaspoon sugar**
**1 tablespoon lemon juice**
**2 tablespoons chopped fresh parsley**

*146*

# TEMPURA

*Recipe must be made close to serving*

**650g uncooked king prawns**
**500g squid hoods**
**2 medium (240g) carrots**
**4 green onions**
**2 egg yolks**
**2 cups (500ml) iced water**
**2 cups (300g) plain flour**
**vegetable oil, for deep-frying**
**2 medium (240g) zucchini, sliced**
**250g broccoli, chopped**

### Chilli dipping sauce

**$1/_4$ cup (60ml) soy sauce**
**$1/_4$ cup (60ml) water**
**1 tablespoon mirin**
**1 small fresh red chilli, sliced**

Shell and devein prawns, leaving the tails intact.

Lightly cut underneath of prawns crossways, flatten out slightly. Cut squid hoods, and carrots into thin strips. Cut onions into 5cm lengths.

Lightly beat egg yolks and water, stir in sifted flour all at once, stir until just combined; do not beat.

Arrange small bundles of combined carrots and onions on a plate, spoon over enough batter to cover, turn bundles, spoon batter over to coat well.

Using a metal spatula, slide the bundles into hot oil, deep-fry until browned lightly; drain on absorbent paper. Repeat using squid and batter.

Dip prawns, zucchini and broccoli in batter, deep-fry until browned lightly; drain on absorbent paper.

Serve hot seafood and vegetables with chilli dipping sauce.

**Chilli dipping sauce** Combine sauce, water and mirin in small bowl, top with chilli.

□ SERVES 6

**Freeze** *Not suitable*
**Microwave** *Not suitable*

Fettuccine with lemon cream sauce, *above left*
Tempura, *left*

147

## Beef and prune CASSEROLE

*Recipe can be made 2 days ahead*

**1kg beef chuck steak**
**plain flour**
**$1/4$ cup (60ml) vegetable oil**
**1 medium (150g) onion, chopped**
**1 clove garlic, crushed**
**1 tablespoon plain flour, extra**
**$2^1/_2$ cups (625ml) water**
**$1/_2$ cup (125ml) dry red wine**
**2 small beef stock cubes, crumbled**
**1 tablespoon Worcestershire sauce**
**2 bay leaves**
**2 cobs corn**
**$3/_4$ cup (85g) seeded prunes**
**300g baby potatoes**

Cut steak into 3cm pieces, toss in flour; shake away excess flour.

Heat 2 tablespoons of the oil in pan, add steak in batches, cook, stirring, until browned all over; remove from pan. Place steak in 2.5 litre (10-cup) ovenproof dish.

Heat remaining oil in same pan, add onion and garlic, cook, stirring, until onion is soft. Add extra flour, cook, stirring, until flour is well browned. Remove from heat, gradually stir in combined water, wine, stock cubes, sauce and bay leaves, stir over heat until mixture boils and thickens. Pour sauce over steak in dish.

Bake, covered, in moderate oven for $1^1/4$ hours.

Cut corn into slices 2cm thick. Add corn, prunes and potatoes to dish; mix well.

Bake, covered, in moderate oven about $1^1/_2$ hours, or until steak is tender. Remove bay leaves before serving.

□ SERVES 6

***Storage*** *Covered, in refrigerator*
***Freeze*** *Not suitable*
***Microwave*** *Not suitable*

## Creole-style PORK casserole

*Recipe can be made 2 days ahead*

**$1/_4$ cup (60ml) vegetable oil**
**750g diced pork**
**1 medium (150g) onion, sliced**
**2 cloves garlic, crushed**
**2 small fresh red chillies, seeded, chopped**
**2 teaspoons ground sweet paprika**
**pinch saffron powder**
**400g can tomatoes, undrained, crushed**
**2 tablespoons tomato paste**
**1 small beef stock cube, crumbled**
**$1^1/_2$ cups (375ml) water**
**100g button mushrooms**
**450g can black-eyed beans, rinsed, drained**

Beef and prune casserole, Creole-style pork casserole, *above, from left*

Heat oil in pan, add pork in batches, cook until browned all over; drain on absorbent paper.

Add onion, garlic and chillies to same pan, cook, stirring, until onion is soft. Stir in paprika and saffron, cook, stirring, until fragrant.

Add tomatoes, paste, stock cube and water, simmer, uncovered, 5 minutes.

Place pork in 2 litre (8-cup) ovenproof dish, add tomato mixture.

Bake, covered, in moderate oven, about 50 minutes or until pork is tender. Add mushrooms and beans. Bake, covered, in moderate oven about 10 minutes or until hot.

□ SERVES 4

**Storage**  *Covered, in refrigerator*
**Freeze**  *Suitable*
**Microwave**  *Not suitable*

## Cheese and leek QUICHE

*Recipe can be made a day ahead*

1$^1/_2$ **cups (225g) plain flour**
**125g butter**
$^1/_4$ **cup (20g) grated parmesan cheese**
**2 egg yolks**
**2 teaspoons lemon juice, approximately**
**20g butter, extra**
**1 medium (350g) leek, sliced**
$^1/_2$ **cup (60g) grated gouda cheese**
$^1/_2$ **cup (50g) grated mozzarella cheese**
$^1/_4$ **cup (40g) grated parmesan cheese, extra**
$^1/_2$ **cup (125ml) cream**
$^1/_2$ **cup (125ml) milk**
**2 eggs, lightly beaten, extra**
**1 tablespoon seeded mustard**

Sift flour into large bowl, rub in butter, stir in parmesan, egg yolks and enough juice to form a firm dough. Knead lightly until smooth, cover and refrigerate for 30 minutes.

Roll out pastry between 2 sheets of baking paper until large enough to line a 23cm flan tin. Lift pastry into tin, gently ease pastry into side of tin; trim edge. Place tin on an oven tray, cover, refrigerate.

Bake pastry, blind, in moderately hot oven, about 20 minutes, or until browned lightly. Cool.

Heat extra butter in a pan, cook leek until soft, cool. Spread into pastry case. Sprinkle with combined remaining cheeses. Pour combined cream, milk, extra eggs and mustard over cheeses.

Bake, uncovered, in moderate oven about 30 minutes or until set.

□ SERVES 6 TO 8

**Storage**  *Covered, in refrigerator*
**Freeze**  *Not suitable*
**Microwave**  *Leek suitable*

Cheese and leek quiche, *below*

## PASTA with tomato sauce and mussels

*Tomato sauce can be made 2 days ahead*

**2 teaspoons olive oil**
**1 large (200g) onion, chopped**
**2 cloves garlic, crushed**
**1 small fresh red chilli,**
**    seeded, chopped**
**3 x 400g cans tomatoes,**
**    undrained, crushed**
**$^1/_4$ cup (60ml) tomato paste**
**1 teaspoon sugar**
**$^1/_3$ cup shredded fresh basil**
**$^1/_2$ cup (125ml) fish stock**
**800g small mussels**
**500g penne pasta**

Heat oil in large pan, add onion and garlic; cook, stirring, until onion is soft. Add chilli, tomatoes, paste, sugar, basil and stock; simmer, uncovered, 15 minutes or until thickened slightly. Add mussels, simmer, covered, about 5 minutes.

Meanwhile, add pasta to large pan of boiling water; boil, uncovered, until just tender; drain. Toss pasta with tomato sauce and mussels.

□ SERVES 6

**Storage** *Sauce, covered, in refrigerator*
**Freeze** *Not suitable*
**Microwave** *Not suitable*

Pasta with tomato sauce and
mussels, *above*
Quick chicken curry, *above right*
Roast beef with horseradish cream, *right*

# Quick chicken CURRY

*Recipe can be made a day ahead*

**1 tablespoon vegetable oil**
**1 medium (150g) onion, chopped**
**2kg chicken thigh fillets, halved**
**2 x 375ml cans Singapore hot**
    **curry sauce**
**1kg packet frozen vegetables,**
    **thawed**

Heat oil in pan, add onion, cook, stirring, until onion is soft.

Add chicken, in batches, cook, stirring, until chicken is browned lightly.

Stir in curry sauce and vegetables, simmer, uncovered, about 30 minutes, or until chicken is cooked through.

☐ SERVES 8

**Storage** *Covered, in refrigerator*
**Freeze** *Not suitable*
**Microwave** *Suitable*

# Roast BEEF with horseradish cream

*Recipe can be prepared a day ahead*

**2 x 900g boned rolled beef sirloins**
**1 tablespoon vegetable oil**
**1 teaspoon seasoned pepper**

### Horseradish cream

**300ml cream**
**$^1/_2$ cup (125ml) sour cream**
**$^1/_3$ cup horseradish cream**
**$^1/_4$ cup chopped fresh parsley**

Brush top of sirloins with oil, sprinkle with seasoned pepper. Place sirloins on wire rack in baking dish.

Bake, uncovered, in moderately hot oven about 50 minutes or until browned and tender.

Serve slices of beef with the horseradish cream.

**Horseradish cream** Combine all ingredients in medium bowl.

☐ SERVES 8 TO 10

**Storage** *Covered, in refrigerator*
**Freeze** *Not suitable*
**Microwave** *Not suitable*

## Chicken, prawn and olive CASSEROLE

*Recipe can be made a day ahead*

2 tablespoons olive oil
40g butter
1kg chicken pieces
1 medium (150g) onion, chopped
2 cloves garlic, crushed
2 x 425g cans tomatoes,
   undrained, crushed
1 small chicken stock
   cube, crumbled
$^1/_2$ cup (125ml) water
$^1/_3$ cup (80ml) madeira
1 tablespoon chopped fresh thyme
250g mushrooms, sliced
500g cooked king prawns,
   shelled, deveined
$3^1/_3$ cups (400g) seeded black olives

Heat oil and butter in large pan, add chicken, cook 3 minutes on each side, or until browned. Stir in onion and garlic, cook until onion is just soft.

Place chicken mixture in 2 litre (8-cup) casserole dish with tomatoes, stock cube, water, madeira and thyme.

Bake, covered, in moderate oven 30 minutes. Remove chicken, blend or process tomato mixture until smooth. Return chicken and pureed sauce to dish. Bake, covered, 30 minutes, or until chicken is cooked. Stir in mushrooms, prawns and olives. Bake, uncovered, 5 minutes, or until hot.

☐ SERVES 6

**Storage** *Covered, in refrigerator*
**Freeze** *Not suitable*
**Microwave** *Not suitable*

## Sesame PORK casserole

*Recipe can be made 2 days ahead*

1kg diced pork
plain flour
2 tablespoons vegetable oil
1 medium (150g) onion
2 cloves garlic, crushed
2 tablespoons sesame seeds
$^1/_4$ cup (60ml) soy sauce
$^1/_4$ cup (60ml) honey
$^1/_4$ cup (60ml) plum jam
1 small chicken stock
   cube, crumbled
1 cup (250ml) water
$^1/_2$ cup (125ml) dry sherry
1 medium (200g) red
   capsicum, chopped
1 medium (200g) green
   capsicum, chopped
1 medium (150g) apple, sliced
2 tablespoons cornflour
$^1/_4$ cup (60ml) water, extra

Toss pork in flour, shake away excess flour. Heat oil in a large pan, stir in pork, cook about 5 minutes or until pork is browned all over. Remove pork from pan, drain excess oil from pan.

Cut onion into wedges, stir onion, garlic and seeds into pan, cook 3 minutes or until seeds are browned lightly. Stir sauce, honey, jam, stock cube, water and sherry into pan, bring to boil; simmer, uncovered, 5 minutes.

Combine pork, capsicums and sesame sauce in 1.5 litre (6-cup) casserole dish.

Bake, covered, in moderate oven about $1^1/_2$ hours, or until the pork is tender. Stir in apple and cornflour blended with extra water. Bake, covered, 15 minutes, or until casserole is thickened.

☐ SERVES 6

**Storage** *Covered, in refrigerator*
**Freeze** *Suitable*
**Microwave** *Not suitable*

## Nutty bean CASSEROLE

*Recipe can be made a day ahead*

445g can soy beans, rinsed, drained
465g can red kidney beans,
   rinsed, drained
$^1/_2$ teaspoon chilli powder
$^1/_2$ teaspoon ground cumin
2 tablespoons tomato paste
3 cups (300g) stale wholemeal
   breadcrumbs
1 cup (60g) unprocessed bran
2 eggs, lightly beaten
$1^1/_2$ cups (150g) packaged
   breadcrumbs
2 tablespoons vegetable oil
3 medium (360g) zucchini, sliced
1 medium (200g) red
   capsicum, sliced
1 medium (200g) green
   capsicum, sliced
2 medium (240g) carrots, chopped
2 celery sticks, chopped
3 medium (600g) potatoes, chopped
1 tablespoon cornflour
2 tablespoons water

### Peanut sauce

1 tablespoon vegetable oil
1 medium (150g) onion, chopped
1 clove garlic, crushed
2 small chicken stock
   cubes, crumbled
2 tablespoons dry sherry
1 tablespoon soy sauce
$^1/_2$ cup (130g) peanut butter
2 tablespoons honey
1 teaspoon ground cumin
1 teaspoon ground coriander

Blend or process beans until smooth. Stir in spices, paste, wholemeal crumbs and bran; mix well. Shape rounded tablespoons of mixture into balls, dip in eggs, toss in packaged crumbs.

Heat oil in large pan, cook balls, in batches, until well browned; drain. Combine vegetables and peanut sauce in 1.5 litre (6-cup) casserole dish.

Bake, covered, in moderate oven 45 minutes. Stir in bean balls and blended cornflour and water.

Bake, covered, in moderate oven 15 minutes, or until casserole is thickened.

**Peanut sauce** Heat oil in medium pan, add onion and garlic, cook until onion is just soft. Stir in stock cubes and remaining ingredients, bring to boil, simmer, uncovered, for 10 minutes.

☐ SERVES 6

**Storage** *Covered, in refrigerator*
**Freeze** *Not suitable*
**Microwave** *Not suitable*

*clockwise from top right, Chicken, prawn and olive casserole, Sesame pork casserole, Nutty bean casserole*

## Spicy prawn and mushroom SALAD

*Recipe can be made 2 hours ahead*

**1kg cooked king prawns**
**250g button mushrooms, quartered**
**1 radicchio lettuce**
**1 butter lettuce**
**1 medium (130g) Lebanese
    cucumber, sliced**
**1 medium (150g) onion, sliced**

### Lemon grass dressing

**$1/4$ cup (60ml) peanut oil**
**2 tablespoons lime juice**
**1 tablespoon chopped fresh
    lemon grass**
**1 tablespoon chopped fresh coriander**
**1 teaspoon sugar**
**1 teaspoon sambal oelek**
**1 clove garlic, crushed**

Shell and devein prawns, leaving
tails intact. Combine all ingredients in
large bowl.

Just before serving, drizzle with lemon
grass dressing.

**Lemon grass dressing** Combine all
ingredients in jar; shake well.

☐ SERVES 4

***Freeze*** *Not suitable*

## CHICKEN breasts with creamy mushroom sauce

*Recipe best made just before serving*

**4 (680g) chicken breast fillets**
**plain flour**
**30g butter**
**150g oyster mushrooms**
**60g button mushrooms, sliced**
**1 tablespoon port**
**$1/2$ cup (125ml) dry white wine**
**$1/2$ cup (125ml) water**
**1 small chicken stock cube, crumbled**
**$1/2$ cup (125ml) cream**
**1 tablespoon chopped fresh chives**

Toss chicken in flour; shake away excess
flour. Heat butter in large pan, add
chicken, cook until browned on both sides.
Remove chicken from pan; drain.

Add mushrooms to same pan, cook,
stirring, until soft. Stir in port, wine, water
and stock cube. Return chicken to pan,
bring to boil, simmer, covered, about
10 minutes or until chicken is tender.
Remove chicken from pan; keep warm.

Add cream to pan, boil 1 minute or
until sauce is reduced slightly. Stir in
chives. Serve chicken with sauce.

☐ SERVES 4

***Freeze*** *Not suitable*
***Microwave*** *Not suitable*

## MUSHROOMS in spicy batter

*Recipe can be prepared 3 hours ahead*

**2 bacon rashers, finely chopped**
**$1/4$ teaspoon ground cumin**
**1 tablespoon sour cream**
**250g button mushrooms**
**vegetable oil, for deep-frying**

### Spicy batter

**2 tablespoons plain flour**
**$1/4$ cup (35g) self-raising flour**
**pinch chilli powder**
**$1/2$ teaspoon garam masala**
**$1/4$ teaspoon ground cumin**
**$1/2$ cup water**

Add bacon and cumin to small pan, cook,
stirring, until bacon is crisp, drain on
absorbent paper; cool.

Combine bacon mixture and cream in
small bowl. Spread around stems of
mushrooms, cover, refrigerate 20 minutes.

Just before serving, dip mushrooms in
spicy batter. Deep-fry, in hot oil, until
browned lightly; drain on absorbent paper.

**Spicy batter** Sift dry ingredients into small
bowl, stir in water, stir until smooth.

☐ MAKES ABOUT 12

***Storage*** *Covered, in refrigerator*
***Freeze*** *Not suitable*
***Microwave*** *Not suitable*

*clockwise from top left*, Spicy prawn and
mushroom salad, Chicken breasts with
creamy mushroom sauce, Mushrooms
in spicy batter

## Beef 'n' bean PANCAKES

*Beef mixture can be made a day ahead*
*Pancakes are best made close to serving*

**2 teaspoons vegetable oil**
**1 medium (150g) onion, chopped**
**250g hamburger mince**
**1/4 teaspoon chilli powder**
**1 teaspoon ground coriander**
**1 teaspoon ground sweet paprika**
**1 small beef stock cube, crumbled**
**410g can tomatoes,**
**undrained, crushed**
**1/2 cup (125ml) water**
**310g can red kidney beans,**
**rinsed, drained**
**1/3 cup (80ml) sour cream**

### Pancakes

**2 cups (300g) self-raising flour**
**1 teaspoon sugar**
**1 egg, lightly beaten**
**1 cup (250ml) milk**
**1/2 cup (125ml) water**

Heat oil in pan, add onion, cook, stirring, until onion is soft. Stir in mince and spices, cook, stirring, until mince is browned. Stir in stock cube, tomatoes and water, simmer, uncovered, about 5 minutes or until sauce is thickened slightly. Add beans, stir over heat until hot. Top pancakes with bean mixture and sour cream.

**Pancakes** Sift flour and sugar into medium bowl, make a well in centre, whisk in combined remaining ingredients; whisk until smooth. Pour 1/4 cup (60ml) of mixture into heated, greased pan, cook until brown underneath. Turn and brown other side, keep warm. Repeat with remaining batter to make 8 pancakes.

□ SERVES 4

***Storage*** *Beef mixture, covered, in refrigerator*
***Freeze*** *Suitable*
***Microwave*** *Beef mixture suitable*

Beef 'n' bean pancakes, *above*

## Spiced CHICKEN with couscous seasoning

*Recipe best made just before serving*

**1.5kg chicken**
**1/2 cup (125ml) plain yogurt**
**1/2 teaspoon ground turmeric**
**2 teaspoons ground sweet paprika**
**2 teaspoons ground cumin**
**2 teaspoons ground coriander**
**1/2 teaspoon ground cinnamon**
**1 2/3 cups (410ml) apricot nectar**
**2 teaspoons cornflour**
**1/3 cup (80ml) chicken stock**

### Couscous seasoning

**1/3 cup (65g) couscous**
**1/3 cup (80ml) boiling water**
**1/4 cup (35g) chopped dried**
**apricots**
**1/3 cup (55g) chopped seeded**
**dates**
**1/4 cup (35g) pistachio kernels,**
**toasted, chopped**
**2 tablespoons apricot nectar**

# LAMB biryani

*Ask the butcher to bone the lamb*
*Recipe can be made a day ahead*

**2 cups (400g) long-grain rice**
**2kg leg of lamb, boned**
**¹/₄ cup (60ml) vegetable oil**
**2 medium (300g) onions, sliced**
**2 cloves garlic, crushed**
**2 teaspoons ground cumin**
**1 tablespoon ground coriander**
**¹/₄ teaspoon ground turmeric**
**410g can tomatoes,**
   **undrained, crushed**
**1 tablespoon tomato paste**
**1 teaspoon sugar**
**2 cups (500ml) coconut milk**
**3cm cinnamon stick**

Lightly oil 3 litre (12-cup) ovenproof dish.

Add rice to pan of boiling water, boil, uncovered, until tender; drain. Rinse well, drain.

Trim lamb, cut into 2cm cubes. Heat 2 tablespoons of the oil in large pan, add lamb in batches, cook, stirring, until well browned all over, remove from pan.

Heat remaining oil in pan, add onions and garlic, cook, stirring, until soft. Add spices, cook, stirring, until fragrant. Add tomatoes, paste, sugar and coconut milk, cook, stirring, 3 minutes.

Return lamb to pan with cinnamon. Simmer, covered, 20 minutes. Remove lid, simmer, uncovered, 30 minutes or until lamb is tender and mixture thickened; discard cinnamon stick.

Spoon half the rice into prepared dish, top with half the lamb mixture, repeat with remaining rice and lamb mixture.

Bake, covered, in moderate oven about 30 minutes or until heated through.

□ SERVES 6

**Storage** *Covered, in refrigerator*
**Freeze** *Suitable*
**Microwave** *Not suitable*

Lamb biryani, *below*

---

**2 tablespoons chopped**
   **fresh coriander**

Fill chicken with couscous seasoning; place chicken in flameproof baking dish. Combine yogurt with spices in small bowl, brush over chicken. Add 1 cup (250ml) of the nectar.

Bake, uncovered, in moderate oven about 1¹/₂ hours or until tender. Remove chicken from dish, cover with foil. Drain fat from dish. Heat pan juices, add remaining nectar and blended cornflour and stock stir until sauce boils and thickens; strain. Serve sauce with chicken.

**Couscous seasoning** Combine couscous and water in heatproof bowl stand 10 minutes or until water is absorbed. Stir in remaining ingredients.

□ SERVES 4 TO 6

**Freeze** *Not suitable*
**Microwave** *Not suitable*

Spiced chicken with couscous seasoning, *above*

# moods
## to be truffled with

*chocolate crackles
with excitement*

# Fruity coffee liqueur TRUFFLES

*Recipe can be made 2 weeks ahead*

$1/3$ cup (80ml) cream
$1^2/3$ cups (250g) white chocolate
  Melts, chopped
$1/3$ cup (50g) dried currants
$1^1/2$ tablespoons Kahlua
1 cup (100g) plain cake crumbs
2 tablespoons finely chopped
  glace figs
$3/4$ cup (65g) desiccated coconut,
  approximately

Heat cream in small pan until boiling; pour over chocolate Melts in a heat proof medium bowl, stir until smooth. Stir in currants, liqueur, crumbs and figs; cool. Cover, refrigerate several hours or until firm.

Roll rounded teaspoons of mixture into balls, roll in coconut; refrigerate until required.

☐ MAKES ABOUT 45

***Storage*** *Airtight container, in refrigerator*
***Freeze*** *Suitable*
***Microwave*** *Suitable*

# Rich amaretti TRUFFLES

*Recipe can be made 2 weeks ahead*

9 (60g) amaretti macaroons
250g dark chocolate, chopped
30g butter
$1/3$ cup (80ml) cream
2 tablespoons Creme de Cacao
1 tablespoon finely chopped
  glace ginger
$1/2$ cup (50g) cocoa powder

Process macaroons until finely crushed.

Combine chocolate, butter and cream in heatproof medium bowl over pan of simmering water; stir until smooth. Remove from heat.

Stir in liqueur, ginger and macaroon crumbs; cool. Cover, refrigerate several hours or until firm.

Roll rounded teaspoons of mixture into balls; drop into bowl of sifted cocoa, toss to coat; cover, refrigerate.

Just before serving, shake away excess cocoa from truffles.

☐ MAKES ABOUT 45

***Storage*** *Airtight container, in refrigerator*
***Freeze*** *Suitable*
***Microwave*** *Suitable*

# Macadamia TRUFFLES

*Recipe can be made 2 weeks ahead*

250g milk chocolate, chopped
30g butter
$1/3$ cup (80ml) cream
$1^1/2$ tablespoons dark rum
$1^1/2$ cups (150g) chocolate
  cake crumbs
$1/2$ cup (75g) unsalted macadamia
  halves, toasted
$1^2/3$ cups (250g) milk
  chocolate Melts
50g Copha, chopped

Combine chocolate, butter and cream in heatproof medium bowl over pan of simmering water; stir until smooth. Remove from heat, stir in rum; cool.

Stir in cake crumbs and nuts. Cover, refrigerate 3 hours or overnight.

Roll rounded teaspoons of mixture into balls, cover; refrigerate until firm.

Combine Melts and Copha in heatproof bowl over pan of simmering water; stir until smooth. Dip balls in Melts mixture, place on baking paper-covered trays; refrigerate until required.

☐ MAKES ABOUT 45

***Storage*** *Airtight container, in refrigerator*
***Freeze*** *Suitable*
***Microwave*** *Suitable*

Rich amaretti truffles, Macadamia truffles, Fruity coffee liqueur truffles, *below left, from left*

# Double chocolate BITES

*Recipe can be made several days ahead*

200g white marshmallows
60g butter
125g white chocolate, chopped
$1^1/2$ cups (285g) Choc Bits, melted

Grease an 8cm x 26cm bar pan, line base and sides with foil; grease foil.

Combine marshmallows and butter in medium pan, stir constantly over

## Triple chocolate
# BROWNIES

*Recipe can be made 3 days ahead*

**125g butter**
**200g dark chocolate, chopped**
**½ cup (110g) caster sugar**
**2 eggs, lightly beaten**
**1¼ cups (185g) plain flour**
**150g white chocolate, chopped**
**100g milk chocolate, chopped**

Grease a deep 19cm square cake pan, cover base and sides with baking paper.

Combine butter and dark chocolate in small pan, stir over heat until smooth; transfer to large bowl, cool 5 minutes.

Stir in sugar and eggs, then sifted flour, fold in white and milk chocolate. Spread mixture evenly into prepared pan.

Bake, uncovered, in moderate oven about 35 minutes or until firm; cool in pan.

Cut into 4cm squares when cold.

☐ MAKES ABOUT 25 SQUARES

***Storage*** *Covered, in refrigerator*
***Freeze*** *Suitable*
***Microwave*** *Not suitable*

Chocolate orange sticks,
Double chocolate bites, *left, from left*
Triple chocolate brownies, *below*

## Chocolate orange
# STICKS

*Recipe can be made 3 days ahead*

**2 large (600g) thick-skinned**
**oranges**
**1 cup (250ml) water**
**1 cup (220g) caster sugar**
**125g dark chocolate**

Cut skin of each orange into quarters by cutting through skin to flesh of orange; peel away orange skin, leaving thick pith intact on orange skin. Cut orange skin into strips 1cm thick.

Drop strips of skin into large pan of boiling water, return to boil; drain. Repeat boiling and draining twice more.

Combine water and sugar in large pan, stir over heat, without boiling, until sugar is dissolved. Add orange strips, bring to boil, simmer, uncovered, about 7 minutes or until strips become translucent. Stir from time to time while simmering.

Using 2 forks or tongs, remove orange strips from pan to wire rack over tray. Allow to dry overnight.

Melt chocolate in small heatproof bowl over simmering water. Dip half of each orange strip into chocolate, place on tray covered with foil. Stand, uncovered, at room temperature until set.

***Storage*** *Airtight container, in refrigerator*
***Freeze*** *Not suitable*
***Microwave*** *Chocolate suitable*

heat until marshmallows are melted; do not boil. Remove pan from heat.

Stir in white chocolate, stir until smooth. Beat for 1 minute with wooden spoon. Spread mixture into prepared pan, cover, refrigerate 3 hours or until set.

Remove mixture from pan, cut into 2cm cubes. Dip cubes in melted chocolate. Place on foil-covered tray, drizzle with any remaining chocolate, refrigerate until firm.

☐ MAKES ABOUT 50

***Storage*** *Airtight container, in refrigerator*
***Freeze*** *Not suitable*
***Microwave*** *Suitable*

# Smoked fish PATTIES

*We used smoked cod for this dish*
*Recipe can be prepared a day ahead*

**1 tablespoon vegetable oil**
**1 medium (150g) onion,**
    **finely chopped**
**2 cloves garlic, crushed**
**500g smoked fish**
**1$\frac{1}{2}$ cups (105g) stale**
    **breadcrumbs**
**1 egg, lightly beaten**
**2 teaspoons grated lemon rind**
**1 tablespoon lemon juice**
**1 tablespoon vegetable oil, extra**

### Mustard mayonnaise

**$\frac{2}{3}$ cup (160ml) mayonnaise**
**1 tablespoon water**
**2 teaspoons hot English mustard**
**$\frac{1}{3}$ cup chopped fresh chives**

Heat oil in pan, add onion and garlic, cook, stirring, until onion is soft; cool. Place fish in food processor, process until smooth.

Combine onion mixture, fish, crumbs, egg, rind and juice in large bowl. Divide mixture into 8 portions, shape into patties.

Heat extra oil in large pan, cook patties, in batches, until well browned and cooked through; drain on absorbent paper. Serve with mustard mayonnaise.

**Mustard mayonnaise** Combine all ingredients in small bowl.

□ SERVES 4

**Storage** *Covered, in refrigerator*
**Freeze** *Not suitable*
**Microwave** *Not suitable*

Smoked fish patties, *above*
Italian veal casserole, *right*
Peppered chicken pasta, *above right*

Heat butter and oil in large pan, add veal, onion and garlic, cook until veal is browned all over.

Place veal mixture in a 2 litre (8-cup) casserole dish, stir in tomatoes and remaining ingredients.

Bake, covered, in moderately slow oven about $1^3/_4$ hours or until veal is tender.

□ SERVES 4

**Storage** *Covered, in refrigerator*
**Freeze** *Suitable*
**Microwave** *Not suitable*

## Peppered CHICKEN pasta

*We used a mixture of spinach and plain fettuccine  Recipe best made just before serving*

**4 (680g) chicken breast fillets**
**1 tablespoon vegetable oil**
**200g pepperoni sausage, sliced**
**2 medium (400g) green capsicums, sliced**
**1 tablespoon canned green peppercorns, drained, rinsed**
**$^1/_2$ cup (125ml) dry white wine**
**300ml cream**
**1 teaspoon cornflour**
**2 teaspoons water**
**500g fresh pasta**

Cut chicken into thin strips. Heat oil in large pan, add chicken, cook about 5 minutes or until chicken is browned and cooked through. Add pepperoni, capsicums and peppercorns, stir over heat for 5 minutes. Stir in wine, cream and cornflour blended with water, stir over heat until sauce boils and thickens.

Meanwhile, cook pasta in large pan of boiling water until tender, serve topped with sauce.

□ SERVES 4

**Freeze** *Not suitable*
**Microwave** *Suitable*

## Italian VEAL casserole

*Recipe can be made 3 days ahead*

**40g butter**
**2 tablespoons olive oil**
**1kg diced veal**
**1 medium (150g) onion, chopped**
**2 cloves garlic, crushed**
**400g can tomatoes, undrained, crushed**
**1 small chicken stock cube, crumbled**
**$^1/_2$ cup (125ml) dry red wine**
**$^1/_2$ cup (125ml) water**
**$1^1/_2$ cups (180g) seeded olives, sliced**
**1 medium (200g) green capsicum, chopped**
**1 medium (200g) red capsicum, chopped**
**$^1/_4$ cup chopped fresh parsley**
**2 tablespoons chopped fresh basil**
**1 tablespoon chopped fresh oregano**
**1 teaspoon dried thyme**

# Pasta-topped beef CASSEROLE

*Recipe can be prepared a day ahead*

250g penne pasta
1kg beef chuck steak
3 medium (450g) onions
$1/4$ cup (60ml) vegetable oil
2 cloves garlic, crushed
1 cup (250ml) beef stock
$1/2$ cup (125ml) dry red wine
$1/2$ cup (125ml) tomato puree
$1/4$ cup (60ml) tomato paste
1 tablespoon chopped
   fresh rosemary
2 teaspoons chopped fresh thyme
400g button mushrooms, halved
$1/4$ cup (35g) plain flour
$1/3$ cup (80ml) water
$1/4$ cup (20g) grated
   parmesan cheese

### Topping

300ml sour cream
1 tablespoon milk
1 cup (125g) grated
   cheddar cheese
$1/4$ cup (20g) grated
   parmesan cheese
1 tablespoon chopped fresh chives

Pasta-topped beef casserole, below

Add pasta to large pan of boiling water, boil, uncovered, until just tender; drain. Trim steak, cut into 2cm cubes. Cut onions into wedges.

Heat half the oil in large pan, add steak in batches, cook, stirring, until well browned; drain on absorbent paper.

Heat remaining oil in same pan, add onions and garlic, cook, stirring, until onions are soft. Return steak to pan with stock, wine, puree, paste and herbs; simmer, covered, 45 minutes, stirring occasionally. Stir in mushrooms, simmer, covered, 30 minutes or until steak is tender.

Stir in blended flour and water, stir until mixture boils and thickens. Stir half the pasta into steak mixture, reserve remaining pasta for topping. Pour mixture into deep 3 litre (12-cup) ovenproof dish. Spoon topping over casserole, sprinkle with cheese.

Bake, uncovered, in moderately hot oven about 25 minutes or until topping is browned lightly.

**Topping** Combine reserved pasta with remaining ingredients in large bowl.

□ SERVES 6

*Storage* Covered, in refrigerator
*Freeze* Suitable
*Microwave* Pasta suitable

# Nutty PORK steaks
## with tomato sauce

*Recipe can be prepared several hours ahead
Sauce can be made a day ahead*

250g packet frozen chopped
   spinach, thawed
4 green onions, chopped
2 cloves garlic, crushed
$1/2$ cup (35g) stale breadcrumbs
2 tablespoons chopped hazelnuts
2 teaspoons seeded mustard
4 pork midloin butterfly steaks
2 teaspoons olive oil

### Tomato sauce

2 teaspoons olive oil
1 small (80g) onion, chopped
2 cloves garlic, crushed
425g can tomatoes,
   undrained, crushed
1 teaspoon mild sweet chilli sauce
$1/2$ teaspoon sugar
1 tablespoon chopped fresh basil

Squeeze excess liquid from spinach. Combine spinach, onions and garlic in small non-stick pan, cook, stirring, until onions are soft. Stir in breadcrumbs, nuts and mustard.

Divide spinach mixture over cut side of pork, fold in half to enclose filling; secure with toothpicks.

Just before serving, place pork on oven tray, brush with oil.

Bake, uncovered, in moderately hot oven, about 20 minutes or until juices just run clear when pork is pierced with a skewer. Remove toothpicks, serve with tomato sauce.

**Tomato sauce** Heat oil in pan, add onion and garlic, cook, stirring, until onion is soft. Add tomatoes, sauce and sugar, simmer, uncovered, about 2 minutes or until thickened slightly. Blend or process tomato mixture until smooth, stir in basil, stir over heat until hot.

□ SERVES 4

*Storage* Covered, in refrigerator
*Freeze* Not suitable
*Microwave* Spinach mixture and Tomato sauce suitable

# Mediterranean-style PORK roast

*Recipe can be cooked in a covered barbecue, following the manufacturer's instructions Recipe can be prepared a day ahead*

**1 medium (200g) red capsicum**
**1.5kg pork neck**
**8 slices prosciutto**
**1 hard-boiled egg, quartered**
**10 pimiento-stuffed green olives**
**1 cup loosely packed fresh basil, roughly chopped**
**2 cloves garlic, crushed**
**1 tablespoon olive oil**

Quarter capsicum, remove and discard seeds and membranes. Roast under grill or in very hot oven, skin-side up, until skin blisters and blackens. Cover capsicum pieces in plastic or paper for 5 minutes, peel away skin.

Place pork on bench, cut lengthways, about 2cm from the base, then continue to roll out and cut pork to create one large 2cm-thick flat piece of pork.

Place prosciutto over pork. Place capsicum, egg and olives across one short end of pork, press basil all over prosciutto.

Roll pork tightly from egg-topped end, secure with string at 3cm intervals, rub all over with garlic.

Heat oil in flameproof baking dish, add pork, cook over heat until browned all over.

Bake, uncovered, in moderate oven, about $1^{1}/_{4}$ hours, or until cooked through.

Let stand 10 minutes before serving.

☐ SERVES 6

**Storage** *Covered, in refrigerator*
**Freeze** *Not suitable*
**Microwave** *Not suitable*

Nutty pork steaks with tomato sauce, Mediterranean-style pork roast *above, from left*

# Spicy beef PIZZA

*Recipe best made just before serving*

1 tablespoon olive oil
500g minced beef
1 large (200g) onion, thinly sliced
1 clove garlic, crushed
2 teaspoons ground cumin
1 teaspoon ground coriander
1 teaspoon ground sweet paprika
$1/4$ teaspoon ground cinnamon
1 medium (120g) carrot, grated
2 small (180g) zucchini, grated
425g can tomatoes,
    undrained, crushed
$1/3$ cup (80ml) tomato paste
2 tablespoons chopped
    fresh coriander
2 x 25cm prepared pizza bases
2 tablespoons pine nuts, toasted

### Yogurt topping

200g plain yogurt
1 tablespoon chopped
    fresh coriander
$1/2$ teaspoon ground cumin
1 teaspoon honey
1 teaspoon lemon juice

Heat oil in large pan, add mince; cook, stirring, until browned. Add onion, garlic and spices; cook, stirring, until onion is soft. Stir in carrot, zucchini, tomatoes, paste and coriander; simmer; covered, about 20 minutes or until thickened; cool slightly. Place pizza bases on oven trays, top with mince mixture.

Bake, uncovered, in very hot oven about 15 minutes or until browned. Place spoonfuls of yogurt topping over mince mixture, sprinkle with pine nuts.
**Yogurt topping** Combine all ingredients in small bowl.

□ SERVES 6 TO 8

*Freeze* Not suitable
*Microwave* Not suitable

# Devilled CHICKEN with caramelised onions

*Recipe best made close to serving*

$1/4$ cup (60ml) olive oil
2 large (400g) onions, sliced
2 medium (400g) red
    capsicums, sliced
1.5kg chicken
$1/4$ cup (50g) firmly packed
    brown sugar
$1/4$ cup (60ml) malt vinegar
$1/4$ cup (60ml) tomato sauce
$1/4$ cup (60ml) Worcestershire sauce
2 x 310g cans chickpeas,
    rinsed, drained

Heat 2 tablespoons of the oil in large flameproof baking dish; add onions, cook, stirring, until soft. Stir in capsicums.

Place chicken on onion mixture, brush remaining oil over chicken.

Bake, uncovered, in moderate oven, 1 hour. Brush chicken with combined sugar, vinegar and sauces.

Bake, uncovered, about 30 minutes or until tender. Brushing chicken occasionally with sauce mixture during baking.

Remove chicken from dish, cover with foil. Add chickpeas to onion mixture simmer; uncovered 5 minutes. Serve onion mixture with chicken.

□ SERVES 4 TO 6

*Freeze* Not suitable
*Microwave* Not suitable

# Lemon thyme POTATO wedges

*Recipe best made close to serving*

6 large (1.8kg) old potatoes
2 tablespoons olive oil
2 tablespoons lemon juice
2 medium (280g) lemons, quartered
1 teaspoon cracked black pepper
2 tablespoons chopped fresh thyme

Cut washed, unpeeled potatoes into thick wedges. Combine potatoes, oil, juice, lemons, pepper and thyme in large shallow baking dish.

Bake, uncovered, in moderate oven about 1 hour or until potatoes are tender, turning occasionally.

□ SERVES 4 TO 6

*Freeze* Not suitable
*Microwave* Not suitable

Lemon thyme potato wedges,
Devilled chicken with caramelised
onions, *left, from top*
Spicy beef pizza, *above*

# Greek LAMB fricassee

*Ask the butcher to bone lamb Recipe can
be prepared a day ahead*

**2kg leg of lamb, boned**

**2 tablespoons olive oil**

**1 medium (150g) onion, chopped**

**1 cup (250ml) dry white wine**

**1 cup (250ml) water**

**2 bay leaves**

**1 large beef stock cube, crumbled**

**2 tablespoons chopped
fresh parsley**

**12 large cos lettuce
leaves, shredded**

**2 eggs, lightly beaten**

**$1/_4$ cup (60ml) lemon juice**

Trim lamb, cut into 2cm cubes.

Heat oil in large pan, add onion,
cook, stirring, until onion is soft. Add
lamb, cook, stirring, until lamb is
browned all over.

Stir in wine, water, bay leaves and
stock cube, bring to boil, simmer,
covered, 1 hour. Remove cover,
simmer further 30 minutes, stirring
occasionally, or until lamb is tender
and most of the liquid is evaporated.

Just before serving, remove bay
leaves, stir in parsley and lettuce. Beat
eggs in small bowl until thick,
gradually add juice, beat until
combined. Add egg mixture to lamb,
stir until heated through; do not boil.
Serve immediately.

□ SERVES 4

*Storage* Covered, in refrigerator
*Freeze* Lamb mixture (excluding parsley,
lettuce and egg mixture) suitable
*Microwave* Not suitable

Greek lamb fricassee, *above*

168

stir-fry 2 minutes. Add noodles, stir-fry until combined. Add onions, coriander and sauces, cook, stirring, until mixture is hot.

□ SERVES 4 TO 6

***Freeze*** *Not suitable*
***Microwave*** *Not suitable*

## Warm vegetable SALAD

*Recipe best made just before serving*

**2 large (700g) red capsicums**
**2 large (500g) tomatoes**
**4 finger (240g) eggplants**
**2 medium (240g) zucchini**
**150g button mushrooms, halved**
**$^1/_3$ cup (60g) small seeded black olives**
**$^1/_4$ cup shredded fresh basil**
**2 tablespoons lemon juice**
**2 tablespoons olive oil**
**2 cloves garlic, crushed**

Quarter capsicums, remove seeds and membranes. Roast under grill or in very hot oven, skin side up, until skin blisters and blackens. Cover capsicum pieces in plastic or paper for 5 minutes, peel away skin, cut into thick strips.

Cut tomatoes in half, remove seeds, cut flesh into thin strips. Cut eggplants and zucchini lengthways into thin strips.

Cook eggplant, zucchini and mushrooms, in batches, on oiled barbecue or pan until well browned and tender; drain on absorbent paper.

Combine capsicums, tomatoes and barbecued vegetables with remaining ingredients in large bowl.

□ SERVES 6

***Freeze*** *Not suitable*
***Microwave*** *Not suitable*

## Barbecued PORK and noodles

*Recipe best made just before serving*

**375g thin fresh egg noodles**
**$^1/_4$ cup (60ml) vegetable oil**
**2 cloves garlic, crushed**
**150g Chinese barbecued pork, sliced**
**150g cooked shelled prawns**
**2 celery sticks, chopped**
**2 green onions, sliced**
**2 tablespoons chopped fresh coriander**
**$^1/_4$ cup (60ml) mild sweet chilli sauce**
**2 tablespoons black bean sauce**
**1 tablespoon soy sauce**

Place noodles into large heatproof bowl, cut into 15cm lengths. Cover noodles with boiling water; drain.

Heat oil in large wok or pan, add garlic, pork, prawns and celery,

Barbecued pork and noodles, *above left*
Warm vegetable salad, *left*

*169*

## Rich beef and mushroom CASSEROLE

*Recipe can be made a day ahead*

2kg beef chuck steak
$1/4$ cup (60ml) vegetable oil
1 medium (150g) onion, chopped
$1/2$ cup (125ml) dry red wine
$1^3/4$ cups (430ml) water
3 teaspoons lemon juice
$1/2$ cup tomato paste
1 large beef stock cube, crumbled
1 bay leaf
1 tablespoon sugar
250g button mushrooms, quartered
2 medium (400g) red
    capsicums, chopped
4 green onions, chopped
$1/4$ cup (35g) cornflour
2 tablespoons water, extra

Trim steak, cut into large cubes. Heat oil in large pan, add steak in batches, cook until well browned all over; remove steak from pan. Add onion to pan, cook, stirring, until browned lightly. Return steak to pan, add wine, water, juice, paste, stock cube, bay leaf and sugar, bring to boil, cover; simmer about $1^1/4$ hours, or until steak is tender.

Add mushrooms, capsicums and green onions to pan, cover and simmer about 15 minutes, or until capsicums are tender.

Stir in cornflour blended with extra water, stir over heat until mixture boils and thickens. Remove bay leaf before serving.

□ SERVES 8 TO 10

***Storage*** *Covered in refrigerator*
***Freeze*** *Suitable*
***Microwave*** *Not suitable*

## Prawn SALAD with citrus dressing

*Croutons and Citrus Dressing can be made a day ahead  Recipe best made close to serving*

1.5kg uncooked medium prawns
$1/2$ loaf (400g) unsliced white bread
2 tablespoons olive oil
500g asparagus, chopped
1 baby (300g) cos lettuce
2 medium (500g) avocados,
    chopped

### Citrus dressing

1 teaspoon grated orange rind
$1/3$ cup (80ml) orange juice
1 teaspoon grated lemon rind
1 tablespoon lemon juice
$1/4$ cup (60ml) mayonnaise
2 tablespoons olive oil
1 tablespoon balsamic vinegar
2 teaspoons sugar
1 clove garlic, crushed

Shell and devein prawns leaving tails intact. Combine prawns and $1/4$ cup (60ml) of the citrus dressing in large bowl, cover, refrigerate 1 hour.

Cut crust from bread, cut bread into 2cm cubes. Combine bread and oil in medium bowl. Place bread in single layer in shallow baking dish.

Bake, uncovered, in moderately hot oven about 15 minutes or until browned and crisp, stirring occasionally.

Add asparagus to pan of boiling water, boil 1 minute; drain. Add prawns to heated oiled griddle pan (or barbecue or frying pan); cook until just tender. Combine prawns with croutons, asparagus, lettuce, avocado and remaining citrus dressing in large bowl; mix gently.

**Citrus dressing**  Blend or process all ingredients until smooth.

□ SERVES 6

***Storage*** *Croutons, airtight container*
*Dressing, airtight container, in refrigerator*
***Freeze*** *Not suitable*
***Microwave*** *Not suitable*

# Chilli SQUID
## and bok choy salad

*Squid can be prepared a day ahead*
*Crisps can be made a day ahead*

**1kg squid hoods**
**1/3 cup (65g) firmly packed**
**brown sugar**
**1/2 cup (125ml) white wine vinegar**
**1/2 cup (125ml) vegetable oil**
**2 tablespoons soy sauce**
**4 small fresh red chillies,**
**seeded, chopped**
**2 medium (400g) yellow capsicums**
**2 bunches (1kg) baby bok choy**
**2 tablespoons sesame**
**seeds, toasted**

### Crisps

**18 gow gee wrappers, halved**
**vegetable oil, for deep-frying**

Cut squid hoods open, score shallow diagonal slashes in criss-cross pattern on inside surface; cut squid into 4cm strips.

Combine sugar, vinegar, oil, sauce and chillies in jug. Reserve half the vinegar mixture for dressing; combine remaining vinegar mixture with squid in large bowl, cover, refrigerate 3 hours.

Quarter capsicums, remove seeds. Place capsicums, skin side down, on board. Cut capsicums horizontally, removing membranes and some of the flesh until 2mm thick; discard membranes and flesh. Slice into 2mm strips, place strips in bowl of iced water, cover, refrigerate about 1 hour or until capsicums curl.

Trim ends from bok choy; shred leaves and stalks.

Drain squid; discard marinade. Add squid, in batches, to heated oiled griddle pan (or barbecue or frying pan); cook until just tender; transfer to bowl, stir in bok choy and reserved vinegar mixture. Serve squid mixture with crisps; top with capsicum curls and sesame seeds.

**Crisps** Deep-fry wrappers in hot oil, in batches, until browned; drain on absorbent paper.

□ SERVES 4 TO 6

**Storage** *Squid, covered, in refrigerator*
*Crisps, in airtight container*
**Freeze** *Marinated squid suitable*
**Microwave** *Not suitable*

Rich beef and mushroom casserole, *above left*
Prawn salad with citrus dressing, Chilli squid and bok choy salad, *above, from top*

Coat chicken in flour, shake away excess flour. Heat butter and oil in large pan, add chicken pieces, cook over high heat until browned; remove from pan.

Add onion, garlic and mushrooms to same pan, cook, stirring, until onions are soft. Add stock, tarragon, paste, sugar, wine and chicken; simmer, covered, about 20 minutes or until chicken is tender. Stir in green onions and parsley just before serving.

□ SERVES 4

**Storage**  Covered, in refrigerator
**Freeze**  Not suitable
**Microwave**  Suitable

## PORK patties with cranberry orange sauce

*Recipe can be prepared a day ahead*

**500g pork and veal mince**
**1 clove garlic, crushed**
**1 medium (150g) onion, grated**
**1 tablespoon chopped**
   **fresh parsley**
**2 teaspoons chopped fresh sage**
**1 egg, lightly beaten**
**$1/_4$ cup (60ml) vegetable oil**
**3 teaspoons grated orange rind**
**$1/_4$ cup (125ml) orange juice**
**$1/_4$ cup (60ml) water**
**1 small chicken stock**
   **cube, crumbled**
**$1/_4$ cup (60ml) cranberry sauce**
**1 tablespoon cream**

Combine mince, garlic, onion, herbs and egg in large bowl. Divide mixture into 8 portions; shape each into a patty. Heat oil in a shallow pan, add patties, cook until cooked through; drain. Remove excess fat from pan. Add rind, juice, water, stock cube, sauce and cream to pan. Return patties to pan, simmer until hot.

□ SERVES 4

**Storage**  Covered, in refrigerator
**Freeze**  Uncooked patties suitable
**Microwave**  Not suitable

## CHICKEN chasseur

*Recipe can be made a day ahead*

**6 (1kg) chicken thigh cutlets**
**2 tablespoons plain flour**
**40g butter**
**1 tablespoon vegetable oil**
**1 medium (150g) onion, chopped**
**1 clove garlic, crushed**

**150g button mushrooms, sliced**
**$1/_2$ cup (125ml) chicken stock**
**$1/_2$ teaspoon dried tarragon**
**2 tablespoons tomato paste**
**1 teaspoon sugar**
**$1/_2$ cup (125ml) dry white wine**
**6 green onions, chopped**
**1 tablespoon chopped**
   **fresh parsley**

# Scalloped potato topped lamb and vegetable HOTPOT

*Recipe can be made a day ahead*

1kg diced lamb forequarter
$1/2$ teaspoon seasoned pepper
$1/2$ cup (75g) plain flour
$1/4$ cup (60ml) vegetable oil
20g butter
1 medium (350g) leek, sliced
$1^1/2$ cups (375ml) beef stock
2 medium (240g) carrots, sliced
1 medium (200g) parsnip, sliced
2 celery sticks, thinly sliced
2 medium (400g) old
    potatoes, sliced
$1/2$ teaspoon ground sweet paprika

Toss lamb in combined pepper and flour, shake away excess flour. Heat 2 tablespoons of the oil and butter in large heavy-based pan, add lamb in batches, cook, stirring until well browned; drain on absorbent paper. Heat remaining oil in same pan, add leek, cook, stirring, until soft. Return lamb to pan with stock, simmer, uncovered, about 10 minutes or until thickened slightly; stir in carrots, parsnip and celery.

Spoon lamb mixture into 2.5 litre (10-cup) ovenproof dish. Top with potato slices, sprinkle with paprika.

Bake, covered, in moderately hot oven about 1 hour or until lamb is tender.

□ SERVES 6

**Storage** *Covered, in refrigerator*
**Freeze** *Suitable*
**Microwave** *Not suitable*

Chicken chasseur, *above left*
Scalloped potato topped lamb and vegetable hotpot, *above right*
Pork patties with cranberry orange sauce, *right*

# Citrus peppered VEAL

*Recipe best prepared a day ahead*

1/2 cup (125ml) dry red wine
2 teaspoons grated orange rind
1/2 cup (125ml) orange juice
1/4 cup (60ml) redcurrant jelly
2 teaspoons chopped fresh sage
2 teaspoons cracked black pepper
8 (1kg) veal cutlets, trimmed
2 tablespoons olive oil
30g butter
3/4 cup (180ml) tomato juice
1 teaspoon cornflour
2 teaspoons water
2 oranges, peeled, sliced
1/2 cup (90g) small seeded
   black olives

Combine wine, rind, orange juice, jelly, sage and pepper in a large bowl. Add cutlets; turn to coat in mixture.

Cover, refrigerate for at least 1 hour, turning occasionally. Remove from marinade; reserve marinade.

Heat oil and butter in pan. Cook cutlets, in batches, on both sides until cooked as desired. Cover to keep warm.

Meanwhile combine reserved marinade and tomato juice in pan; bring to boil, simmer 5 minutes. Add blended cornflour and water, stir over heat until mixture boils and thickens slightly.

Place orange slices on oven tray, cook under hot grill until just warmed.

Serve cutlets with orange slices, olives and sauce.

□ SERVES 4

**Storage** *Covered, in refrigerator*
**Freeze** *Not suitable*
**Microwave** *Sauce suitable*

# LINGUINE with zucchini sauce

*Recipe best made just before serving*

500g linguine pasta
1 cup (250ml) olive oil
3 cloves garlic, crushed
4 large (600g) zucchini, grated
1 teaspoon cracked black pepper
1/3 cup shredded fresh basil
1/3 cup (50g) pine nuts, toasted
1/2 cup (40g) grated
   parmesan cheese

Add pasta to large pan of boiling water, boil, uncovered, until just tender; drain, keep warm.

Heat oil in pan, add garlic and zucchini, cook, stirring, about 10 minutes or until softened. Stir in pepper and basil.

Combine pasta and zucchini sauce in large serving bowl; sprinkle with nuts and cheese.

□ SERVES 4 TO 6

**Freeze** *Not suitable*
**Microwave** *Suitable*

# Vegetable CANNELLONI

*Recipe can be made a day ahead*

2 medium (600g) eggplants
salt
2 tablespoons olive oil
2 medium (300g) onions,
   finely chopped
1 large (350g) red capsicum,
   finely chopped
3 cloves garlic, crushed
2 tablespoons chopped
   fresh oregano
2 x 425g cans tomatoes,
   undrained, crushed
2 tablespoons tomato paste
2 teaspoons sugar
1 teaspoon cracked black pepper
250g packaged instant cannelloni
   pasta tubes
1/2 cup (40g) grated
   parmesan cheese

### Cheese sauce

**40g butter**
**¹/₄ cup (35g) plain flour**
**3 cups (750ml) milk**
**³/₄ cup (75g) grated mozzarella cheese**

Oil a rectangular 2.25 litre (9-cup) ovenproof dish. Cut eggplant into slices 1cm thick, place on rack. Sprinkle with salt, stand 30 minutes. Rinse, under cold running water; drain, chop into 1cm cubes.

Heat oil in pan, add onions, cook, stirring, until onions are very soft. Add eggplant, capsicum, garlic and oregano, cook, stirring, about 10 minutes or until vegetables are very soft. Add tomatoes, paste, sugar and pepper. Simmer, uncovered, about 20 minutes or until thick. Refrigerate until cold.

Spoon eggplant mixture into piping bag fitted with large plain tube, pipe into cannelloni tubes. Spread ¹/₂ cup (125ml) cheese sauce over base of dish, top with half the cannelloni. Repeat with cheese sauce and cannelloni, ending with cheese sauce; sprinkle with cheese.

Bake, uncovered, in moderate oven 1 hour or until pasta is tender.

**Cheese sauce** Melt butter in pan, add flour, cook, stirring, until bubbling. Remove from heat, gradually stir in milk. Stir over heat until sauce boils and thickens; stir in cheese.

□ SERVES 4

**Storage** *Covered, in refrigerator*
**Freeze** *Suitable*
**Microwave** *Cheese sauce suitable*

Citrus peppered veal, *left*
Linguine with zucchini sauce,
Vegetable cannelloni, *above, from left*

# Rich fruit STRUDELS

*Filling can be made 2 days ahead*
*Strudels best made just before serving*

**¹/₃ cup (50g) chopped**
    **dried apricots**
**¹/₃ cup (70g) chopped**
    **seeded prunes**
**¹/₃ cup (50g) dried currants**
**¹/₄ cup (20g) chopped dried apples**
**¹/₃ cup (55g) chopped dried dates**
**¹/₃ cup (65g) chopped dried figs**
**¹/₂ cup (80g) sultanas**
**¹/₄ teaspoon ground cinnamon**
**¹/₄ teaspoon ground cloves**
**¹/₂ teaspoon grated lemon rind**
**¹/₄ cup (60ml) Grand Marnier**
**¹/₄ cup (50g) firmly packed**
    **brown sugar**
**6 sheets fillo pastry**
**60g butter, melted**

**¹/₂ cup (60g) ground walnuts**
**²/₃ cup (160ml) Grand**
    **Marnier, extra**

Combine fruit, spices, rind, liqueur and sugar in large bowl; stand 2 hours.

Brush one pastry sheet with some of the butter, top with another pastry sheet, brush with some of the remaining butter, sprinkle with half the nuts, top with another pastry sheet, brush with some of the remaining butter; cut in half to form 2 large squares. Repeat with remaining pastry, some of the butter and nuts.

Spoon a quarter of the fruit mixture onto the centre of each pastry square, fold in sides, roll up squares to form small parcels.

Place strudels on an oven tray, brush with any remaining butter.

Bake in moderately hot oven 30 minutes or until browned lightly.

Meanwhile, heat extra liqueur in small pan, bring to the boil, simmer 3 minutes, or until reduced by a third; cool slightly. Serve strudels with warm extra liqueur.

□ MAKES 4

**Storage** *Covered, in refrigerator*
**Freeze** *Not suitable*
**Microwave** *Not suitable*

Rich fruit strudels, *above*

# White chocolate banana TORTE

*You will need 2 large over-ripe bananas*
*Recipe can be made a day ahead*

- 1¹/₂ cups (225g) self-raising flour
- ¹/₂ cup (75g) plain flour
- 1 cup (220g) caster sugar
- ¹/₂ teaspoon bicarbonate of soda
- 90g white chocolate Melts, melted
- 125g butter, melted
- 2 eggs
- ¹/₂ cup (125ml) milk
- 1 cup mashed banana
- 300ml cream
- 1 cup (80g) flaked almonds, toasted

### White chocolate cream

- 300ml cream
- 100g white chocolate Melts, melted

Grease a deep 22cm round cake pan, line base with baking paper. Combine sifted flours, sugar, soda, Melts, butter, eggs, milk and banana in medium bowl of electric mixer, beat on low speed until ingredients are combined. Then beat until mixture is smooth and changed in colour. Spoon into prepared pan.

Bake in moderate oven 1 hour. Turn onto wire rack to cool.

Split cold cake horizontally into three layers, sandwich layers together with white chocolate cream.

Beat cream in small bowl until firm peaks form. Spread cream over top and side of cake, press nuts around side of cake.

**White chocolate cream** Beat cream and cooled Melts in small bowl with electric mixer until soft peaks form.

□ SERVES 6 TO 8

**Storage** *Covered, in refrigerator*
**Freeze** *Unfilled cake suitable*
**Microwave** *Melts and butter suitable*

White chocolate banana torte, *below*

# Hot RHUBARB butternut pie

*Recipe can be made a day ahead*

150g butternut cookies
1 cup (100g) plain cake crumbs
60g butter, melted
1/3 cup (25g) flaked almonds

### Rhubarb filling

750g bunch rhubarb,
 trimmed, chopped
2 large (400g) apples,
 peeled, grated
1/2 cup (110g) caster sugar
1 teaspoon grated orange rind
1/4 cup (35g) cornflour
1/4 cup (60ml) water
3/4 cup (75g) plain cake crumbs

### Crumble

1/3 cup (50g) self-raising flour
50g cold butter, chopped
1/4 cup (15g) shredded coconut
1/4 cup (50g) firmly packed
 brown sugar

Grease a 23cm pie dish. Process cookies until finely crushed. Combine cookie crumbs, cake crumbs and butter in bowl. Press over base and side of prepared dish; refrigerate 30 minutes.

Spread rhubarb filling into prepared dish, top with crumble, sprinkle with almonds.

Bake in moderate oven 30 minutes or until pie is browned. Serve hot.

**Rhubarb filling** Combine rhubarb, apples, sugar and rind in large pan, simmer, covered, 5 minutes, stirring occasionally, or until rhubarb is soft. Simmer, uncovered, stirring occasionally for 10 minutes. Stir in blended cornflour and water, continue stirring until mixture boils and thickens. Remove from heat, stir in crumbs; cool.

**Crumble** Sift flour into small medium bowl, rub in butter; stir in remaining ingredients.

□ SERVES 6

**Storage** *Covered, in refrigerator*
**Freeze** *Not suitable*
**Microwave** *Not suitable*

# Warm BERRY tart

*Recipe can be made a day ahead*

1 cup (90g) desiccated coconut
2/3 cup (150g) caster sugar
1/2 cup (75g) plain flour
125g butter, melted
4 eggs
1 cup (250ml) milk
1 cup (250ml) cream
1 teaspoon vanilla essence
1/2 cup (80g) sliced strawberries
425g can blueberries, drained

Grease 24cm pie dish. Combine coconut, sugar and flour in large bowl. Whisk in butter, eggs, milk, cream and essence until combined. Fold in berries, pour into prepared dish.

Bake in moderate oven 50 minutes or until firm.

□ SERVES 6

**Storage** *Covered, in refrigerator*
**Freeze** *Not suitable*
**Microwave** *Not suitable*

# Lime quince CAKE

*Cake can be made a day ahead*

1 large (500g) quince
1 cup (220g) caster sugar
1/2 cup (125ml) orange juice
1 1/2 cups (375ml) water
10cm cinnamon stick

### Cake mixture

125g butter
1 tablespoon grated lime rind
3/4 cup (165g) caster sugar
2 eggs
2 cups (300g) self-raising flour
1/4 cup (60ml) milk
1 tablespoon lime juice

Peel quince, cut into eighths, remove core. Place quince in shallow ovenproof dish. Combine remaining ingredients in pan, stir over heat, without boiling, until sugar is dissolved. Pour sugar mixture over quince.

Bake, covered, in moderately slow oven 1 1/2 hours, or until quince is rosy pink and tender; cool. Drain quince on absorbent paper; discard syrup.

Grease a 20cm round cake pan, line base with baking paper. Spread cake mixture over base of prepared pan, arrange quince over top.

Bake in moderate oven 45 minutes. Stand in pan 10 minutes, turn onto wire rack to cool. Serve warm or cold.

**Cake mixture** Beat butter, rind, and sugar in bowl until light and fluffy. Add eggs, one at a time, beat well. Fold in sifted flour, milk and juice in 2 batches.

□ SERVES 6

**Storage** *Airtight container*
**Freeze** *Not suitable*
**Microwave** *Not suitable*

## QUINCES in syrup

*Recipe can be made a day ahead*

- **2 large (1kg) quinces**
- **1 cup (220g) caster sugar**
- **1¹/₂ cups (375ml) water**
- **¹/₂ cup (125ml) dry white wine**
- **1 teaspoon grated lemon rind**
- **2 tablespoons lemon juice**
- **¹/₂ teaspoon ground cinnamon**

Peel quinces, cut into quarters, remove cores. Cut each quarter lengthways into 4 slices.

Combine remaining ingredients in pan, stir over heat, without boiling, until sugar is dissolved. Place quinces into 2 litre (8-cup) ovenproof dish. Pour sugar mixture over quinces.

Bake, covered, in moderately slow oven 2 hours or until quinces are rosy pink and tender.

Serve warm quince slices with syrup.

□ SERVES 6

**Storage** *Covered, in refrigerator*
**Freeze** *Not suitable*
**Microwave** *Not suitable*

Hot rhubarb butternut pie,
Warm berry tart, *above, from top*

Quinces in syrup, Lime quince cake,
*below, from top*

## Dried fruit COMPOTE

*Recipe can be made 3 days ahead*

$1^1/_4$ **cups (310ml) dry white wine**
$^1/_2$ **cup (125ml) port**
$^1/_2$ **cup (110g) caster sugar**
$^1/_3$ **cup (50g) dried apricots**
**8 (160g) dried figs, halved**
$^1/_2$ **cup (85g) seeded prunes**
**8 (125g) dried peaches, halved**
**10cm cinnamon stick**

Combine wine, port and sugar in
medium pan, stir over heat without
boiling until sugar is dissolved.
Simmer, uncovered, without stirring,
5 minutes. Add fruit and cinnamon to
pan, simmer, uncovered, 10 minutes
or until fruit is soft. Serve warm or
cold with yogurt, if desired.

□ SERVES 4

**Storage** *Covered, in refrigerator*
**Freeze** *Not suitable*
**Microwave** *Not suitable*

## Poached PEARS with
## cinnamon cream

*Recipe can be made a day ahead*

**4 medium (720g) firm pears**
**1 cup (250ml) dry red wine**
**1 cup (250ml) water**
$^1/_2$ **cup (110g) caster sugar**
**10cm cinnamon stick**

### Cinnamon cream

**300ml cream**
**1 tablespoon caster sugar**
**1 teaspoon ground cinnamon**

Trim base of pears to sit flat;
peel pears. Combine remaining
ingredients in medium pan, stir over
heat, without boiling, until sugar is
dissolved. Place pears upright in pan,
bring to boil, cover with foil, then
lid, simmer 15 minutes or until pears
are just tender.

Transfer pears and sugar syrup to
large bowl, cover, refrigerate 3 hours
or overnight, turning occasionally.

Remove pears from sugar syrup, strain syrup into medium pan; boil, uncovered, until reduced to about ³/₄ cup; cool. Serve pears with syrup and cinnamon cream.

**Cinnamon cream** Beat ingredients in small bowl until soft peaks form.

□ SERVES 4

**Storage** *Covered, in refrigerator*
**Freeze** *Not suitable*
**Microwave** *Suitable*

Dried fruit compote, *above left*
Poached pears with cinnamon cream, *left*
Sago steamed pudding, *above*

# Sago steamed
# PUDDING

*Recipe can be made 3 days ahead*

²/₃ cup (130g) sago (seed tapioca)
2 cups (500ml) milk
2 cups (320g) sultanas
1 cup (170g) raisins, chopped
2¹/₂ cups (175g) stale
   breadcrumbs
1¹/₂ cups (300g) firmly packed
   brown sugar
2 tablespoons plain flour
2 teaspoons bicarbonate of soda
2 eggs, lightly beaten
60g butter, melted

Combine sago and milk in small bowl, stir well, cover; refrigerate overnight.

Grease 2.25 litre (9-cup) pudding steamer, line base with baking paper.

Place sago mixture in small pan, stir constantly over low heat for 15 minutes or until sago is clear. Combine sago mixture with remaining ingredients in large bowl. Spoon into prepared steamer, cover with baking paper then foil, secure with string or lid. Crush surplus foil around rim of lid to form a good seal.

Place steamer in large pan with enough boiling water to come halfway up side of steamer. Boil, covered with tight-fitting lid, 3 hours. Replenish boiling water as necessary. Stand 5 minutes before turning out. Serve hot or cold.

□ SERVES 8

**Storage** *Covered, in refrigerator*
**Freeze** *Suitable*
**Microwave** *Not suitable*

# Banana SOUFFLES

*You will need about 1 over-ripe banana*
*Recipe must be made just before serving*

- 2$^1/_2$ **tablespoons caster sugar**
- 2 **tablespoons cornflour**
- $^1/_4$ **cup mashed banana**
- 2 **egg yolks**
- $^1/_2$ **cup (125ml) milk**
- 6 **egg whites**
- 2 **tablespoons caster sugar, extra**

Grease 4 x 1$^1/_4$ cup (310ml) souffle dishes, sprinkle bases and sides with about 1 tablespoon of the caster sugar, shake away excess sugar. Whisk remaining sugar, cornflour, banana and egg yolks in medium bowl until combined. Bring milk to boil, gradually whisk hot milk into banana mixture. Return mixture to pan, whisk over heat until mixture boils and becomes very thick. Transfer banana mixture to large bowl, cover surface with plastic wrap; cool for 5 minutes.

Beat egg whites in medium bowl with electric mixer until soft peaks form, gradually add extra sugar, beat until firm peaks form. Gently fold egg white mixture into banana mixture in 2 batches. Spoon mixture into prepared dishes, smooth tops. Place a thin slice of banana on each souffle, if desired. Lightly run a knife around edge of souffles. Place dishes on an oven tray.

Bake in moderately hot oven about 20 minutes or until browned and well risen. Serve immediately.

□ SERVES 4

**Freeze** *Not suitable*
**Microwave** *Not suitable*

Banana souffles, *above*
Peach and pear cake, *above right*
Pumpkin strudel, *right*

# Pumpkin STRUDEL

*Recipe best made just before serving*

- 800g **pumpkin, chopped**
- $^2/_3$ **cup (50g) stale breadcrumbs**
- 2 **tablespoons caster sugar**
- $^1/_2$ **teaspoon ground cinnamon**
- 1 **tablespoon apricot jam**
- 1 **cup (125g) chopped pecans**
- 3 **sheets fillo pastry**
- 40g **butter, melted**
- $^1/_4$ **cup (15g) stale**
  **breadcrumbs, extra**

Boil, steam or microwave pumpkin until soft, mash pumpkin with a fork until smooth. Combine pumpkin, breadcrumbs, sugar, cinnamon, jam and pecans in medium bowl.

Layer pastry sheets together, lightly brushing each with some of the butter and sprinkling one-third of the extra breadcrumbs over each sheet.

Spoon pumpkin filling along one long edge of pastry, leaving a 4cm border at ends. Fold in ends, roll up to form a log, brush with any remaining butter, place strudel on an oven tray.

Bake in moderate oven 20 minutes or until well browned.

□ SERVES 6

**Freeze** *Not suitable*
**Microwave** *Pumpkin suitable*

## Peach and pear CAKE

*This cake contains plain flour only*
*Recipe can be made a day ahead*

**2 x 415g cans peach slices**
**in light syrup**
**415g can pear halves**
**in light syrup**
**250g soft butter**
**³/₄ cup (165g) caster sugar**
**2 eggs**
**1 cup (150g) plain flour**
**¹/₃ cup (80ml) milk**
**³/₄ cup (90g) ground almonds**

### Cinnamon topping

**80g butter, melted**
**¹/₄ cup (55g) caster sugar**
**2 teaspoons ground cinnamon**
**2 eggs, lightly beaten**

Grease a 24cm springform tin, line base with baking paper. Drain fruit, pat dry; slice pears. Beat butter and sugar in medium bowl with electric mixer until light and fluffy; beat in eggs, one at a time, until combined. Fold in sifted flour and milk. Spread mixture into prepared tin. Sprinkle with almonds, top with fruit; pour cinnamon topping over fruit. Place tin on oven tray, place another oven tray on top of tin.

Bake in moderate oven 1¹/₂ hours, remove top tray and bake another 15 minutes. Stand cake 30 minutes before removing from tin.

**Cinnamon topping** Combine all ingredients in medium bowl.

***Storage*** *Airtight container*
***Freeze*** *Not suitable*
***Microwave*** *Not suitable*

# Frangipani PIE

*Pie case can be made 4 days ahead*
*Pie is best filled just before serving*

**1 cup (150g) plain flour**
**1 tablespoon icing sugar mixture**
**90g butter**
**1 egg yolk**
**1 tablespoon lemon juice,**
   **approximately**
**3 egg whites**
**¹/₂ cup (110g) caster sugar**

### Coconut filling

**¹/₃ cup (75g) caster sugar**
**¹/₄ cup (35g) cornflour**
**1¹/₂ cups (375ml) milk**
**¹/₄ cup (60ml) water**
**1 cup (70g) desiccated coconut**
**¹/₂ teaspoon coconut essence**

### Pineapple filling

**450g can crushed pineapple**
**2 egg yolks**
**¹/₄ cup (35g) cornflour**
**¹/₄ cup (60ml) water**

Sift flour and icing sugar into small bowl, rub in butter, add egg yolk and enough juice to make ingredients cling together. Knead pastry on floured surface until smooth; cover, refrigerate 30 minutes.

Roll pastry between two pieces of baking paper until large enough to line greased 23cm pie dish. Lift pastry into dish, trim edge of pastry, refrigerate 20 minutes.

Bake pastry, blind, in moderately hot oven 20 minutes; cool.

Spread half coconut filling into pie case, top with pineapple filling then remaining coconut filling.

Beat egg whites in a small bowl until soft peaks form, gradually beat in sugar until dissolved. Spread meringue over pie. Bake in moderate oven 10 minutes.

**Coconut filling** Combine sugar and cornflour in pan, stir in milk and water. Stir over heat until mixture boils; stir in coconut and essence.

**Pineapple filling** Combine undrained pineapple, egg yolks and blended cornflour and water in pan, stir over heat until mixture boils and thickens.

□ SERVES 6 TO 8

*Storage* *Fillings, in airtight containers, in refrigerator Pie case, in airtight container*
*Freeze* *Not suitable*
*Microwave* *Not suitable*

# Bee-sting CAKE

*It is important to have topping ready when cake has been cooked for 30 minutes Cake best made on day of serving*

**2 teaspoons (7g) dried yeast**
**$^1/_3$ cup (75g) caster sugar**
**$^3/_4$ cup (180ml) warm milk, approximately**
**$2^1/_2$ cups (375g) plain flour**
**60g butter, melted**

### Topping

**20g butter**
**2 tablespoons caster sugar**
**1 tablespoon honey**
**$^1/_2$ cup (40g) flaked almonds**

### Filling

**2 tablespoons custard powder**
**$^1/_4$ cup (55g) caster sugar**
**1 cup (250ml) milk**
**$^1/_2$ cup (125ml) cream, whipped**

Grease 22cm springform tin. Combine yeast, 1 teaspoon of the sugar and $^1/_4$ cup (60ml) of the milk in small bowl. Cover, stand in warm place about 10 minutes or until frothy.

Sift flour into large bowl, stir in remaining sugar. Make well in centre, stir in yeast mixture, butter and enough of the remaining milk to mix to a soft dough.

Knead dough on floured surface about 3 minutes or until dough is smooth and elastic. Place dough in large greased bowl. Cover, stand in warm place about 1 hour or until dough is nearly doubled in size.

Knead dough on lightly floured surface, until smooth. Press dough into 15cm circle, place in prepared tin, cover, stand in warm place about 1 hour or until dough reaches top of tin.

Bake in moderate oven 30 minutes. Quickly spread cake with topping, return to oven 5 minutes or until cake is firm and brown. Remove cake from tin, place on wire rack to cool.

Just before serving, split cold cake horizontally, sandwich with filling – do not refrigerate. Cut into wedges with serrated knife.

**Topping** Combine butter, sugar and honey in small heavy-based pan, cook, stirring, without boiling, until sugar is dissolved. Boil, without stirring, about $1^1/_2$ minutes or until light caramel in colour; gently stir in nuts.

**Filling** Combine custard powder and sugar in small pan, stir in enough of the milk to make a smooth paste; gradually stir in remaining milk. Stir over heat until mixture boils, simmer, stirring, 1 minute or until very thick.

Cover surface of custard with plastic wrap, refrigerate until cold. Beat custard until smooth; fold in cream, refrigerate before using.

□ SERVES 6 TO 8

***Freeze*** *Not suitable*
***Microwave*** *Not suitable*

Frangipani pie, *left*
Bee-sting cake, *below*

## BANANA and orange cake

*You will need about 2 large over-ripe bananas  Recipe can be made 1 week ahead*

**125g butter, chopped**
**2 teaspoons grated orange rind**
**$^3/_4$ cup (165g) caster sugar**
**2 eggs**
**1$^1/_2$ cups (225g) self-raising flour**
**$^1/_4$ cup (35g) plain flour**
**$^1/_2$ teaspoon bicarbonate of soda**
**$^1/_4$ cup (60ml) orange juice**
**$^1/_2$ cup (80g) sultanas**
**$^1/_2$ cup (60g) chopped walnuts**
**1 cup mashed banana**

Grease deep 22cm round cake pan, line base with baking paper.

Beat butter, rind and sugar in small bowl with electric mixer until light and fluffy; beat in eggs one at a time, beat

until combined. Transfer mixture to large bowl, stir in sifted flours and soda with remaining ingredients; mix well. Spread mixture into prepared pan.

Bake in moderate oven about 45 minutes. Stand cake 10 minutes before turning onto wire rack to cool.

**Storage** *Airtight container, in refrigerator*
**Freeze** *Suitable*
**Microwave** *Not suitable*

# Caramelised apple TART

*Golden delicious apples will give the best result  Recipe best made close to serving*

- **2 sheets frozen ready-rolled puff pastry, thawed**
- **1 egg yolk, lightly beaten**
- **4 medium (800g) apples, peeled**
- **40g butter**
- **1/2 cup (100g) firmly packed brown sugar**
- **2 tablespoons water**

Brush one pastry sheet with egg yolk, top with remaining sheet. Cut a 24cm circle from pastry; place pastry on lightly greased oven tray.

Bake in hot oven 15 minutes or until puffed and browned.

Meanwhile, halve apples; cut each half into 3 wedges, remove cores. Heat butter in large heavy-based pan, add apples, cook, 8 minutes or until lightly browned, stirring occasionally. Add sugar and water, stir gently until combined. Simmer, stirring, 5 minutes or until caramel mixture thickens slightly.

Place hot pastry on serving plate. Remove apples from caramel mixture with slotted spoon. Using two forks carefully arrange apples over pastry. Drizzle with remaining caramel mixture.

□ SERVES 6

**Freeze** *Not suitable*
**Microwave** *Not suitable*

Banana and orange cake, *above left*
Caramelised apple tart, *left*
Sweet sherry zabaglione with finger biscuits, *right*

# Sweet sherry ZABAGLIONE with finger biscuits

*Biscuits can be made a day ahead  Zabaglione must be made just before serving*

- **6 egg yolks**
- **1/4 cup (60ml) sweet sherry**
- **1/4 cup (55g) caster sugar**

### Finger biscuits

- **30g butter**
- **1/4 cup (55g) caster sugar**
- **1 egg white**
- **2 1/2 tablespoons plain flour**
- **1 tablespoon finely chopped pecans**

Combine all ingredients in small heatproof bowl, over a pan of simmering water, beat with rotary beater, or hand-held electric mixer for about 10 minutes or until thick and creamy. Pour into six individual serving dishes, serve with finger biscuits.

**Finger biscuits** Beat butter and sugar in a small bowl with electric mixer until light and fluffy, stir in egg white. Fold in sifted flour and pecans, spoon mixture into a piping bag fitted with a plain tube. Pipe 5cm lengths of mixture, onto lightly greased oven trays allowing room for spreading between each.

Bake in hot oven 5 minutes or until browned lightly. Stand biscuits on trays for 1 minute, carefully remove from trays; cool on wire racks.

□ SERVES 6

**Storage** *Biscuits, in airtight container*
**Freeze** *Not suitable*
**Microwave** *Not suitable*

# Golden syrup PUDDINGS with chocolate sauce

*If sauce thickens on standing, heat gently before serving Sauce can be made a day ahead Puddings best made just before serving*

**$1/3$ cup (80ml) golden syrup**
**2 eggs**
**$1/2$ cup (100g) firmly packed brown sugar**
**$1/3$ cup (80ml) evaporated milk**
**60g butter, melted**
**$3/4$ cup (110g) self-raising flour**
**$1/2$ teaspoon bicarbonate of soda**

### Chocolate sauce

**300ml cream**
**$1/4$ cup (55g) caster sugar**
**125g dark chocolate, chopped**
**1 tablespoon Grand Marnier**

Lightly grease 4 x 250ml (1-cup) ovenproof moulds; pour 1 tablespoon golden syrup over base of each mould. Beat eggs and sugar in small bowl with electric mixer, about 5 minutes or until thick. Stir in milk and butter; fold in sifted flour and soda.

Spoon mixture into prepared moulds, cover with greased greaseproof paper, then foil; secure with string. Place moulds in large shallow pan or boiler. Pour in enough boiling water to come halfway up sides of moulds. Cover pan, boil 20 minutes or until puddings are firm. Turn out puddings, serve warm with chocolate sauce.

**Chocolate sauce** Combine cream and sugar in pan; stir over heat until sugar is dissolved. Bring to boil, remove from heat. Add chocolate and liqueur, stir until chocolate is melted.

□ SERVES 4

***Freeze*** *Puddings suitable*
***Microwave*** *Sauce suitable*

Plum and apple cobbler, *above left*
Golden syrup puddings with chocolate sauce, *left*

# Plum and apple COBBLER

*Recipe best made just before serving*

**825g can dark plums in syrup**
**1 medium (150g) apple, sliced**
**$1/2$ teaspoon grated orange rind**
**2 tablespoons caster sugar**
**$1/2$ cup (75g) self-raising flour**
**$1/4$ cup (35g) plain flour**
**60g butter, chopped**
**2 tablespoons brown sugar**
**1 egg**
**2 tablespoons cream**
**$1/4$ teaspoon ground cinnamon**

Drain plums, reserve 2 tablespoons syrup. Halve plums, remove stones. Combine apple, rind, caster sugar and reserved syrup in small pan; simmer, covered, about 8 minutes, stirring occasionally. Stir in plums, spoon into 1.5 litre (6-cup) ovenproof dish.

Sift flours into bowl, rub in butter, stir in brown sugar, egg and cream. Drop heaped tablespoons of mixture around edge of dish, sprinkle lightly with cinnamon.

Bake in moderate oven 30 minutes or until browned.

□ SERVES 6

***Freeze*** *Not suitable*
***Microwave*** *Not suitable*

# Unbelievably rich CHOCOLATE cake

*Cake can be made 1 week ahead*

370g packet rich chocolate cake mix
1 cup (250ml) vegetable oil
2½ cups (625ml) water
300g dark chocolate, melted
1 cup (200g) firmly packed
   brown sugar
2 cups (300g) plain flour
½ cup (50g) cocoa
1 teaspoon bicarbonate of soda
2 eggs

### Filling

500g dark chocolate, chopped
360g unsalted butter, chopped
1 cup (250ml) sour cream

Grease a deep 25cm round or deep 23cm square cake pan, line base and sides with baking paper, bringing paper 5cm above edge of pan.

Combine cake mix (but not the ingredients listed on packet) with remaining cake ingredients in large bowl of electric mixer, beat on low speed until ingredients are combined. Beat on medium speed 2 minutes, or until mixture is smooth and changed in colour. Pour into prepared pan.

Bake in moderate oven 1⅔ hours. Stand cake 10 minutes before turning onto wire rack to cool.

Trim top of cold cake to make level, carefully split cake horizontally into 3 even layers. Divide filling into 3 portions; reserve 2 portions for decorating cake.

Place one layer of cake on serving plate, spread with half of remaining filling. Repeat layers once more, top with remaining cake layer.

Spread half the reserved filling all over cake, use remaining filling to decorate top of cake.

**Filling** Melt chocolate and butter in medium heatproof bowl over pan of simmering water. Remove from heat, stir in cream; cool to room temperature, stirring occasionally with wooden spoon, until thick and spreadable.

□ SERVES ABOUT 20

***Storage*** *Covered in refrigerator*
***Freeze*** *Unfilled cake suitable*
***Microwave*** *Filling suitable*

Unbelievably rich chocolate cake, *below*

*t*ouched by winter's chill,

cheeks become rosy like apples, and brisk walks

are an exhilarating pleasure... this is the time of year

comfort foods and convivial groups around a laden

table come into their own.

winter
*comfort ye*

This is the season when cocooning in front of

a crackling fire becomes one of life's great pleasures,

especially when coupled with a fragrant bowl of soup or

a steaming casserole or baked apples just like

mother used to make. The cold plays wonderful

havoc with our appetites... in the selection of these winter

recipes, there are ways to indulge each and every one.

# winter

*Feast of the season*

Port and chicken liver PATE  *(page 200)*

MELBA toast  *(page 201)*

Roast TURKEY with macadamia
seasoning  *(page 216)*

Loin of PORK with apple seasoning  *(page 216)*

Herb and garlic VEGETABLES  *(page 216)*

Parmesan POTATOES  *(page 216)*

Quick-mix Christmas PUDDING  *(page 248)*

Cinnamon brandy CUSTARD  *(page 249)*

Orange LIQUEUR hard sauce  *(page 249)*

SERVES 10

curries

puddings & pies

soups

## Retreat to the hearth

Ham and split pea SOUP
*(page 203)*

Steak and kidney PIE
*(page 208)*

Roast POTATOES with parsnips
and bacon rolls  *(page 232)*

Steamed green VEGETABLES

Sticky fruit PUDDING
with caramel sauce  *(page 238)*

SERVES 6

cakes

## An Indian affair

Cauliflower FRITTERS
with yogurt dip  *(page 194)*

BEEF Masala  *(page 212)*

Light and spicy FISH  *(page 215)*

Tomato chilli LENTILS  *(page 218)*

TANDOORI chicken
with coconut rice and
yogurt sauce *(page 230)*

Fresh FRUIT

SERVES 6 to 8

# Cauliflower FRITTERS
## with yogurt dip

*Recipe best made close to serving*

$1/2$ small (600g) cauliflower,
   chopped
1 cup (125g) chickpea flour
1 cup (150g) self-raising flour
2 teaspoons curry powder
2 teaspoons ground coriander
$1/4$ teaspoon chilli powder
$1^1/2$ teaspoons brown
   mustard seeds
$1^1/2$ teaspoons cumin seeds
$1^1/4$ cups (310ml) water,
   approximately
vegetable oil, for deep-frying

### Yogurt dip

1 cup (250ml) plain yogurt
1 tablespoon chopped fresh mint
1 tablespoon chopped
   fresh coriander
$1/2$ teaspoon sambal oelek
$1/4$ teaspoon garam masala
2 teaspoons water
$1/2$ teaspoon sugar

Boil, steam or microwave cauliflower
until tender, rinse under cold water;
drain well.

Sift flours and spices into medium
bowl, stir in seeds and enough water to
mix to a smooth batter.

Dip cauliflower into batter. Deep-
fry in hot oil until browned lightly;
drain on absorbent paper.

Serve cauliflower fritters with
yogurt dip.

**Yogurt dip** Combine all ingredients in
small bowl.

□ SERVES 4 TO 6

*Freeze* Not suitable
*Microwave* Cauliflower suitable

Cauliflower fritters with
yogurt dip, Sesame eggplant salad,
*above right, from left*

Heat combined oils in pan, add eggplants, cook in batches until browned lightly.

Combine eggplants and sesame seeds in medium bowl; cool. Add tomatoes, onions, artichokes and dressing; mix well.

**Dressing** Combine all ingredients in jar; shake well.

□ SERVES 4

***Storage*** *Covered, in refrigerator*
***Freeze*** *Not suitable*
***Microwave*** *Not suitable*

## Asian-flavoured PUMPKIN soup

*Recipe can be made a day ahead*

**1kg pumpkin**
**1 tablespoon peanut oil**
**2 cloves garlic, crushed**
**1 large (200g) onion, chopped**
**1 teaspoon sambal oelek**
**2 tablespoons chopped fresh lemon grass**
**1 litre (4 cups) water**
**1 teaspoon chicken stock powder**
**1 tablespoon fish sauce**
**3 teaspoons lime juice**
**1 cup (250ml) coconut cream**
**2 tablespoons chopped fresh basil**
**2 tablespoons chopped fresh coriander**

Peel and seed pumpkin, cut pumpkin into 1.5cm cubes.

Heat oil in large pan, add garlic, onion, sambal oelek and lemon grass, cook, stirring, until onion is soft.

Add pumpkin, cook, stirring, 1 minute. Add water, stock powder, sauce and juice, simmer, covered, until pumpkin is just tender.

Blend or process half the mixture until smooth, return puree to mixture in pan. Add coconut cream and herbs, stir over heat until hot.

□ SERVES 4 TO 6

***Storage*** *Covered, in refrigerator*
***Freeze*** *Suitable*
***Microwave*** *Suitable*

## Sesame eggplant SALAD

*Recipe can be made 3 hours ahead*

**8 small (500g) eggplants**
**2 medium (260g) tomatoes**
**2 teaspoons sesame oil**
**2 tablespoons olive oil**
**1 tablespoon sesame seeds**
**2 green onions, chopped**
**1 cup (190g) artichoke hearts, drained, halved**

### Dressing

**$^1/_4$ cup olive oil**
**2 tablespoons balsamic vinegar**
**1 clove garlic, crushed**

Cut eggplants into, slices 1.5cm thick. Cut tomatoes into wedges.

## DAMPER with olives and herbs

*Recipe best made on day of serving*

**$2^1/_2$ cups (375g) self-raising flour**
**30g butter**
**2 tablespoons chopped fresh rosemary**
**2 tablespoons chopped fresh oregano**
**$^1/_2$ cup (80g) chopped seeded black olives**
**$^1/_2$ cup (40g) grated parmesan cheese**
**$^3/_4$ cup (180ml) milk**
**$^1/_3$ cup (80ml) water, approximately**
**2 tablespoons grated parmesan cheese, extra**

Sift flour into bowl; rub in butter. Stir in herbs, olives and cheese; mix well.

Make well in mixture, stir in milk and enough water to mix to a soft, sticky dough (use a knife for best results).

Turn dough onto lightly floured surface, knead lightly until smooth, press into 15cm circle.

Place dough on oiled oven tray, cut a 1cm-deep cross on top of dough. Brush dough with a little milk, sprinkle with extra cheese.

Bake, uncovered, in moderately hot oven, 30 minutes or until damper sounds hollow when tapped.

***Storage*** *In airtight container*
***Freeze*** *Suitable*
***Microwave*** *Not suitable*

Asian-flavoured pumpkin soup, Damper with olives and herbs, *left*

## Curried beef TRIANGLES with mango sauce

*Recipe can be prepared a day ahead*

1 tablespoon peanut oil
1 small (80g) onion, chopped
2 cloves garlic, crushed
2 tablespoons curry paste
1 teaspoon chilli powder
400g minced beef
1/4 cup chopped fresh mint
1 small (120g) potato,
    finely chopped
1/4 cup (60ml) water
1 small beef stock cube, crumbled
1 teaspoon sugar
4 sheets frozen ready-rolled
    puff pastry, thawed
1 egg, lightly beaten

### Mango sauce

300g plain yogurt
1/4 cup (60ml) mango chutney
1/4 cup loosely packed fresh mint
1/4 cup loosely packed
    fresh coriander

Heat oil in medium pan, add onion, garlic, paste and chilli; cook, stirring, until onion is soft.

Add mince, mint, potato, water, stock cube and sugar; cook, stirring, until potato is tender and most of the liquid is evaporated; cool.

Cut each pastry sheet into quarters. Place rounded tablespoons of mince mixture diagonally across each pastry square, fold pastry over to form a triangle and enclose filling; press edges together. Place triangles on oiled oven trays, make small decorative cuts in pastry edges, brush with egg.

Bake, uncovered, in hot oven about 10 minutes or until browned. Serve with mango sauce.

**Mango sauce** Blend or process all ingredients until smooth.

□ MAKES 16

**Storage** *Covered, in refrigerator*
**Freeze** *Uncooked triangles suitable*
**Microwave** *Not suitable*

Curried beef triangles with mango sauce, *below*

## SILVERBEET pots with green peppercorn sauce

*Recipe can be made 3 hours ahead*
*Green peppercorn sauce best made just before serving*

6 leaves (480g) spinach (silverbeet)
1/3 cup (65g) Calrose rice
30g butter
1 clove garlic, crushed
1 teaspoon cumin seeds
250g minced chicken
1 teaspoon lemon
    pepper seasoning
2 teaspoons plain flour
1/3 cup (80ml) water
1 small chicken stock
    cube, crumbled
125g packet cream
    cheese, chopped
2 tablespoons chopped fresh mint
1 teaspoon dried thyme
1/3 cup (25g) stale breadcrumbs
1 egg, lightly beaten

### Green peppercorn sauce

1 cup (250ml) dry white wine
1 tablespoon lemon juice
2 teaspoons canned green
    peppercorns, rinsed, drained
200g butter, chopped

Oil 6 x 1-cup (250ml) ovenproof dishes. Remove stalks from silverbeet, add leaves to pan of boiling water; drain immediately. Rinse under cold water; drain, pat dry.

Line base and sides of prepared dishes with leaves, allowing ends to extend over sides.

Add rice to pan of boiling water, boil, uncovered, until just tender; drain.

Heat butter in pan, add garlic, seeds and chicken, stir over heat until changed in colour. Add seasoning and flour, stir until combined. Remove from heat, gradually stir in water, stock cube and cheese, stir over heat until mixture boils and thickens. Stir in rice, herbs, crumbs and egg.

Spoon chicken mixture evenly into prepared dishes, fold leaves over to cover filling; cover with foil. Place dishes in baking dish, pour in enough

boiling water to come halfway up sides of dishes.

Bake in moderate oven about 45 minutes, or until firm.

Serve silverbeet pots with green peppercorn sauce.

**Green peppercorn sauce** Combine wine, juice and peppercorns in small pan, simmer, uncovered, 5 minutes, or until mixture is reduced to about 2 tablespoons. Quickly whisk in butter, over low heat.

□ SERVES 6

*Storage  Covered, in refrigerator*
*Freeze  Not suitable*
*Microwave  Rice and silverbeet suitable*

# Chicken and tomato
## ROLLS with sesame
## mayonnaise

*Filling can be prepared 3 hours ahead*
*Assemble and cook rolls close to serving*

**90g rice vermicelli noodles**
**250g minced chicken**
**2 tablespoons soy sauce**
**2 tablespoons mild sweet**
**   chilli sauce**
**1 teaspoon dried oregano leaves**
**2 tablespoons chopped**
**   sun-dried tomatoes**
**32 small spring-roll wrappers**
**vegetable oil, for deep-frying**

### Sesame mayonnaise

**1 cup (250ml) mayonnaise**
**$1/_4$ teaspoon sesame oil**
**2 teaspoons sesame seeds, toasted**

Place noodles in a heatproof bowl, cover with hot water, stand 10 minutes; drain well.

Combine noodles, chicken, sauces, oregano and tomatoes in a large bowl.

Place a level tablespoon of mince mixture on one corner of each wrapper; brush edges with water. Fold in sides, roll up to enclose filling.

Deep-fry rolls in hot oil, until browned lightly; drain on absorbent paper.

Serve hot with sesame mayonnaise.

**Sesame mayonnaise** Combine all ingredients in a small bowl.

□ MAKES 32

*Storage  Covered, in refrigerator*
*Freeze  Uncooked rolls suitable*
*Microwave  Not suitable*

Silverbeet pots with green peppercorn sauce, Chicken and tomato rolls with sesame mayonnaise, *above, from top*

## Spicy AVOCADO dip

*Recipe can be made 3 hours ahead*

$1/2$ medium (125g) avocado
1 tablespoon mild sweet
   chilli sauce
2 tablespoons lemon juice
2 teaspoons ground cumin
1 tablespoon water
3 medium (360g) tomatoes,
   seeded, chopped
130g can corn kernels, drained
2 teaspoons chopped
   fresh coriander

Blend or process avocado, sauce, juice, cumin and water until smooth. Transfer mixture to medium bowl, add tomatoes and corn; mix well.

Cover surface of dip with plastic wrap; refrigerate. Just before serving, sprinkle with coriander.

□ MAKES $2^{1}/_{2}$ CUPS

**Storage** *Covered, in refrigerator*
**Freeze** *Not suitable*

## Chicken kumara CROQUETTES

*Recipe can be made a day ahead*

1 large (500g) kumara, chopped
2 medium (400g) potatoes, chopped
3 green onions, chopped
1 teaspoon Cajun seasoning
$1/2$ cup (40g) grated
   parmesan cheese
40g butter, chopped
1 cup (200g) finely chopped
   cooked chicken
plain flour
2 eggs, lightly beaten
$3/4$ cup (75g) packaged breadcrumbs
vegetable oil, for shallow-frying

Boil, steam or microwave kumara and potatoes until tender, drain into large bowl; mash. Stir in onions, seasoning, cheese, butter and chicken; mix well. Shape mixture into 16 croquettes. Cover, refrigerate 30 minutes.

Toss croquettes in flour, shake away excess. Dip croquettes in eggs, then crumbs.

Shallow-fry croquettes, in batches, in hot oil until browned; drain on absorbent paper.

□ MAKES 16

**Storage** *Covered, in refrigerator*
**Freeze** *Not suitable*
**Microwave** *Kumara and potatoes suitable*

Spicy avocado dip, *above left*
Chicken kumara croquettes, *left*
Quick tomato and bacon soup, *above*

# Quick tomato and bacon SOUP

*Recipe can be made a day ahead*

2 teaspoons vegetable oil
1 small (80g) onion, finely chopped
2 bacon rashers, finely chopped
4 medium (520g) tomatoes, finely chopped
125g button mushrooms, finely chopped
1/2 small (75g) red capsicum, finely chopped
2 tablespoons coconut cream
2 tablespoons tomato paste
1 teaspoon ground ginger
1/4 teaspoon cayenne pepper
1/4 teaspoon ground turmeric
1/4 teaspoon dried basil leaves
2 cups (500ml) water

Heat oil in pan, add onion and bacon, cook, stirring, until onion is soft. Add tomatoes, mushrooms and capsicum; simmer, covered, 2 minutes. Stir in coconut cream, paste, spices, basil and water, simmer, covered, about 10 minutes, or until vegetables are soft. Do not boil.

□ SERVES 4

**Storage** *Covered, in refrigerator*
**Freeze** *Not suitable*
**Microwave** *Suitable*

# Port and chicken liver PATE

*Recipe can be made 2 days ahead*

1/2 small (75g) red capsicum
500g chicken livers
125g butter
2 cloves garlic, crushed
1 small (80g) onion, chopped
2 teaspoons canned green
    peppercorns, rinsed, drained
2 tablespoons port
1/2 cup (125ml) cream
1 teaspoon chopped fresh sage
125g butter, melted, extra
6 fresh sage leaves, extra

## Aspic

2 teaspoons gelatine
1/2 cup (125ml) water
3 teaspoons port
1/4 teaspoon chicken stock powder

Cut capsicum into thin strips, place in bowl, cover with cold water, refrigerate 1 hour, or until capsicum is curled; drain, pat dry.

Trim and chop chicken livers.

Heat butter in pan, add garlic and onion, cook, stirring, until onion is soft. Add livers, cook, stirring, until changed in colour. Stir in peppercorns, port, cream and sage.

Blend or process liver mixture until smooth, push through a fine sieve into a small bowl; return to processor. With motor operating, pour in extra butter. Pour mixture into 2 x 1 1/4 cup (310ml) dishes, arrange capsicum and extra sage on surface, spoon aspic over top. Refrigerate 3 hours or until firm.

**Aspic** Combine gelatine and water in cup, stand in small pan of simmering water, stir until dissolved. Stir in port and stock powder.

□ MAKES ABOUT 2 1/2 CUPS

**Storage** *Covered, in refrigerator*
**Freeze** *Not suitable*
**Microwave** *Not suitable*

## MELBA toast

*Recipe can be made 2 weeks ahead*

**1 square unsliced loaf bread**

Remove all crusts from bread. Cut bread in half, giving two half-loaves (this way, it is easier to handle the cutting of individual slices). Cut each loaf diagonally in half, giving four thick triangle-shaped bread pieces. Place flat side down on board. Using a serrated knife, cut into wafer-thin slices. Place slices on unoiled oven trays.

Bake, uncovered, in moderate oven about 15 minutes or until crisp, turning frequently.

**Storage**  *Airtight container*
**Freeze**  *Suitable*
**Microwave**  *Not suitable*

## Seafood CHOWDER

*Recipe best made just before serving*

**300g small mussels**
**200g calamari tubes**
**2 tablespoons olive oil**
**2 medium (300g) onions,**
  **finely chopped**
**2 cloves garlic, crushed**
**150g sliced ham, chopped**
**1 large (300g) potato, chopped**
**1¹/₂ cups (375ml) fish stock**
**¹/₂ cup (125ml) water**
**¹/₃ cup (80ml) dry white wine**
**¹/₂ cup (50g) full-cream**
  **powdered milk**
**2 tablespoons instant mashed**
  **potato powder**
**250g white fish fillets, chopped**
**150g bottled oysters, drained**
**500g uncooked medium**
  **prawns, peeled**
**2 teaspoons dried parsley leaves**
**few drops Tabasco sauce**
**2 teaspoons grated lemon rind**
**2 teaspoons cornflour**
**375ml can evaporated milk**

Scrub mussels, remove beards; cut calamari into rings. Heat oil in large pan, add onions, garlic and ham, cook, stirring, until onions are soft. Add potato, stock, water and wine; simmer, uncovered, about 8 minutes or until potato is tender; stir in powders (mixture can look curdled at this stage).

Stir in fish and seafood; simmer, uncovered, 4 minutes or until just tender. Add parsley, sauce, rind and blended cornflour and milk; stir over heat until sauce comes to the boil.

□ SERVES 4 TO 6

**Freeze**  *Not suitable*
**Microwave**  *Not suitable*

Port and chicken liver pate,
Melba toast, *left, from top*
Seafood chowder, *above*

## Garlic bread BOWLS

*We used petit cottage rolls  Recipe can be made 3 hours ahead  Reheat before serving*

**6 round bread rolls
  (about 12cm diameter)
125g butter, melted
3 cloves garlic, crushed**

Cut tops from bread rolls, brush cut sides of tops with some of the combined butter and garlic.

Pull bread out of rolls to leave shells 2cm thick. Brush insides of bread shells with butter mixture, place on oven trays with tops.

Bake, uncovered, in moderate oven 20 minutes or until crisp and firm.

☐ MAKES 6

***Storage***  *Airtight container*
***Freeze***  *Suitable*
***Microwave***  *Not suitable*

## Corn and SALMON chowder

*Recipe must be made just before serving*

**30g butter
4 bacon rashers, finely chopped
2 medium (300g) onions, chopped
1 tablespoon plain flour
1$^1/_2$ cups (375ml) milk
1 cup (250ml) water
1 small chicken stock
  cube, crumbled
1 medium (150g) potato,
  finely chopped
440g can corn kernels, drained
440g can creamed corn
415g can red salmon,
  drained, flaked**

Heat butter in pan, add bacon and onions, cook, stirring, until onions are very soft.

Stir in flour, cook, stirring, 1 minute. Remove from heat, gradually stir in combined milk, water and stock cube. Add potato, corn kernels, creamed corn and salmon, stir over high heat until mixture boils and thickens. Reduce heat, simmer, covered, about 15 minutes or until potato is tender.

Spoon soup into hot garlic bread bowls, place bowl tops to one side.

☐ SERVES 6

***Freeze***  *Not suitable*
***Microwave***  *Suitable*

## Ham and split pea SOUP

*Recipe can be made 4 days ahead*

**800g ham bone**
**1 medium (150g) onion, chopped**
**2 cups (320g) yellow split peas**
**2 celery sticks, chopped**
**2 medium (240g) carrots, chopped**
**2 bay leaves**
**2.5 litres (10 cups) water**

Combine all ingredients in large pan, simmer, covered, 2 hours or until split peas are soft, stirring occasionally.

Carefully remove ham bone, remove ham from bone; discard bone. Chop ham finely, return to pan, stir over heat until hot.

Remove bay leaves before serving.

☐ SERVES 6

**Storage** *Covered, in refrigerator*
**Freeze** *Suitable*
**Microwave** *Not suitable*

## Lamb GOULASH soup

*Recipe can be made a day ahead*

**8 small (1.8kg) lamb shanks**
**plain flour**
**$1/_4$ cup (60ml) olive oil**
**2 medium (300g) onions, chopped**
**2 tablespoons ground sweet paprika**
**$1/_2$ teaspoon caraway seeds**
**4 medium (800g) potatoes,**
   **chopped**
**2 large (700g) red**
   **capsicums, chopped**
**5 large (1.25kg) tomatoes, peeled,**
   **seeded, chopped**
**1 litre (4 cups) beef stock**
**$1/_4$ cup (60ml) tomato paste**
**1 tablespoon chopped**
   **fresh oregano**

Toss shanks in flour, shake away excess flour. Heat oil in large pan, add shanks in batches, cook until well browned all over; drain on absorbent paper.

Reserve 2 teaspoons oil in pan, add onions, paprika and seeds to same pan; cook, stirring, until onions are soft. Return shanks to pan with remaining ingredients. Simmer, covered, 2 hours or until shanks are tender.

☐ SERVES 4

**Storage** *Covered, in refrigerator*
**Freeze** *Suitable*
**Microwave** *Not suitable*

Corn and salmon chowder
in Garlic bread bowls, *above left*
Ham and split pea soup, *left*
Lamb goulash soup, *above*

## Quick mushroom RISOTTO

*Recipe best made just before serving*

- **1 tablespoon olive oil**
- **1 medium (150g) onion, chopped**
- **2 cloves garlic, crushed**
- **1¹/₂ cups (300g) Calrose rice**
- **3¹/₂ cups (875ml) vegetable stock**
- **2 teaspoons olive oil, extra**
- **125g button mushrooms, sliced**
- **2 medium (240g) zucchini, sliced**
- **1 medium (200g) green capsicum, chopped**
- **1 medium (200g) red capsicum, chopped**
- **2 medium (260g) tomatoes, chopped**
- **¹/₄ cup (30g) seeded black olives**
- **¹/₂ cup (40g) flaked parmesan cheese**

Heat oil in large pan, add onion and garlic; cook stirring, until onion is soft. Add rice, stir to coat with oil. Stir in stock; simmer, covered, 10 minutes. Remove from heat, stand 10 minutes.

Heat extra oil in separate pan, add mushrooms, zucchini, capsicums and tomatoes; cook, stirring, until vegetables are tender. Return rice to heat, stir in vegetables and olives, stir until hot. Serve topped with cheese.

□ SERVES 4

***Freeze*** *Not suitable*
***Microwave*** *Suitable*

## Hearty SAUSAGE soup with pesto

*Recipe can be made a day ahead*

- **16 large (1.5kg) egg tomatoes, quartered**
- **2 large (400g) onions, quartered**
- **1 large (350g) red capsicum, quartered**
- **6 cloves garlic, peeled**
- **4 small fresh red chillies, seeded**
- **2 tablespoons olive oil**
- **2 tablespoons balsamic vinegar**
- **2 tablespoons brown sugar**
- **600g thick spicy Italian sausages**
- **1.5 litres (6 cups) beef stock**

## Mexican MEATBALL soup

*Soup and meatballs can be made a day ahead*

**1 tablespoon olive oil**
**1 medium (150g) onion, chopped**
**2 cloves garlic, crushed**
**1 teaspoon bottled chopped chilli**
**2 x 425g cans tomatoes, undrained, crushed**
**1.5 litres (6 cups) beef stock**
**1 tablespoon chopped fresh parsley**
**290g can red kidney beans, rinsed, drained**
**¹/₂ cup (125ml) sour cream**
**2 green onions, thinly sliced**

### Meatballs

**500g minced beef**
**2 green onions, chopped**
**1 egg, lightly beaten**
**¹/₄ cup (25g) packaged breadcrumbs**
**35g packet taco seasoning mix**
**1 tablespoon olive oil**

Heat oil in large pan, add onion and garlic; cook, stirring, until onion is soft. Add chilli; cook, stirring, 1 minute. Stir in tomatoes and stock; simmer, covered, 15 minutes. Add parsley, beans and meatballs to pan, simmer, covered, until meatballs are cooked through. Serve soup topped with sour cream and onions.

**Meatballs** Combine mince, onions, egg, crumbs and seasoning mix in bowl. Roll level tablespoons of mixture into balls. Heat oil in large shallow pan, add meatballs; cook until well browned all over; drain on absorbent paper.

□ SERVES 4

***Storage*** *Covered, separately, in refrigerator*
***Freeze*** *Meatballs and soup suitable, separately*
***Microwave*** *Soup suitable*

Quick mushroom risotto, *above, far left*
Hearty sausage soup with pesto
Mexican meatball soup, *above left, from left*

### Pesto

**2 cups firmly packed fresh basil**
**1 clove garlic**
**¹/₄ cup (60ml) olive oil**
**¹/₄ cup (40g) pine nuts, toasted**
**¹/₄ cup (20g) grated parmesan cheese**

Combine tomatoes with onions, capsicum, garlic, chillies, oil, vinegar and sugar in baking dish.

Bake, uncovered, in moderately hot oven about 30 minutes or until tomatoes are soft. Blend or process vegetables and pan juices until smooth.

Add sausages to large dry pan; cook until browned and cooked through; drain on absorbent paper. Slice sausages thinly.

Combine stock, vegetable mixture and sausages in large pan, stir over heat until hot. Serve topped with pesto.

**Pesto** Blend or process basil, garlic, oil, nuts and cheese until smooth. Cover surface of pesto tightly with plastic wrap until required.

□ SERVES 6

***Storage*** *Covered, separately, in refrigerator*
***Freeze*** *Soup and pesto suitable separately*
***Microwave*** *Not suitable*

# Pasta and vegetable MORNAY

*Recipe best made on day of serving*

30g butter
1 small (80g) onion, chopped
2 tablespoons plain flour
1 cup (250ml) milk
$^1/_4$ cup (60ml) dry white wine
$^1/_2$ cup (125ml) cream
2 cups (160g) cooked pasta

1 cup (125g) grated cheddar cheese
$^1/_3$ cup (25g) grated
    parmesan cheese
1 medium (120g) carrot, grated
1 medium (120g) zucchini, grated
2 hard-boiled eggs, finely chopped
1 tablespoon chopped fresh parsley
$^1/_2$ teaspoon celery salt
$^3/_4$ cup (50g) stale breadcrumbs

Melt butter in small pan, add onion, cook, stirring, until soft. Stir in flour, stir until mixture is dry and grainy. Remove from heat, gradually stir in combined milk and wine, stir over heat until sauce boils and thickens. Transfer to large bowl, stir in cream, pasta, cheeses, carrot, zucchini, eggs, parsley and salt; mix well.

Spoon mixture into 1.5 litre (6-cup) ovenproof dish, sprinkle with crumbs.

Bake, uncovered, in moderate oven, 30 minutes or until browned lightly.

□ SERVES 4

**Storage** *Covered, in refrigerator*
**Freeze** *Not suitable*
**Microwave** *Suitable*

*clockwise from top left*, Pasta and vegetable mornay, Sun-dried tomato and artichoke fettuccine, Baked vegetarian pasta

# Baked vegetarian PASTA

*Recipe can be made a day ahead*

**2 cups (320g) cooked spiral pasta**

### Sauce

**1 tablespoon olive oil**
**1 large (150g) onion, chopped**
**$1/2$ teaspoon chilli powder**
**1 clove garlic, crushed**
**750g can red kidney beans, rinsed, drained**
**400g can tomatoes, undrained, crushed**
**$1/4$ cup (60ml) tomato paste**
**2 teaspoons sugar**

### Topping

**1 cup (125g) grated cheddar cheese**
**1 cup (70g) stale breadcrumbs**
**1 teaspoon ground sweet paprika**

Oil a 1.25 litre (5-cup) shallow ovenproof dish. Place half the pasta over base of dish, top with half of sauce, remaining pasta, then remaining sauce. Sprinkle topping over sauce.

Bake, uncovered, in moderately hot oven, 20 minutes or until hot and browned lightly.

**Sauce** Heat oil in pan, add onion, chilli powder and garlic, cook, stirring, until onion is soft. Stir in beans, tomatoes, paste and sugar.

**Topping** Combine all ingredients in medium bowl.

□ SERVES 4

**Storage** *Covered, in refrigerator*
**Freeze** *Suitable*
**Microwave** *Not suitable*

# Sun-dried tomato and artichoke FETTUCCINE

*Recipe best made close to serving*

**1 tablespoon olive oil**
**6 bacon rashers, chopped**
**2 cloves garlic, crushed**
**6 green onions, chopped**
**1 cup (190g) halved canned or bottled artichoke hearts**
**$1/2$ cup (60g) seeded black olives, halved**
**$1/2$ cup (75g) sliced sun-dried tomatoes**
**$1/2$ cup shredded fresh basil**
**$1/2$ bunch (20 leaves) English spinach, shredded**
**2 cups (320g) cooked fettuccine**

Heat oil in large pan, add bacon, garlic and onions, cook, stirring, until bacon is crisp. Stir in artichokes, olives, tomatoes, basil, spinach and fettuccine, cook, stirring, until spinach is wilted and fettuccine is heated through.

□ SERVES 2

**Freeze** *Not suitable*
**Microwave** *Suitable*

207

# STEAK and kidney pie

*Recipe can be made 2 days ahead*

**250g ox kidney**
**1kg beef chuck steak, chopped**
**2 medium (300g) onions, chopped**
**1 tablespoon soy sauce**
**2 cups (500ml) water**
**2 small beef stock cubes, crumbled**
**$^1/_3$ cup (50g) plain flour**
**$^1/_2$ cup (125ml) water, extra**
**2 tablespoons chopped**
  **fresh parsley**
**375g block frozen puff**
  **pastry, thawed**
**1 egg yolk**

Trim kidney, remove skin, chop kidney into 2cm cubes. Combine kidney, steak, onions, sauce, water and stock cubes in a large pan, bring to boil; simmer, covered, 1$^1/_2$ hours or until steak is tender. Stir in blended flour and extra water, stir over heat, steak or until mixture boils and thickens. Stir in parsley; cool.

Spoon mixture into lightly oiled 1.5 litre (6-cup) ovenproof pie dish.

Roll out pastry to 3mm in thickness. Measure around top edge of dish, cut strips from edges of pastry to equal this measurement, with each strip having the width of the top edge of dish. Place pastry strips around rim of dish, brush with water.

Place remaining pastry on top of pie, trim excess pastry with a sharp knife. Cut through both layers of pastry around rim of dish. Cut small slits into top of pie, decorate with pastry trimmings if desired. Brush pastry with egg yolk.

Bake, uncovered, in moderately hot oven, 20 minutes or until pastry is puffed and well browned and pie is heated through.

□ SERVES 4

**Storage** *Covered, in refrigerator*
**Freeze** *Suitable*
**Microwave** *Not suitable*

# Chicken-filled nugget
## PUMPKINS with spinach sauce

*Recipe can be prepared 2 days ahead*

1 tablespoon vegetable oil
2 cloves garlic, crushed
2 tablespoons pine nuts
$^1/_4$ teaspoon ground fennel seeds
$^1/_2$ teaspoon ground turmeric
1 teaspoon ground cumin
500g minced chicken
$^1/_4$ cup (35g) dried currants
425g can tomatoes, undrained, crushed
4 medium golden nugget pumpkins

### Spinach sauce

30g butter
1 small (80g) onion, sliced
1 teaspoon cumin seeds, crushed
$^1/_4$ bunch (10 leaves) English spinach, shredded
1 small chicken stock cube, crumbled
300ml cream
1 teaspoon cornflour
$^1/_2$ cup (125ml) water

Heat oil in pan, add garlic, pine nuts, and spices, cook, stirring, until fragrant.

Add chicken, cook, stirring, until changed in colour. Stir in currants and tomatoes; remove from heat.

Cut tops from pumpkins, carefully scoop out and discard seeds. Fill pumpkins with mince mixture; replace tops. Place pumpkins in ovenproof dish, add enough boiling water to come 1cm up sides of pumpkins.

Bake, covered, in moderately hot oven about 50 minutes or until pumpkins are tender.

Serve hot pumpkins with spinach sauce.

**Spinach sauce** Heat butter in medium pan, add onion and seeds, cook, stirring, until onion is soft. Add spinach, stock cube and cream, bring to boil. Stir in blended cornflour and water, stir over heat until mixture boils and thickens.

□ SERVES 4

**Storage** *Covered, in refrigerator*
**Freeze** *Not suitable*
**Microwave** *Suitable*

Steak and kidney pie, *far left*
Chicken-filled nugget pumpkins with spinach sauce, *left*

# LAMB, potato and spinach hotpot

*Recipe can be made a day ahead*

2 tablespoons olive oil
1.5kg diced lamb
2 medium (300g) onions,
    thinly sliced
3 cloves garlic, crushed
2 teaspoons cumin seeds
$1/2$ teaspoon ground cinnamon
$1/2$ teaspoon ground sweet paprika
2 x 425g cans tomatoes,
    undrained, crushed
$3/4$ cup (180ml) chicken stock
4 medium (800g) potatoes, chopped
1 bunch (40 leaves) English spinach
$1/4$ cup chopped fresh mint
1 tablespoon lemon juice

Heat half the oil in large pan, add lamb in batches; cook, stirring, until browned all over. Remove from pan, drain on absorbent paper.

Heat remaining oil in same pan, add onions, garlic and spices; cook, stirring, until onions are soft. Return lamb to pan with tomatoes and stock; simmer, covered, 45 minutes. Add potatoes to pan; simmer, covered, 40 minutes or until lamb and potatoes are tender. Add spinach, mint and juice to pan; simmer, uncovered, until spinach is just wilted.

□ SERVES 6

***Storage*** *Covered, in refrigerator*
***Freeze*** *Suitable*
***Microwave*** *Not suitable*

Lamb, potato and spinach hotpot, *above*

# Lamb SHANKS and barley in red wine

*Ask the butcher to trim ends from lamb shanks  Recipe can be made a day ahead*

$1/3$ cup (50g) plain flour
1 teaspoon ground cumin
$1/2$ teaspoon ground coriander
8 small (1.8kg) lamb shanks
$1/4$ cup (60ml) olive oil
2 medium (300g) onions, chopped
1 clove garlic, crushed
$1/3$ cup (55g) pearl barley
1 medium (125g) carrot,
    finely chopped
1 medium (200g) parsnip,
    finely chopped
2 teaspoons chopped fresh rosemary
2 teaspoons chopped fresh thyme
1 cup (250ml) dry red wine
2 cups (500ml) beef stock
425g can tomatoes,
    undrained, crushed
2 tablespoons tomato paste

Combine flour, cumin and coriander in plastic bag. Add lamb shanks, one at a time, shake to coat; shake away excess flour.

Heat oil in large pan, add lamb in batches, cook until well browned all over. Remove lamb from pan, reserve 1 tablespoon oil in pan. Add onions and garlic, cook, stirring, until soft. Add barley, vegetables and herbs, cook, stirring, 5 minutes or until vegetables are browned lightly. Return lamb to pan with wine, stock, tomatoes and paste. Simmer, covered, $1^{1}/4$ hours or until lamb is tender, turning lamb twice during cooking.

Remove lamb from pan, keep warm. Simmer vegetable mixture, uncovered, 5 minutes or until thickened slightly. Serve over lamb.

□ SERVES 4

***Storage*** *Covered, in refrigerator*
***Freeze*** *Suitable*
***Microwave*** *Not suitable*

# Spicy VEGETABLE parcels

*Vegetable mixture can be made a day ahead*

1 medium (300g) eggplant
1 large (500g) kumara, chopped
2 tablespoons olive oil
1 medium (170g) red
   onion, chopped
1 clove garlic, crushed
1 teaspoon ground cumin
1/2 teaspoon ground coriander
2 tablespoons pine nuts
1 large (180g) carrot,
   finely chopped
125g finely chopped broccoli
125g finely chopped cauliflower
2 tablespoons water
1 egg, lightly beaten
1 teaspoon sambal oelek
1 tablespoon mango chutney
16 sheets fillo pastry
125g butter, melted

Place whole eggplant on oven tray. Bake, uncovered, in hot oven about 1 hour or until soft. Peel eggplant, mash flesh. Boil, steam or microwave kumara until soft; drain, mash.

Heat oil in large pan, add onion, garlic, cumin, coriander, pine nuts and carrot, cook, stirring, 5 minutes or until carrot is tender. Add broccoli, cauliflower and water, cook, covered, 3 minutes or until broccoli is just tender. Combine eggplant, kumara, broccoli mixture, egg, sambal oelek and chutney in large bowl. Cover, refrigerate until cold.

Layer 2 sheets of pastry together, brushing each with butter; fold in half to form a square. Place 1/2 cup (125ml) of vegetable mixture in centre of pastry, gather edges together to form a parcel, brush lightly with some of the remaining butter. Repeat with the remaining pastry, butter and vegetable mixture. Place pastry parcels on an oiled oven tray.

Bake, uncovered, in moderate oven about 25 minutes or until browned.

□ MAKES 8

**Storage**  *Covered, in refrigerator*
**Freeze**  *Suitable*
**Microwave**  *Vegetable mixture suitable*

Spicy vegetable parcels,
Lamb shanks and barley in red wine,
*below, from left*

211

Cut steak, potatoes and pumpkin into 3cm cubes. Heat oil in large pan, add onions, garlic, spices and steak, cook, stirring, until steak is well browned all over. Add half the water, simmer, covered, 40 minutes.

Add potatoes, pumpkin, carrots and remaining water, simmer, uncovered, 15 minutes. Add celery, broccoli, beans, corn, raisins and extra water, simmer, 10 minutes or until vegetables are tender. Sprinkle with parsley.

□ SERVES 4

**Storage** *Covered, in refrigerator*
**Freeze** *Suitable*
**Microwave** *Not suitable*

## CHICKPEA curry

*Recipe can be made a day ahead*

1 tablespoon vegetable oil
1 medium (150g) onion, chopped
1 medium (200g) green
   capsicum, chopped
2 cloves garlic, crushed
1$^1/_2$ tablespoons curry powder
1 tablespoon brown malt vinegar
400g can tomatoes,
   undrained, crushed
2 x 300g cans chickpeas,
   rinsed, drained
3 medium (600g) potatoes,
   peeled, chopped
$^1/_3$ cup (80ml) plain yogurt

Heat oil in large pan, add onion, capsicum, garlic and curry powder; cook, stirring, until onion is soft. Add vinegar, tomatoes, chickpeas and potatoes; simmer, covered, about 20 minutes or until potato is tender, stirring occasionally. Top with yogurt.

□ SERVES 4

**Storage** *Covered, in refrigerator*
**Freeze** *Not suitable*
**Microwave** *Suitable*

## BEEF masala

*Recipe can be made a day ahead*

500g beef blade steak
4 medium (800g) potatoes
240g pumpkin
$^1/_4$ cup (60ml) olive oil
2 medium (300g) onions, chopped
2 cloves garlic, crushed
1 teaspoon garam masala
1 teaspoon ground turmeric
1 teaspoon ground cumin

1 teaspoon curry powder
2 cloves
3 cups (750ml) water
2 medium (240g) carrots, sliced
3 celery sticks, chopped
300g broccoli, chopped
120g green beans, trimmed
$^1/_2$ cup corn kernels
$^1/_2$ cup raisins
$^1/_2$ cup water, extra
2 teaspoons chopped
   fresh parsley

Beef masala, *above left*
Chickpea curry, *above right*
Vegetable goulash with herbed
dumplings, *right*

# Vegetable GOULASH
## with herbed dumplings

*Recipe best made close to serving*

**20g butter**
**2 medium (300g) onions, chopped**
**1 clove garlic, crushed**
**2 tablespoons plain flour**
**$\frac{1}{2}$ cup (125ml) water**
**400g new potatoes, halved**
**1 medium (120g) carrot, sliced**
**400g can tomatoes, undrained, crushed**
**2 tablespoons tomato paste**
**2 teaspoons chopped fresh thyme**
**1 bay leaf**
**1 small vegetable stock cube, crumbled**
**1$\frac{1}{2}$ cups (375ml) water, extra**
**2 medium (120g) zucchini, sliced**
**200g broccoli, chopped**
**$\frac{1}{2}$ cup (125ml) cream**

### Herbed dumplings

**1 cup (150g) self-raising flour**
**20g butter**
**1 tablespoon chopped fresh parsley**
**2 tablespoons milk**
**$\frac{1}{3}$ cup (80ml) water, approximately**

Heat butter in medium pan, add onions and garlic, stir over heat until onions are soft. Stir in flour, stir over heat for 1 minute. Remove pan from heat, gradually stir in water, stir over heat until mixture boils and thickens.

Combine onion mixture with potatoes, carrot, tomatoes, paste, herbs and combined stock cube and extra water in a 3 litre (12-cup) ovenproof dish.

Bake, uncovered, in moderate oven for 45 minutes. Stir in zucchini and broccoli, bake, covered, 15 minutes or until vegetables are just soft. Remove bay leaf, stir in cream. Place heaped teaspoons of herbed dumpling mixture around edge of casserole, bake, uncovered, 20 minutes or until dumplings are cooked through.

**Herbed dumplings** Sift flour into medium bowl, rub in butter, stir in parsley. Stir in milk and enough water to mix to soft dough.

□ SERVES 4

***Freeze*** *Not suitable*
***Microwave*** *Not suitable*

213

Heat oil in large pan, add garlic, onions and bacon, cook, stirring, 5 minutes or until onions are soft. Add chicken, cook; stirring, until changed in colour.

Stir in tomatoes, basil and sugar, simmer, uncovered, about 1 hour or until the mixture is thick, stirring occasionally.

Place 6 lasagne sheets over base of oiled, shallow 3 litre (12-cup) ovenproof dish, top with half the mince mixture and 1 cup (250ml) of the cheese sauce.

Repeat layers, then top with remaining pasta sheets and cheese sauce; sprinkle top with cheese.

Bake, uncovered, in moderate oven 40 minutes or until top is browned and pasta is tender.

**Cheese sauce** Melt butter in pan, stir in flour, stir over heat until bubbling. Remove from heat, gradually stir in combined milk and cream, stir over heat until mixture boils and thickens slightly. Remove from heat, stir in nutmeg and cheese.

□ SERVES 8

*Storage* Covered, in refrigerator
*Freeze* Suitable
*Microwave* Cheese sauce suitable

## Creamy tomato chicken LASAGNE

*Recipe can be made a day ahead*

1 tablespoon olive oil
1 clove garlic, crushed
2 medium (300g) onions, chopped
2 bacon rashers, chopped
1kg minced chicken
2 x 825g cans tomatoes, undrained, crushed
1 tablespoon chopped fresh basil
2 tablespoons sugar
18 instant lasagne pasta sheets
1/2 cup (40g) grated parmesan cheese

### Cheese sauce

40g butter
2 tablespoons plain flour
2 1/2 cups (625ml) milk
300ml cream
1/4 teaspoon ground nutmeg
1/2 cup (40g) grated parmesan cheese

## Spinach and bacon PENNE

*Recipe best made close to serving*

800g penne pasta
1 tablespoon olive oil
1 medium (150g) onion, chopped
4 bacon rashers, sliced
2 cloves garlic, crushed
1 medium (200g) green capsicum, chopped
750g tomato pasta sauce
1/2 cup (125ml) cream
1 bunch (40 leaves) English spinach, shredded
250g cherry tomatoes, halved
1/4 cup (40g) pine nuts, toasted
1/4 cup shredded fresh basil
1/4 cup (40g) flaked parmesan cheese

Add pasta to large pan of boiling water; boil, uncovered, until just tender; drain, keep warm.

Heat oil in large pan, add onion, bacon and garlic; cook, stirring, until bacon is browned. Add capsicum; cook, stirring until soft. Stir in pasta sauce and cream; simmer, uncovered, until sauce thickens slightly. Stir in spinach and tomatoes. Combine pasta with sauce and remaining ingredients in large bowl; toss well.

□ SERVES 4

**Freeze** *Not suitable*
**Microwave** *Suitable*

# Light and spicy FISH

*Recipe best made close to serving*

**1 tablespoon vegetable oil**
**1 medium (150g) onion, chopped**
**2 cloves garlic, crushed**
**2 teaspoons ground sweet paprika**
**pinch cayenne pepper**
**2 teaspoons ground cumin**
**1 teaspoon ground coriander**
**2 x 400g cans tomatoes,**
   **undrained, crushed**
**1 large potato, chopped**
**1 teaspoon sugar**
**350g white fish fillets, chopped**
**2 tablespoons chopped**
   **fresh parsley**
**2 tablespoons flaked**
   **almonds, toasted**

Heat oil in medium pan, add onion and garlic, cook, stirring, until onion is soft. Add spices, cook, stirring, until fragrant.

Add tomatoes, potato and sugar, simmer, covered, 15 minutes or until potato is tender. Stir in fish, simmer, covered, 7 minutes or until fish is just cooked through. Sprinkle with parsley and almonds.

□ SERVES 4

**Freeze** *Not suitable*
**Microwave** *Suitable*

Creamy tomato chicken lasagne, above *left*
Spinach and bacon penne, *above right*
Light and spicy fish, *right*

215

# Roast TURKEY with macadamia seasoning

*Seasoning can be prepared a day ahead*
*Fill turkey with seasoning close to cooking*

**4kg turkey**
**1/2 cup (125ml) water**
**1/4 cup (60ml) vegetable oil**

### Macadamia seasoning

**1/4 cup (45g) wild rice**
**1 cup (200g) long-grain**
   **white rice**
**1 cup (150g) roasted macadamias,**
   **coarsely chopped**
**5 green onions, chopped**
**1/4 cup chopped fresh basil**
**2 teaspoons vegetable oil**
**1 small (80g) onion,**
   **finely chopped**
**2 cloves garlic, crushed**
**2 teaspoons chopped fresh ginger**
**1 tablespoon grated lemon rind**
**1 1/2 tablespoons lemon juice**
**1 teaspoon seeded mustard**
**2 tablespoons honey**

### Gravy

**2/3 cup (100g) plain flour**
**1.25 litres (5 cups) water**
**1/2 cup (125ml) port**
**1/4 cup (60ml) dry red wine**
**3/4 cup (180ml) orange juice**
**1 small chicken stock cube**

Place neck and giblets from turkey in base of large flameproof baking dish.

Rinse turkey under cold water; pat dry. Tuck wings under body, spoon macadamia seasoning into cavity. Place wire rack over neck and giblets in baking dish, add water to dish.

Place turkey on rack, tuck trimmed neck flap under body, tie legs together securely. Brush turkey evenly with oil.

Bake, uncovered, in moderate oven about 2 1/2 hours or until tender, basting every 20 minutes with pan juices (cover turkey breast and legs with foil after 1 hour to prevent over-browning). Remove turkey from dish, reserve pan drippings for gravy.

Place turkey on oven tray, cover with foil, keep warm while making gravy.

**Macadamia seasoning** Add wild rice and white rice to separate pans of boiling water, boil, uncovered, until just tender, drain, rinse under cold water; drain well. Combine rices, macadamias, green onions and basil in large bowl. Heat oil in pan, add onion, garlic and ginger, cook, stirring, until onion is soft. Stir in rind, juice, mustard and honey, bring to boil, simmer, uncovered, about 1 minute, or until mixture thickens and darkens slightly; stir into rice mixture.

**Gravy** Remove neck and giblets from baking dish; discard. Heat pan juices in dish, stir in flour, cook, stirring, until browned lightly. Remove from heat, gradually stir in combined water, port, wine, juice and crumbled stock cube, stir over heat until gravy boils. Simmer, uncovered, until thickened slightly; strain.

☐ SERVES 8

***Storage*** *Covered, in refrigerator*
***Freeze*** *Not suitable*
***Microwave*** *Not suitable*

# Herb and garlic VEGETABLES

*Recipe best made close to serving*

**1.5 kg broccoli, chopped**
**36 spears asparagus, halved**
**3 medium (600g) red**
   **capsicums, sliced**
**125g butter**
**2 cloves garlic, crushed**
**1/2 cup chopped fresh parsley**
**1/4 cup chopped fresh basil**
**1/4 cup chopped fresh chives**
**1 teaspoon seeded mustard**

Boil, steam or microwave vegetables separately until just tender; drain well. Heat butter in large pan, add garlic, herbs and mustard, cook, stirring, until fragrant. Add vegetables, stir to coat in butter mixture.

☐ SERVES 8

***Freeze*** *Not suitable*
***Microwave*** *Suitable*

# Parmesan POTATOES

*Recipe can be prepared 2 hours ahead*

**10 (2kg) large potatoes**
**60g butter, melted**
**2/3 cup (50g) grated**
   **parmesan cheese**

Peel potatoes, cut in half, place cut-side down on board. Using a sharp knife, carefully slice almost through potatoes at 3mm intervals, leaving bases intact.

Place potatoes, base-down, in lightly oiled baking dish, brush well with butter.

Bake, uncovered, in moderate oven 40 minutes, brushing occasionally with butter from dish. Sprinkle with cheese, bake in moderately hot oven further 40 minutes, or until potatoes are crisp outside and tender inside (do not turn potatoes while baking).

☐ SERVES 8

***Storage*** *Covered, at room temperature*
***Freeze*** *Not suitable*
***Microwave*** *Not suitable*

# Loin of PORK with apple seasoning

*Ask the butcher to bone pork*
*Recipe best made close to serving*

**2.25kg loin of pork, boned**
**1 tablespoon vegetable oil**
**salt**
**1 tablespoon plain flour**
**1 cup (250ml) apple juice**
**1/2 cup (125ml) water**
**1 large vegetable stock**
   **cube, crumbled**
**1 teaspoon seeded mustard**

### Apple seasoning

**1 1/2 cups (130g) finely chopped**
   **dried apples**
**1/2 cup thinly sliced dried figs**
**3/4 cup apple juice**
**1 medium (150g) onion, chopped**
**2 teaspoons chopped fresh thyme**
**2 teaspoons seeded mustard**
**1 1/2 cups (100g) stale**
   **breadcrumbs**

Score pork rind at 1cm intervals. Place pork, rind-side down on bench. Horizontally slice through thickest part of meat (without cutting all the way through to the side), open out to form one large piece; press flat.

Spread apple seasoning evenly over pork, roll up, secure with string at 2cm intervals. Rub oil and salt into rind of pork, place on rack over flameproof baking dish.

Bake, uncovered, in hot oven 20 minutes, reduce heat to moderate, bake further 1¹/₂ hours or until tender.

Remove pork from dish; reserve pan drippings for gravy. Cut string from pork, keep pork warm.

Drain all but 1 tablespoon of drippings from dish, add flour, cook, stirring, over heat, 1 minute. Remove dish from heat, gradually stir in combined apple juice, water and stock cube, stir over heat until boiling. Simmer, stirring, about 2 minutes, or until gravy has thickened slightly; strain.

Stir mustard into gravy. Serve sliced pork with gravy.

**Apple seasoning**  Combine apples, figs and juice in bowl, cover, refrigerate 3 hours or overnight. Combine undrained fruit with remaining ingredients in medium bowl.

☐ SERVES 8

***Storage***  *Covered, in refrigerator*
***Freeze***  *Not suitable*
***Microwave***  *Not suitable*

*clockwise from top left*, Herb and garlic vegetables, Roast turkey with macadamia seasoning, Parmesan potatoes, Loin of pork with apple seasoning

# Tomato CHILLI lentils

*Recipe can be made a day ahead*

1 tablespoon olive oil

1 clove garlic, crushed

1 teaspoon grated fresh ginger

1 small fresh red chilli,
   finely chopped

1 teaspoon garam masala

2 medium (360g) onions,
   thinly sliced

300g pumpkin, chopped

2 (120g) finger
   eggplants, chopped

150g button mushrooms, halved

1 large (350g) red
   capsicum, chopped

2 small (180g) zucchini, chopped

3 x 400g cans tomatoes,
   undrained, crushed

2 tablespoons seeded mustard

1 tablespoon chopped
   fresh parsley

3/4 cup (150g) red lentils

Heat oil in pan, add garlic, ginger, chilli, garam masala, onions, pumpkin and eggplants; cook, stirring, until onions are soft. Add mushrooms, capsicum, zucchini and tomatoes; simmer, covered, 45 minutes. Stir in mustard, parsley and lentils, simmer, uncovered, for 25 minutes or until the lentils are tender.

□ SERVES 6

*Storage* Covered, in refrigerator
*Freeze* Not suitable
*Microwave* Not suitable

## Moroccan-style VEGETABLES

*Recipe can be made a day ahead*

3 small (700g) eggplants
1 large (350g) red capsicum
2 medium (300g) onions
2 small (180g) zucchini
2 tablespoons olive oil
2 cloves garlic, crushed
1 tablespoon ground cumin
1 tablespoon ground coriander
2 x 400g cans tomatoes,
    undrained, crushed
10cm cinnamon stick
1 tablespoon lemon juice
1 tablespoon sugar
3/4 cup (120g) blanched almonds,
    toasted, chopped

### Burghul

1 cup (160g) burghul
30g butter, chopped
1/4 cup (35g) dried currants

Cut eggplants and capsicum into 2cm pieces, cut onions into wedges, cut zucchini into slices 1cm thick.

Heat oil in large pan, add eggplant, capsicum, onion, zucchini, garlic, cumin and coriander; cook, stirring, until onions are soft. Add tomatoes, cinnamon stick and juice; simmer, covered, about 45 minutes or until eggplant is soft.

Discard cinnamon stick, stir in sugar. Serve with burghul and sprinkle with almonds.

**Burghul** Place burghul in medium heatproof bowl, cover with boiling water, stand 15 minutes, drain. Rinse under cold water, drain well, pat dry. Add the burghul to heated pan, stir over low heat until burghul is dry; add butter and currants, stir gently until the butter is melted.

□ SERVES 4 TO 6

***Storage*** *Covered, in refrigerator*
***Freeze*** *Not suitable*
***Microwave*** *Vegetable mixture suitable*

Tomato chilli lentils, Moroccan-style vegetables, *above left, from top*
Peppered beef pot roast, *right*

## Peppered beef POT ROAST

*Recipe best made just before serving*

2 tablespoons olive oil
2kg piece beef rump roast
3 medium (360g) carrots, halved
3 medium (375g) parsnips, halved
1 large (200g) onion, sliced
6 cloves garlic, peeled
3/4 cup (180ml) dry red wine
3/4 cup (180ml) port
3 sprigs fresh rosemary
1 1/2 tablespoons cracked
    black pepper

Heat oil in large pan, add beef; cook until browned all over. Remove from pan. Add carrots, parsnips, onion and garlic to same pan; cook, stirring, until onion is soft.

Return roast and any juices to pan with remaining ingredients; simmer, covered, about 45 minutes or until roast is tender. Remove roast from pan; cover to keep warm. Simmer sauce in pan, uncovered, about 5 minutes or until sauce thickens slightly. Serve sauce and vegetables with roast.

□ SERVES 6

***Freeze*** *Not suitable*
***Microwave*** *Not suitable*

# the bottle
# department
*cooking for keeps*

## No-cook CHILLI SAUCE

*Recipe best made a week ahead*

**500g small fresh red chillies**
**125g fresh ginger, peeled, chopped**
**6 cloves garlic, chopped**
**2 teaspoons grated lemon rind**
**¼ cup (55g) caster sugar**
**1 cup (250ml) white vinegar**

Using tight-fitting rubber gloves, wash chillies; remove and discard stalks but do not remove membranes or seeds. Quarter chillies.

Blend or process chillies with remaining ingredients until the consistency of a thick sauce.

Pour into hot sterilised jars; seal immediately.

MAKES ABOUT 3 CUPS (750 ML)

***Storage*** *Refrigerator, for one month*
***Freeze*** *Not suitable*

## Spiced mango CHUTNEY

*Recipe best made a week ahead*

**4 medium (1.75 kg) mangoes, peeled, chopped**
**1 medium (150g) onion, chopped**
**1 small fresh red chilli, finely chopped**
**1½ cups (250g) sultanas**
**2½ cups (625ml) brown vinegar**
**2 teaspoons salt**
**1 tablespoon grated fresh ginger**
**1¾ cups (385g) caster sugar**
**1 teaspoon ground cinnamon**
**1 teaspoon mixed spice**
**1 teaspoon ground ginger**
**¼ teaspoon cayenne pepper**
**2 cloves garlic, crushed**

Combine mangoes, onion, chilli, sultanas, vinegar, salt and ginger in large bowl. Cover, stand at room temperature 3 hours or overnight.

Transfer mango mixture to large pan, add sugar, stir over heat until sugar is dissolved.

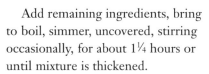

Add remaining ingredients, bring to boil, simmer, uncovered, stirring occasionally, for about 1¼ hours or until mixture is thickened.

Pour into hot sterilised jars; seal while hot.

MAKES ABOUT 1.5 LITRES (6 CUPS)

***Storage*** *Cool, dark place for about 6 months; refrigerate after opening*
***Freeze*** *Not suitable*
***Microwave*** *Not suitable*

## Marinated ARTICHOKE HEARTS

*Recipe best made a week ahead*

**10 medium (2kg) globe artichokes**
**3 medium (420g) lemons, halved**
**1 clove garlic, crushed**
**1 teaspoon black peppercorns**
**1 litre (4 cups) white vinegar**
**2 cups (500ml) water**
**2 cups (500ml) hot olive oil, approximately**

Marinated mushrooms, *above right*
Marinated capsicums, *above centre*
Marinated artichoke hearts, *above left*

Spiced mango chutney, *far left*
No-cook chilli sauce, *left*

Remove and discard stems from each artichoke; snap off and discard tough outer leaves until just a centre core of leaves remains.

Trim away any dark green parts, cut away tops of cores, rub all over artichokes with a lemon half.

Place artichokes in large bowl with another lemon half; cover with water.

Heat garlic, peppercorns, vinegar and the 2 cups (500ml) of water in large pan; do not boil.

Add drained artichokes and remaining lemons, simmer, uncovered, 15 minutes. Drain; discard vinegar mixture and lemon halves. Cool.

Remove and discard centre leaves and chokes with spoon; cut artichoke hearts in half. Place hearts in hot sterilised 1 litre (4-cup) jar, pour in enough oil (taking care as it will bubble) to leave 1cm space between artichoke hearts and top of jar. Seal while hot.

***Storage*** *Refrigerator, for 3 months*
***Freeze*** *Not suitable*
***Microwave*** *Not suitable*

## Marinated CAPSICUMS

*Recipe best made a week ahead*

**3 medium (600g) red capsicums**
**3 medium (600g) yellow capsicums**
**1 litre (4 cups) white vinegar**
**2 cups (500ml) water**
**2 teaspoons salt**
**1 clove garlic, finely sliced**
**1 teaspoon dried thyme leaves**
**3 dried bay leaves**
**½ teaspoon ground black pepper**
**2 cups (500ml) hot olive
   oil, approximately**

Cut off and remove both ends of capsicums, remove and discard seeds and membranes; cut capsicums lengthways into 4 cm pieces.
Heat vinegar, water and salt in large pan, do not boil. Add capsicum pieces; simmer gently, uncovered, 15 minutes; drain. Discard vinegar mixture.

Combine hot capsicum pieces, both leaves, garlic and pepper in hot sterilised 1 litre (4 cup) jar; pour in enough oil (taking care as it will bubble) to leave 1cm space between capsicum pieces and top of jar. Seal while hot.

***Storage*** *In refrigerator, for 3 months*
***Freeze*** *Not suitable*
***Microwave*** *Not suitable*

## Marinated MUSHROOMS

*Recipe best made a week ahead*

**1 litre (4 cups) white vinegar**
**2 cups (500ml) water**
**2 teaspoons salt**
**800g button mushrooms, trimmed**
**1 tablespoon chopped fresh parsley**
**1 teaspoon dried thyme leaves**
**1 clove garlic, finely sliced**
**½ teaspoon ground black pepper**
**2 cups (500ml) hot olive oil,
   approximately**

Heat vinegar, water and salt in large pan, do not boil. Add mushrooms, simmer gently, uncovered, 5 minutes. Drain; discard vinegar mixture.

Combine hot mushrooms, herbs, garlic and pepper in hot sterilised 1 litre (4 cup) jar; pour in enough hot oil (taking care as it will bubble) to leave 1cm space between mushrooms and top of jar. Seal while hot.

***Storage*** *In refrigerator, for 3 months*
***Freeze*** *Not suitable*
***Microwave*** *Not suitable*

## Thick-cut MARMALADE

*Recipe best made a week ahead*

**6 medium (1.25kg) Seville oranges**
**2 litres (8 cups) water**
**8 cups (1.75kg) sugar,
   approximately**

Cut unpeeled oranges in half lengthways, remove seeds, tie seeds in piece of muslin. Cut halves into 8mm slices.

Combine oranges, water and muslin bag in bowl, cover, stand overnight to soften rind.

Transfer fruit mixture to large pan, discard muslin bag. Bring to boil, simmer, covered, about 45 minutes or until rind is soft.

Measure fruit mixture and allow 1 cup sugar to each cup of fruit mixture. Return fruit mixture to pan, add sugar, stir over heat, without boiling until sugar is dissolved.

Boil, uncovered, stirring occasionally, about 30 minutes or until marmalade jells when tested.

Pour into hot sterilised jars; seal while hot.

MAKES ABOUT 2.5 LITRES (10 CUPS)

***Storage*** *Cool place, for 12 months*
***Freeze*** *Not suitable*
***Microwave*** *Not suitable*

## Lemon and lime CURD

*Recipe best made a day ahead*

**185g butter, chopped**
**2 cups (440g) caster sugar**
**½ cup (125ml) lemon juice**
**1 teaspoon grated lime rind**
**⅓ cup (80ml) lime juice**
**4 eggs, beaten, strained**

Combine all ingredients in top half of double saucepan or in heatproof bowl. Stir over simmering water until mixture coats the back of a wooden spoon. Pour into hot sterilised jars; seal while hot.

MAKES ABOUT 3 CUPS (750ML)

***Storage*** *Refrigerator, for 3 weeks*
***Freeze*** *Not suitable*
***Microwave*** *Not suitable*

Lemon and lime curd, *right*
Thick-cut marmalade, *left*

## Creamy coriander and CHICKEN curry

*Recipe can be made a day ahead*

1 small (80g) onion,
  finely chopped
2 cloves garlic, crushed
1 teaspoon bottled
  chopped chillies
2 teaspoons grated lime rind
$^1/_4$ cup (60ml) lime juice
1 teaspoon ground turmeric
2 teaspoons ground sweet paprika
1 teaspoon ground cumin
1 tablespoon chopped fresh
  coriander roots
2 teaspoons chopped
  fresh coriander

1 tablespoon peanut oil
8 (1kg) chicken thigh
  fillets, sliced
$^3/_4$ cup (180ml) coconut cream

Process onion, garlic, chillies, rind, juice, spices and coriander roots and leaves until mixture forms a paste.

Heat oil in large pan, add spice mixture, cook, stirring, until fragrant. Add chicken, cook, stirring, until tender. Add coconut cream, stir over heat until hot.

☐ SERVES 4

***Storage*** *Covered, in refrigerator*
***Freeze*** *Not suitable*
***Microwave*** *Not suitable*

Creamy coriander and chicken curry, *above*

## Ricotta RAVIOLI with
## tomato sauce

*Sauce can be made a day ahead*
*Recipe best made close to serving*

**200g packet (about 30 sheets)**
**gow gee pastry rounds**

### Filling

**2 tablespoons olive oil**
**1 small (80g) onion, chopped**
**1 clove garlic, crushed**
**250g flat mushrooms, chopped**
**2 tablespoons grated**
**parmesan cheese**
**125g ricotta cheese**
**1 tablespoon chopped fresh basil**

### Tomato sauce

**1 tablespoon olive oil**
**1 small (80g) onion, chopped**
**1 clove garlic, crushed**
**400g can tomatoes,**
**undrained, crushed**
**2 tablespoons dry red wine**
**1 teaspoon sugar**

Place rounded teaspoons of filling on centre of each pastry round. Brush edges of rounds with a little water, fold rounds over to enclose filling; press edges firmly to seal and form ravioli.

Add ravioli to large pan of boiling water, boil, uncovered, 2 minutes or until just tender; drain.

Serve ravioli with tomato sauce.

**Filling** Heat oil in large pan, add onion and garlic, cook, stirring, until onion is soft. Add mushrooms, cook stirring, until liquid has evaporated. Remove from heat stir in cheeses and basil.

**Tomato sauce** Heat oil in medium pan; add onion and garlic, cook, stirring, until onion is soft. Stir in tomatoes, wine and sugar, bring to boil. Blend or process mixture until smooth, strain into medium pan, simmer, uncovered until sauce has reduced to 1 cup (250ml).

□ SERVES 4

***Storage*** *Sauce, covered, in refrigerator*
***Freeze*** *Sauce suitable*
***Microwave*** *Not suitable*

## STEAKS with
## mushroom pockets

*Recipe can be prepared a day ahead*

**6 (1.2kg) beef Scotch fillet steaks**
**6 bacon rashers**
**2 tablespoons olive oil**

### Mushroom filling

**60g butter**
**1 medium (150g) onion,**
**finely chopped**
**300g mushrooms, finely chopped**
**2 tablespoons dry white wine**
**1/2 cup (35g) stale breadcrumbs**
**2 tablespoons chopped**
**fresh parsley**
**1 tablespoon seeded mustard**

Cut a pocket in side of each steak, fill pockets with mushroom filling. Wrap a bacon rasher around side of each steak; secure with toothpicks.

Heat oil in large pan, add steaks, cook, turning once, until well browned and cooked as desired. Remove toothpicks before serving.

**Mushroom filling** Heat butter in medium pan, add onion and mushrooms, cook, stirring, until onion is soft. Add wine, stir over heat until almost all the liquid has evaporated; remove from heat. Stir in crumbs, parsley and mustard; cool.

□ SERVES 6

***Storage*** *Covered, in refrigerator*
***Freeze*** *Not suitable*
***Microwave*** *Not suitable*

Ricotta ravioli with tomato sauce,
Steaks with mushroom pockets,
*left, from top*

## Vegetable FRITTATA

*Recipe can be made a day ahead*

- 3 medium (600g) potatoes
- 1 tablespoon olive oil
- 1 medium (170g) red onion, sliced
- 250g broccoli, chopped
- 2 medium (400g) red capsicums, sliced
- 8 eggs, lightly beaten
- $1/4$ cup (20g) grated parmesan cheese
- $1/4$ cup (30g) grated cheddar cheese
- $1/4$ cup chopped fresh chives

Oil a deep 22cm round cake pan, cover base with baking paper. Cut potatoes into 2cm cubes. Heat oil in large non-stick pan, add potato and onion, cook, stirring, 10 minutes or until potato is just tender; cool slightly.

Place broccoli and capsicums in medium heatproof bowl, cover with boiling water, stand 2 minutes; drain, pat dry. Combine potato mixture with capsicums and broccoli in prepared pan; pour over combined remaining ingredients.

Bake, uncovered, in moderate oven 45 minutes or until set. Stand frittata 10 minutes before turning out.

□ SERVES 6

**Storage** *Covered, in refrigerator*
**Freeze** *Not suitable*
**Microwave** *Not suitable*

## MEDITERRANEAN vegetables

*Recipe best made just before serving*

- $1/4$ cup (60ml) olive oil
- 5 (300g) finger eggplants, sliced
- 3 cloves garlic, crushed
- 3 medium (600g) red capsicums, sliced
- 1 medium (200g) yellow capsicum, sliced
- 300g button mushrooms, halved
- 200g green beans
- 5 small (450g) green zucchini, chopped
- 1 bunch (40 leaves) English spinach, coarsely chopped
- $1/2$ cup firmly packed flat-leaf parsley, chopped
- $1/4$ cup (60ml) balsamic vinegar

Vegetable frittata, Mediterranean vegetables, *below, from left*

Heat half the oil in wok or large pan, add eggplant, stir-fry until just tender; remove from wok. Heat remaining oil in wok, add garlic, capsicums and mushrooms, stir-fry 1 minute. Add beans and zucchini, stir-fry until vegetables are just tender.

Return eggplants to wok with spinach, parsley and vinegar, cook, stirring, until hot.

□ SERVES 6

*Freeze*  Not suitable
*Microwave*  Not suitable

## Citrus mint LAMB chops

*Recipe best prepared a day ahead*

**¹/₂ cup (125ml) orange juice**
**¹/₄ cup (60ml) cranberry sauce**
**2 tablespoons grated lemon rind**
**2 tablespoons chopped fresh mint**
**8 (1kg) lamb loin chops**

Combine juice, sauce, rind and mint in shallow dish, add chops, turn to coat; cover, refrigerate 3 hours or overnight.

Drain chops from marinade, reserve marinade. Add chops to heated oiled griddle pan (or barbecue or grill); cook on both sides, brushing occasionally with reserved marinade, until browned and tender.

□ SERVES 4

*Storage*  Covered, in refrigerator
*Freeze*  Marinated chops suitable
*Microwave*  Not suitable

## Italian GNOCCHI salad

*Recipe best made close to serving*

**1kg fresh potato gnocchi**
**400g can artichoke hearts, drained, quartered**
**¹/₂ cup (75g) drained sun-dried tomatoes in oil, halved**
**1 cup (160g) seeded black olives**
**¹/₄ cup shredded fresh basil**
**¹/₄ cup (40g) pine nuts, toasted**

### Balsamic vinegar dressing
**2 tablespoons white vinegar**
**2 tablespoons balsamic vinegar**
**¹/₃ cup (80ml) olive oil**
**1 teaspoon sugar**
**2 cloves garlic, crushed**

Add gnocchi to large pan of boiling water, simmer, uncovered, until tender; drain. Rinse gnocchi under cold water; drain well.

Combine gnocchi with remaining ingredients in large bowl, add balsamic vinegar dressing; mix gently.

**Balsamic vinegar dressing** Combine all ingredients in jar; shake well.

□ SERVES 6 TO 8

*Freeze*  Not suitable
*Microwave*  Gnocchi suitable

Italian gnocchi salad, Citrus mint lamb chops, above, from left

227

# Herbed beef SAUSAGES in tomato sauce

*Recipe can be prepared a day ahead*

1kg minced beef
1¹/₂ cups (100g) stale
    breadcrumbs
1 medium (150g) onion,
    finely chopped
2 cloves garlic, crushed
2 teaspoons seasoned pepper
1 tablespoon chopped
    fresh oregano
1 tablespoon chopped fresh thyme
2 eggs, lightly beaten
2 tablespoons olive oil

### Tomato sauce

2 tablespoons olive oil
1 medium (150g) onion, chopped
2 cloves garlic, crushed

¹/₂ cup (125ml) dry red wine
810g can tomatoes,
    undrained, crushed
425g can tomato puree
¹/₄ cup (60ml) tomato paste
¹/₃ cup (80ml) water
2 teaspoons sugar
1 small beef stock
    cube, crumbled
2 tablespoons chopped
    fresh oregano
2 tablespoons chopped fresh mint

Combine mince, crumbs, onion, garlic, pepper, herbs and eggs in large bowl. Shape heaped tablespoons of mixture into sausage shapes.

Heat oil in large pan, cook sausages in batches, turning until well browned; drain on absorbent paper.

Place sausages in pan with tomato sauce, simmer, covered, about

10 minutes or until cooked through.

**Tomato sauce** Heat oil in large pan, add onion and garlic, cook, stirring, until onion is soft. Add wine, simmer, uncovered, until most of the liquid is evaporated. Stir in tomatoes, puree, paste, water, sugar, stock cube and oregano, simmer, uncovered, about 15 minutes or until slightly thickened. Stir in mint.

□ SERVES 6 TO 8

*Storage* Covered, in refrigerator
*Freeze* Suitable
*Microwave* Not suitable

Herbed beef sausages in tomato sauce, Chicken pie, *above, from left*

# Chicken PIE

*Recipe can be made a day ahead*

**60g butter**
**4 bacon rashers, chopped**
**6 green onions, chopped**
**2 cloves garlic, crushed**
**2 tablespoons plain flour**
**1¹/₂ cups (375ml) milk**
**3¹/₂ cups (525g) chopped**
    **cooked chicken**
**¹/₂ cup (25g) grated**
    **parmesan cheese**
**2 eggs, lightly beaten**
**10 sheets fillo pastry**
**80g butter, melted, extra**

Lightly oil 23cm pie dish.

Heat butter in medium pan, add bacon, onions and garlic, cook, stirring, until bacon is browned lightly. Add flour, stir until combined. Remove pan from heat, gradually stir in milk, stir over heat until mixture boils and thickens; cool. Stir in chicken, cheese and eggs.

Layer 2 pastry sheets together, brushing each with some of the extra butter, fold in half lengthways. Repeat with another 2 pastry sheets and some of the extra butter. Arrange strips in the form of a cross, place into prepared pie dish, letting ends overhang edge of dish. Repeat with another 4 pastry sheets and some of the extra butter, placing this cross diagonally on top of other cross so base of dish is completely covered.

Spoon chicken mixture into dish, fold overhanging pastry edges back onto filling; brush with some of the remaining extra butter.

Layer remaining 2 pastry sheets with some of the remaining extra butter, fold in half crossways to form a square. Place pastry on top of pie; trim edge.

Brush top lightly with remaining extra butter.

Bake, uncovered, in moderate oven about 35 minutes or until browned lightly and heated through (cover pie with foil if it begins to over-brown).

□ SERVES 6

***Storage*** *Covered, in refrigerator*
***Freeze*** *Not suitable*
***Microwave*** *Filling suitable*

# Winter vegetable CASSEROLE

*Recipe can be made a day ahead*

**2 tablespoons vegetable oil**
**2 medium (300g) onions, chopped**
**1 clove garlic, crushed**
**2 medium (240g) carrots, chopped**
**500g pumpkin, chopped**
**4 small (480g) potatoes, chopped**
**2 cups (500ml) chicken stock**
**1 tablespoon tomato paste**
**1 tablespoon seeded mustard**
**¹/₂ teaspoon dried thyme leaves**
**2 large (300g) zucchini, chopped**
**3 teaspoons cornflour**
**1 tablespoon water**

Heat oil in pan, add onions and garlic, cook, stirring, until onion is soft. Add carrots, pumpkin, potatoes, stock, paste, mustard and thyme; simmer, covered, 15 minutes. Stir in zucchini and blended cornflour and water; stir until mixture boils and thickens. Simmer, uncovered, until vegetables are just tender.

□ SERVES 4

***Storage*** *Covered, in refrigerator*
***Freeze*** *Not suitable*
***Microwave*** *Suitable*

Winter vegetable casserole, *below*

# TANDOORI chicken with coconut rice and yogurt sauce

*Coconut rice and yogurt sauce can be made a day ahead  Chicken can be prepared a day ahead*

**10 (1.7kg) chicken breast fillets**
**¹/₂ cup (125ml) plain yogurt**
**¹/₄ cup (60ml) lemon juice**
**¹/₄ cup (60ml) tandoori paste**

### Coconut rice

**3 cups (600g) basmati rice**
**425ml can coconut milk**
**2 cups (500ml) chicken stock**
**³/₄ cup (50g) shredded coconut, toasted**

### Yogurt sauce

**1³/₄ cups (430ml) plain yogurt**
**1 small (130g) green cucumber, peeled, seeded, chopped**
**¹/₄ cup chopped fresh mint**
**2 teaspoons lemon juice**
**2 teaspoons sugar**

Place chicken in shallow glass dish, add combined remaining ingredients; turn to coat chicken. Cover, refrigerate 3 hours or overnight.

Remove chicken from yogurt mixture; discard excess yogurt mixture. Place chicken on wire racks in baking dishes.

Bake, uncovered, in moderately hot oven about 30 minutes or until just tender, alternating positions halfway through cooking time. Serve chicken sliced with coconut rice and yogurt sauce.

**Coconut rice**  Combine rice, milk and stock in large heavy-based pan; bring to boil, stirring. Simmer, covered, about 20 minutes or until rice is tender. Remove from heat; gently stir in coconut.

**Yogurt sauce**  Combine all ingredients in medium bowl.

□ SERVES 8 TO 10

***Storage***  *Covered, separately, in refrigerator*
***Freeze***  *Rice suitable*
***Microwave***  *Rice suitable*

## VEAL ratatouille casserole

*Recipe can be prepared a day ahead*

12 (1.5kg) veal cutlets
plain flour
$1/4$ cup (60ml) olive oil
1 medium (350g) leek,
   coarsely chopped
2 cloves garlic, crushed
1 medium (200g) red
   capsicum, chopped
1 medium (200g) green
   capsicum, chopped
4 (240g) finger eggplants, chopped
$1/3$ cup (80ml) dry white wine
250g button mushrooms
3 medium (360g) zucchini, chopped
3 x 400g cans tomatoes,
   undrained, crushed
425g can tomato puree
$1/4$ cup chopped fresh oregano
$1^1/4$ cups (200g) seeded black olives
1 tablespoon sugar

Toss cutlets in flour, shake away excess flour. Heat half the oil in large pan, add cutlets in batches, cook until browned on both sides; drain on absorbent paper. Heat remaining oil in same pan, add leek and garlic; cook, stirring, until leek is soft. Add capsicum and eggplant; cook, stirring, until softened. Add wine, mushrooms and zucchini, cook, stirring, until liquid is reduced by half.

Stir in tomatoes, puree and oregano, simmer, covered, 20 minutes. Return cutlets to pan, simmer, uncovered, further 30 minutes or until cutlets are tender. Stir in olives and sugar.

☐ SERVES 6

**Storage**  *Covered, in refrigerator*
**Freeze**  *Not suitable*
**Microwave**  *Not suitable*

## Garlic thyme CHICKEN

*Recipe best made close to serving*

1 tablespoon olive oil
8 (900g) chicken thigh
   fillets, quartered
1 medium (200g) onion, sliced
4 cloves garlic, crushed
$1/4$ cup (60ml) lemon juice
$1/2$ cup (125ml) cream
$1/2$ cup (125ml) chicken stock
1 tablespoon chopped fresh thyme
1 bunch (40 leaves) English spinach
2 teaspoons cornflour
2 teaspoons water

Heat oil in non-stick pan, add chicken in batches, cook, stirring, until browned and just tender; remove from pan.

Add onion, garlic and juice to pan, cook, stirring, until onion is soft. Add cream, stock, thyme, spinach and blended cornflour and water, cook, stirring, until sauce thickens slightly. Return chicken to pan, stir over heat until hot.

☐ SERVES 6

**Freeze**  *Not suitable*
**Microwave**  *Not suitable*

Tandoori chicken with coconut rice and yogurt sauce, *far left*
Veal ratatouille casserole, *above left*
Garlic thyme chicken, *left*

# Roast potatoes with parsnips and bacon ROLLS

*Recipe best made just before serving*

- 8 small (960g) old potatoes, peeled
- $^1/_4$ cup (60ml) olive oil
- 30g butter, melted
- 3 medium (375g) parsnips, halved
- 2 large (400g) onions, quartered
- 6 bacon rashers
- 2 teaspoons chopped fresh sage

Boil, steam or microwave potatoes until almost cooked; drain. Combine oil, butter, potatoes, parsnips and onions in large baking dish. Bake, uncovered, in very hot oven 30 minutes.

Cut each bacon rasher in half lengthways, roll up and secure with toothpicks. Add to potato mixture, bake further 15 minutes or until bacon is crisp. Remove toothpicks. Sprinkle vegetables with sage.

□ SERVES 6

***Freeze*** *Not suitable*
***Microwave*** *Potatoes suitable*

Roast potatoes with parsnips and bacon rolls, *above*
Creamy mushroom veal,
Roast pork with caramel ginger pears, *right, from top*

# Creamy mushroom VEAL

*Ask the butcher to bone veal shoulder  Recipe can be made a day ahead*

1 tablespoon olive oil
1.5kg boned rolled shoulder of veal
8 (80g) spring onions, quartered
4 cloves garlic, crushed
250g button mushrooms, halved
$1/2$ cup (125ml) dry white wine
440g can cream of mushroom soup
$1/2$ cup (125ml) chicken stock
2 teaspoons French mustard
1 tablespoon chopped fresh rosemary
2 tablespoons cornflour
2 tablespoons water

Heat oil in large pan, add veal; cook until well-browned; remove.

Add onions and garlic to same pan; cook, stirring, until onions are softened. Return veal to pan with mushrooms, wine, undiluted soup, stock, mustard and rosemary. Bring to boil, simmer, covered, about 1 hour or until veal is tender. Remove veal from pan, keep warm. Stir blended cornflour and water into mushroom mixture, stir until mixture boils and thickens. Serve sauce with veal.

□ SERVES 4 TO 6

**Storage**  *Covered, in refrigerator*
**Freeze**  *Suitable*
**Microwave**  *Not suitable*

# Roast PORK with caramel ginger pears

*Recipe best prepared a day ahead*

1.2kg pork foreloin (neck) roast
20g piece fresh ginger, peeled
1 tablespoon whisky
$1/4$ cup (60ml) maple syrup
2 teaspoons vegetable oil
4 medium (720g) pears, peeled, cored, sliced
$1/2$ cup (125ml) dry white wine

Roll up pork, secure with string at 2cm intervals. Cut ginger into thin strips. Combine ginger, whisky and syrup in dish, add pork; turn to coat well. Cover, refrigerate 3 hours or overnight.

Drain pork from marinade, reserve marinade. Heat oil in flameproof baking dish, add pork; cook until well-browned all over.

Bake, uncovered, in moderate oven 45 minutes. Add pears and reserved marinade to dish. Bake, uncovered, further 30 minutes or until pork and pears are tender, stirring occasionally. Remove pork from dish. Add wine to dish, simmer, uncovered, until sauce thickens slightly. Serve with pork.

□ SERVES 6

**Freeze**  *Not suitable*
**Microwave**  *Not suitable*

## Curried EGGPLANT with yogurt

*Eggplants can be baked a day ahead*

- 2 large (1kg) eggplants
- 1 tablespoon vegetable oil
- 2 cloves garlic, crushed
- 1 medium (150g) onion, finely chopped
- 1 teaspoon ground cumin
- 1/4 teaspoon chilli powder
- 2 tablespoons Korma curry paste
- 1 tablespoon mango chutney
- 1/4 cup chopped fresh coriander
- 200g plain yogurt

Pierce skin of eggplants once with knife. Place unpeeled eggplants on oven tray. Bake in moderately hot oven about 1 hour or until soft. Cool eggplants 10 minutes, peel, chop flesh.

Heat oil in large pan, add garlic and onion; cook, stirring, until onion is soft. Add cumin, chilli and paste; cook, stirring, until fragrant. Add eggplant, chutney and half the coriander, stir over heat until hot. Remove from heat; stir in yogurt. Serve warm, sprinkled with remaining coriander.

□ SERVES 6

**Storage** *Covered, in refrigerator*
**Freeze** *Not suitable*
**Microwave** *Not suitable*

## Chilli BOK CHOY

*Recipe best made close to serving*

- 1 tablespoon sesame oil
- 1 small fresh red chilli, thinly sliced
- 2 teaspoons grated fresh ginger
- 2 medium (300g) onions, quartered
- 2 cloves garlic, crushed
- 2 bunches (800g) bok choy, roughly chopped
- 1 medium (200g) red capsicum, sliced
- 2 tablespoons soy sauce
- 2 tablespoons mild sweet chilli sauce

Heat oil in wok or large pan, add chilli, ginger, onions and garlic, stir-fry until onions are soft. Add bok choy, capsicum and soy sauce; stir-fry until bok choy is just wilted. Serve drizzled with chilli sauce.

□ SERVES 4

**Freeze** Not suitable
**Microwave** Suitable

Curried eggplant with yogurt, Chilli bok choy, *below, from left* Osso bucco, *right*

## OSSO BUCCO

*Ask the butcher to cut veal into pieces 4cm to 5cm thick
Recipe can be made 2 days ahead*

**650g veal shanks (osso bucco)**
**plain flour**
**2 tablespoons olive oil**
**2 medium (300g) onions, sliced**
**2 cloves garlic, crushed**
**1 large (180g) carrot, sliced**
**1 small chicken stock**
  **cube, crumbled**
**2$^1/_2$ cups (625ml) water**
**2 tablespoons tomato paste**
**1 bay leaf**
**$^1/_2$ teaspoon dried thyme leaves**
**$^1/_2$ teaspoon dried rosemary leaves**
**8 (320g) baby new**
  **potatoes, halved**

Toss veal in flour, shake away excess flour. Heat oil in large pan, add veal in batches, cook until well browned all over; drain on absorbent paper. Add onions, garlic and carrot to same pan, cook, stirring, until onions are soft.

Return veal to pan with stock cube, water, paste and herbs; simmer, covered, 45 minutes. Add potatoes, simmer, covered, further 20 minutes or until veal is tender.

□ SERVES 4

**Storage** Covered, in refrigerator
**Freeze** Suitable
**Microwave** Not suitable

235

## CREPES with banana
## pecan caramel sauce

*Crepes can be made a day ahead*
*Sauce best made close to serving*

**375g bottle pancake shake mix**
**60g butter**
**$^3/_4$ cup (150g) firmly packed**
   **brown sugar**
**$^1/_4$ cup (60ml) maple syrup**
**$^1/_2$ cup (125ml) cream**
**$^1/_2$ cup (125ml) sour cream**
**2 medium (200g) bananas, sliced**
**$^1/_2$ cup pecans, roughly chopped**

Make 8 crepes according to directions on bottle; keep warm.

Heat butter in heavy-based pan, add sugar, cook, stirring, until sugar is dissolved. Stir in syrup, simmer, uncovered, 2 minutes. Stir in creams, simmer, uncovered, further 2 minutes.

Stir in bananas and nuts, cook, stirring, until heated through.

Serve crepes with sauce.

☐ SERVES 4

**Storage** *Covered, in refrigerator*
**Freeze** *Crepes suitable*
**Microwave** *Not suitable*

Crepes with banana pecan caramel sauce, *above*

# COFFEE hazelnut layer cake

*Recipe can be made a day ahead*

1 tablespoon dry instant coffee

1 tablespoon hot water

2 x 340g packets buttercake mix (plus cake
  ingredients listed on packets)

1 cup (110g) ground hazelnuts

2 tablespoons caster sugar

$1/4$ cup (60ml) water, extra

2 tablespoons Kahlua

$3/4$ cup (80g) ground hazelnuts, extra

## Coffee cream

1 tablespoon dry instant coffee

1 tablespoon hot water

1 tablespoon Kahlua

600ml cream

$1/3$ cup (80ml) icing sugar mixture

## Chocolate topping

100g dark chocolate, chopped

50g unsalted butter, chopped

Grease a deep 22cm round cake pan, line base and side with baking paper, bringing paper 5cm above edge of pan.

Combine coffee and water in small bowl, stir until coffee is dissolved; cool.

Combine cake mixes, ingredients listed on cake packets, coffee mixture and hazelnuts in large bowl of electric mixer. Make according to directions on packet. Pour mixture into prepared pan.

Bake in moderate oven 1 hour 10 minutes. Stand cake in pan 5 minutes, turn onto rack to cool.

Combine sugar, extra water and liqueur in pan, stir over heat until sugar is dissolved; cool.

Trim top of cake, split cake into 5 layers, brush each layer with liqueur syrup. Reserve 1 cup (250ml) coffee cream, join cake layers with remaining coffee cream. Spread chocolate topping over top of cake. Spread reserved coffee cream around side of cake, press extra hazelnuts around side of cake.

**Coffee cream** Combine coffee and water in small bowl, stir until dissolved, stir in liqueur; cool. Beat cream, icing sugar and coffee mixture in small bowl of electric mixer until firm peaks form.

**Chocolate topping** Combine chocolate and butter in heatproof bowl, place over pan of simmering water, stir until melted; cool to room temperature. Stir until thick.

***Storage*** *Covered, in refrigerator*
***Freeze*** *Unfilled cake suitable*
***Microwave*** *Syrup and chocolate topping suitable*

Coffee hazelnut layer cake, *left*

## Aniseed BAVAROIS
### with red wine pears

*Recipe can be made 2 days ahead*

**2 cups (500ml) milk**
**5 star anise**
**8 egg yolks**
**³/₄ cup (165g) caster sugar**
**1 tablespoon gelatine**
**2 tablespoons water**
**2 cups (500ml) cream**

#### Red wine pears

**2 cups (500ml) dry red wine**
**2 cups (440g) caster sugar**
**2 x 10cm cinnamon sticks**
**2 star anise**
**4 medium (720g) pears,
    peeled, quartered**

Lightly grease a 14cm x 21cm loaf pan. Combine milk and star anise in pan, bring to boil, remove from heat, cover, stand 20 minutes.

Beat egg yolks and sugar in medium bowl with electric mixer until creamy, gradually whisk in milk mixture. Return mixture to pan, stir over heat, without boiling, until mixture

## Sticky fruit PUDDING
### with caramel sauce

*Recipe can be made a day ahead*

**410g jar fruit mince**
**³/₄ cup (180ml) boiling water**
**1 teaspoon bicarbonate of soda**
**60g butter, chopped**
**¹/₂ cup (100g) firmly packed
    brown sugar**
**2 eggs, lightly beaten**
**1 cup (150g) self-raising flour**
**¹/₂ cup (75g) plain flour**

#### Caramel sauce

**250g butter, chopped**
**1 cup (200g) firmly packed
    brown sugar**
**300ml cream**

Grease a deep 20cm round cake pan, line base and side with baking paper. Combine fruit mince, water and soda in large bowl, mix well; stand 5 minutes. Process mince mixture and butter until almost smooth. Return mixture to same bowl, stir in sugar, eggs and sifted flours; mix well. Pour mixture into prepared pan.

Bake in moderate oven about 1 hour, stand 15 minutes before turning out.

Serve pudding warm with warm caramel sauce.

**Caramel sauce** Combine all ingredients in medium pan, stir over heat until sugar is dissolved. Simmer, uncovered, about 5 minutes or until sauce is thickened slightly.

***Storage*** *Covered, in refrigerator*
***Freeze*** *Suitable*
***Microwave*** *Sauce suitable*

thickens. Strain into clean large bowl; discard star anise.

Sprinkle gelatine over water in cup, stand cup in pan of simmering water, stir until gelatine is dissolved. Stir gelatine mixture into egg mixture. Cover, refrigerate, stirring occasionally, until partially set.

Beat cream in small bowl until soft peaks form, fold into egg mixture in 2 batches. Pour mixture into prepared pan, cover, refrigerate several hours until set.

Serve sliced bavarois with red wine pears and strained syrup.

**Red wine pears** Combine wine, sugar, cinnamon and star anise in large pan, stir over heat, without boiling, until sugar is dissolved. Simmer, uncovered, without stirring, 10 minutes. Add pears, simmer, uncovered, about 10 minutes, or until just tender; cool pears in syrup. Cover, refrigerate 3 hours or overnight.

☐ SERVES 8

*Storage* Covered, in refrigerator
*Freeze* Not suitable
*Microwave* Not suitable

# Pear and port
# CHEESECAKE

*Recipe can be made 3 days ahead*

**2 cups (200g) plain sweet
  biscuit crumbs**
**2¹/₂ teaspoons ground ginger**
**1¹/₂ tablespoons brown sugar**
**90g butter, melted**
**2 teaspoons gelatine**

### Filling

**125g packet cream cheese**
**250g ricotta cheese**
**¹/₃ cup (75g) caster sugar**
**2 eggs**
**¹/₄ cup (60ml) cream**

### Spiced pears

**2 cups (500ml) port**
**1 cup (250ml) water**
**¹/₂ cup (110g) caster sugar**
**10cm cinnamon stick**
**2 x 6cm pieces lemon rind**
**2 medium (360g) pears,
  peeled, quartered**

Grease a deep 23cm flan tin. Combine crumbs, ginger, sugar and butter in medium bowl. Press over base and side of prepared tin, refrigerate 30 minutes.

Place tin on oven tray, spoon filling into crumb crust.

Bake in moderately slow oven, about 40 minutes or until firm; cool.

Drain spiced pears; reserve liquid. Slice pears thinly, arrange over top of cheesecake. Place reserved liquid in pan, boil, uncovered, until reduced to 1 cup (250ml). Discard cinnamon stick and rind. Sprinkle gelatine over hot liquid, stir until dissolved; strain, refrigerate until thick and syrupy. Pour gelatine mixture over pears, refrigerate until set.

**Filling** Beat cheeses and sugar in small bowl until smooth, add eggs one at a time. Add cream, beat until combined.

**Spiced pears** Combine port, water, sugar, cinnamon and rind in pan, stir over heat until sugar is dissolved. Add pears, simmer about 10 minutes; cool.

☐ SERVES 6 TO 8

*Storage* Covered, in refrigerator
*Freeze* Not suitable
*Microwave* Pears and gelatine suitable

Sticky fruit pudding with caramel sauce, *above left*
Aniseed bavarois with red wine pears, *left*
Pear and port cheesecake, *above*

## KUMQUAT puddings
### with custard cream

*Kumquat mixture and custard
cream can be made a day ahead
Puddings best made just before serving*

**350g kumquats**
**2 cups (500ml) water**
**1 cup (220g) caster sugar**

### Cake mixture

**125g butter**
**1 teaspoon vanilla essence**
**$1/2$ cup (110g) caster sugar**
**2 eggs**
**2 cups (300g) self-raising flour**
**$1/2$ cup (125ml) milk**

### Custard cream

**$3/4$ cup (180ml) cream**
**$3/4$ cup (180ml) milk**
**4 egg yolks**
**$1/4$ cup (55g) caster sugar**
**2 tablespoons Grand Marnier**

Grease 6 x 1 cup (250ml) ovenproof
dishes. Cut kumquats into quarters
lengthways, discard seeds. Combine
kumquats and water in medium pan,
simmer, uncovered, stirring
occasionally, about 1 hour or until
kumquats are very tender.

Add sugar to pan, stir over heat,
without boiling, until sugar is
dissolved. Simmer, uncovered, without
stirring, about 10 minutes or until
mixture is like the consistency of a
soft-setting jam.

Divide kumquat mixture
among dishes, top with cake
mixture. Cover with greased foil,
secure with string or rubber bands.
Place dishes in large baking dish, pour
in enough boiling water to come
halfway up sides.

Bake in moderate oven 30 minutes.
Turn puddings onto serving plates,
serve with custard cream.

**Cake mixture** Beat butter, essence and
sugar in small bowl with electric mixer
until thick and creamy, beat in eggs,
one at a time. Transfer mixture to
medium bowl, stir in sifted flour and
milk in 2 batches.

**Custard cream** Bring cream and milk to boil in medium pan. Beat egg yolks and sugar in medium bowl with electric mixer until thick and creamy, gradually whisk into hot milk mixture. Stir over heat, without boiling, until mixture thickens slightly; add liqueur.

□ SERVES 6

*Storage Kumquat mixture, covered, in cool, dry place Custard, covered, in refrigerator*
*Freeze Not suitable*
*Microwave Not suitable*

## PEARS with brandy butter and cinnamon ice-cream

*Ice-cream can be made 3 days ahead*
*Pears can be prepared a day ahead*

**6 medium (1.4kg) Corella pears**
**10cm cinnamon stick**
**$^1/_2$ cup finely chopped fresh ginger**
**$2^1/_2$ cups dessert wine**
**2 cups (440g) caster sugar**
**2 cups (500ml) water**
**3cm piece vanilla bean**

### Brandy butter

**$^1/_4$ cup (40g) icing sugar mixture**
**60g butter**
**2 tablespoons Cognac**
**2 tablespoons cream**

### Cinnamon ice-cream

**600ml thickened cream**
**10cm cinnamon stick**
**$^1/_2$ teaspoon ground cinnamon**
**6 egg yolks**
**$^1/_2$ cup caster sugar**

Peel pears, leaving stems intact. Combine remaining ingredients in large pan, stir over heat, without boiling, until sugar is dissolved. Add pears, simmer, covered, about 35 minutes, or until pears are just tender.

Cut pears in half, brush rounded sides with brandy butter, cook under hot grill until hot. Serve with cinnamon ice-cream.

**Brandy butter** Combine all the ingredients in small pan, cook, stirring,

until mixture thickens slightly.

**Cinnamon ice-cream** Combine cream, cinnamon stick and ground cinnamon in medium pan, bring to boil. Cool slightly; discard cinnamon stick. Beat egg yolks and sugar in small bowl with electric mixer until pale and thick, slowly whisk in cream mixture. Return mixture to pan, stir over heat, without boiling, until mixture coats the back of a wooden spoon; cool. Cover, refrigerate until cold.

Pour mixture into a 20cm x 30cm lamington pan; cover freeze until firm.

Beat or process ice-cream until light and fluffy, place in 14cm x 21cm loaf pan; cover, freeze until firm.

□ SERVES 6

*Freeze Ice-cream suitable*
*Microwave Not suitable*

Kumquat puddings with custard cream, *left*
Pears with brandy butter and cinnamon ice-cream, *below left*
Lemon delicious, *below*

## LEMON delicious

*Recipe must be made just before serving*

**4 eggs, separated**
**$^3/_4$ cup (165g) caster sugar**
**2 tablespoons self-raising flour**
**$^3/_4$ cup (180ml) lemon juice**
**$1^1/_2$ cups (375ml) milk**

Beat egg yolks and sugar in small bowl with electric mixer until thick and creamy. Gradually beat in sifted flour and juice, then beat in milk. Transfer mixture to a large bowl.

Beat egg whites in a clean small bowl with electric mixer until soft peaks form. Fold egg whites into yolk mixture in 2 batches. Pour mixture into a deep, 1.5 litre (6-cup) ovenproof dish. Stand dish in a baking dish, pour in enough boiling water to come halfway up the side of ovenproof dish.

Bake in moderate oven about 50 minutes or until firm to touch.

□ SERVES 4

*Freeze Not suitable*
*Microwave Not suitable*

# Spicy almond ROULADE with apricot sauce

*Recipe can be made a day ahead*

2 tablespoons caster sugar
5 eggs
$^3/_4$ cup (165g) caster sugar, extra
1 cup (150g) self-raising flour
1 teaspoon ground ginger
2 teaspoons ground cardamom
1 teaspoon ground cinnamon
1 teaspoon mixed spice
1 tablespoon hot water
50g butter, melted

### Almond filling

$^3/_4$ cup (180ml) thickened cream
$^1/_2$ cup (125ml) sour cream
$^1/_4$ cup (40g) icing sugar mixture
$^1/_2$ teaspoon ground cardamom
few drops almond essence
$^1/_3$ cup (35g) slivered
   almonds, toasted

### Apricot sauce

2 x 425g cans apricots in syrup
1 tablespoon brandy

Grease a 26cm x 32cm Swiss roll pan, line base and sides with baking paper.

Cover wire rack with baking paper; sprinkle with sugar. Beat eggs in medium bowl with electric mixer until thick and creamy (about 3 minutes). Beat in extra sugar, a tablespoon at a time, beat until dissolved between additions. Gently fold in sifted flour and spices and combined water and butter. Spread mixture into prepared pan.

Bake in moderately hot oven about 15 minutes, or until firm to touch. Immediately turn cake onto prepared wire rack, trim edges, roll up from long side using paper to lift and guide roll; stand 2 minutes. Carefully unroll cake; cool.

Spread cake with almond filling, roll up; cover, refrigerate several hours or until almond filling is firm. Serve with apricot sauce.

**Almond filling** Beat creams, icing sugar, cardamom and essence in small bowl with electric mixer until soft peaks form; fold in almonds.

**Apricot sauce** Drain apricots, reserve $^1/_3$ cup (80ml) syrup. Blend or process apricots and reserved syrup until smooth; strain. Stir in brandy, refrigerate until cold.

☐ SERVES 8

***Storage*** *Covered, in refrigerator*
***Freeze*** *Suitable*
***Microwave*** *Not suitable*

# Poached TAMARILLOS

*Tamarillos can be prepared 3 hours ahead*
*Pour wine over fruit just before serving*

4 medium (440g) tamarillos
$^3/_4$ cup (165g) caster sugar
$1^1/_4$ cups (310ml) water
1 cup (250ml) pink sparkling wine

Make a small slit in skin of tamarillos, around the stem end. Place tamarillos in a medium heatproof bowl, cover with boiling water, let stand for 5 minutes. Remove tamarillos from water; cool. Discard skins, leaving stems intact.

Combine sugar and water in a large pan, stir over heat, without boiling, until sugar is dissolved. Add tamarillos to syrup, simmer 5 minutes, or until tamarillos are just soft; cool in syrup. Remove tamarillos from the syrup, reserve syrup. Cut tamarillos to form petal shapes, leaving stem ends intact. Open out petals, pressing seeds from petals towards the centre. Place tamarillos in serving dishes with some of the reserved syrup, pour wine over fruit, serve immediately.

☐ SERVES 4

***Storage*** *Covered, in refrigerator*
***Freeze*** *Not suitable*
***Microwave*** *Not suitable*

Spicy almond roulade with apricot sauce, *above left*
Poached tamarillos, *right*

## APPLE crunch

*Recipe can be prepared several hours ahead*

**4 medium (600g) apples**
**1 teaspoon grated lemon rind**
**1 tablespoon lemon juice**
**$^1/_2$ cup (125ml) apple juice**
**$^1/_4$ cup chopped pitted prunes**
**$^1/_2$ loaf (450g) unsliced white bread**
**100g butter**
**$^1/_4$ cup (60ml) golden syrup**
**$^1/_4$ cup (55g) caster sugar**
**$1^1/_2$ teaspoons ground cinnamon**

Grease 1.5 litre (6-cup) shallow
ovenproof dish. Thinly slice apples,
combine with rind, juices and prunes
in medium bowl. Spread half apple
mixture into prepared dish. Trim
crusts from bread, cut into 1cm cubes.
Combine butter, golden syrup and

sugar in medium pan, stir over heat, without boiling, until sugar is dissolved. Add bread and cinnamon; mix well. Sprinkle half the bread mixture over apples in dish, repeat with remaining apple and bread mixtures.

Bake in moderately slow oven about 1 hour or until browned.

□ SERVES 4 TO 6

**Storage** *Covered, in refrigerator*
**Freeze** *Not suitable*
**Microwave** *Not suitable*

## Easy lemon TART

*Recipe can be made a day ahead*

**4 eggs**
**1/2 cup (75g) plain flour**
**1 cup (220g) caster sugar**
**1 cup (90g) desiccated coconut**
**125g butter, melted**
**1 cup (250ml) cream**
**3/4 cup (180ml) milk**
**1 tablespoon grated lemon rind**
**1/4 cup (60ml) lemon juice**

Grease straight-sided 25cm pie dish. Whisk eggs in medium bowl. Gradually whisk in sifted flour, then remaining ingredients until well combined. Pour mixture into prepared pie dish.

Bake in moderate oven about 45 minutes or until set and browned lightly. Serve warm or cold.

□ SERVES 6 TO 8

**Storage** *Covered, in refrigerator*
**Freeze** *Not suitable*
**Microwave** *Not suitable*

## PEAR and pecan pie

*Recipe can be made a day ahead*

**2 1/2 cups (375g) plain flour**
**1/3 cup (55g) icing sugar mixture**
**125g butter, chopped**
**1/4 cup (30g) finely chopped, toasted pecans**
**1 egg, lightly beaten**
**1/4 cup (60ml) water**

### Pear filling

**8 medium (1.5kg) pears**
**1 cup (250ml) water**
**1/3 cup (65g) firmly packed brown sugar**
**1 tablespoon grated orange rind**
**1 teaspoon ground cinnamon**
**3/4 cup (110g) dried apricots**
**1/4 cup (15g) stale breadcrumbs**

Sift flour and sugar into medium bowl, rub in butter. Add nuts, half the egg and water. Knead dough gently on lightly floured surface until smooth. Divide in half, cover, refrigerate 30 minutes.

Roll half the pastry between sheets of baking paper until large enough to line 23cm pie plate. Lift pastry into plate, ease into side; trim edge. Prick base, refrigerate 30 minutes.

Bake pastry case, blind, in moderately hot oven 20 minutes; cool.

Spoon pear filling into pastry case, brush edge with remaining egg. Roll remaining pastry large enough to cover filling. Press edges together with a fork, trim edge. Brush pastry with more egg.

Bake in hot oven 15 minutes, reduce heat to moderate; bake 25 minutes.

**Pear filling** Peel, core and thinly slice pears, combine with water in shallow pan; simmer, covered, about 5 minutes or until tender. Drain pears, discard liquid. Dry pears with absorbent paper; cool. Transfer pears to large bowl, stir in remaining ingredients.

□ SERVES 6 TO 8

**Storage** *Covered, in refrigerator*
**Freeze** *Suitable*
**Microwave** *Pears suitable*

Easy lemon tart, *above left*
Apple crunch, *left*
Pear and pecan pie, *right*

## Rhubarb SOUFFLES
## with vanilla bean
## ice-cream

*Vanilla bean ice-cream can be
made 3 days ahead
Souffles must be made just before serving*

**3 cups (350g) chopped
fresh rhubarb**
**1¹/₂ tablespoons water**
**¹/₂ cup (110g) caster sugar**
**¹/₄ cup (60ml) water, extra**

**2 teaspoons potato flour**
**2 teaspoons milk**
**6 egg whites**
**¹/₄ cup (55g) caster sugar, extra**

Vanilla bean ice-cream

**2 vanilla beans**
**1 cup (250ml) milk**
**300ml cream**
**4 egg yolks**
**²/₃ cup (150g) caster sugar**

Grease 6 x 1-cup (250ml) souffle
dishes sprinkle bases and sides with a
little caster sugar.

Place rhubarb in medium pan of
water, simmer, covered, 10 minutes or
until soft; mash until smooth.

Combine sugar and extra water in
small pan, stir over heat, without
boiling, until sugar is dissolved. Boil,
uncovered, until syrup reaches 115°C
on candy thermometer or when a
teaspoon of syrup forms a soft ball
when dropped into cold water.

Stir rhubarb puree into sugar syrup, bring to boil, remove from heat, stir in blended potato flour and milk, simmer 2 minutes or until thick.

Beat egg whites in medium bowl with electric mixer until soft peaks form. Gradually add extra sugar, beat until dissolved between additions.

Gently fold egg white mixture into warm rhubarb mixture in 2 batches spoon into prepared dishes; level tops. Place dishes on oven tray.

Bake in moderately hot oven 12 minutes or until well risen and browned. Serve immediately with vanilla bean ice-cream.

**Vanilla bean ice cream** Split beans lengthways, scrape out seeds with small knife. Combine milk, cream, vanilla seeds and pods in medium pan, bring to boil, remove from heat, cover, stand 10 minutes.

Beat egg yolks and sugar in small bowl with electric mixer until creamy, gradually beat in strained cream mixture. Pour mixture into shallow tray, cover, freeze about 3 hours, or until firm. Spoon mixture into large bowl, beat with electric mixer until smooth and creamy. Pour into 14cm x 21cm loaf pan, cover, freeze overnight, or until firm.

□ SERVES 6

**Freeze** *Ice-cream suitable*
**Microwave** *Not suitable*

# DATE, ricotta and polenta cake

*Recipe can be made 3 days ahead*

**1 cup (160g) chopped seeded dates**
**$1/3$ cup (80ml) Grand Marnier**
**2 cups (300g) self-raising flour**
**1 teaspoon baking powder**
**$2/3$ cup (110g) polenta**
**1 cup (220g) caster sugar**
**$1\frac{1}{4}$ cups (250g) ricotta cheese**
**125g butter, melted**
**$3/4$ cup (180ml) water**
**$1/2$ cup (60g) chopped
    hazelnuts, toasted**

### Filling

**$1\frac{1}{4}$ cups (250g) ricotta cheese**
**2 tablespoons Grand Marnier**
**2 tablespoons icing sugar mixture**
**1 tablespoon grated orange rind**

Grease a deep 22cm round cake pan, line base and side with baking paper. Combine dates and liqueur in small bowl, stand 15 minutes.

Sift flour and baking powder into a large bowl, add polenta, sugar, cheese butter and water; beat with electric mixer until just combined. Stir in undrained dates and nuts. Spread half the polenta mixture into prepared pan, spread with filling, then remaining polenta mixture.

Bake in moderately slow oven 45 minutes, cover tightly with foil, bake further 1 hour or until firm.

Stand cake 10 minutes before turning onto wire rack to cool.

**Filling** Combine all ingredients in medium bowl.

□ SERVES 6 TO 8

**Storage** *Covered, in refrigerator*
**Freeze** *Not suitable*
**Microwave** *Not suitable*

Rhubarb souffles with vanilla bean ice-cream, *above left*
Date, ricotta and polenta cake, *left*

# Quick-mix CHRISTMAS pudding

*Recipe can be cooked in a cloth (boiled) or steamed*

- 1¹/₂ cups (240g) sultanas
- 1¹/₂ cups (225g) currants
- 1¹/₂ cups (250g) raisins, chopped
- ³/₄ cup (125g) mixed peel
- 2¹/₄ cups (450g) firmly packed brown sugar
- 1 tablespoon grated lemon rind
- ¹/₄ cup (60ml) brandy
- 3 eggs, lightly beaten
- ¹/₂ cup (75g) plain flour
- 1 tablespoon mixed spice
- 4 cups (280g) stale breadcrumbs
- 185g butter, melted

Combine all ingredients in large bowl; mix well.

**Steamed pudding** Grease 2.25 litre (9-cup) pudding steamer, line base with baking paper. Spoon mixture into prepared steamer. Place a 30cm x 40cm sheet of foil on bench, top with a sheet of baking paper. Fold a 5cm pleat crossways through centre of both sheets. Place paper sheets, baking-paper side-down over steamer, secure firmly with string or lid. Crush surplus foil and baking paper firmly around rim to help form a good seal.

Place pudding in a large boiler with enough boiling water to come halfway up side of steamer. Cover boiler with a tight-fitting lid; boil 6 hours. Replenish with boiling water as necessary. Stand pudding 15 minutes before turning out.

**Boiled pudding** First prepare pudding cloth. Use a 60cm square of unbleached calico; if calico is new, soak in cold water overnight. Next day, boil calico for 20 minutes; rinse. Have a large boiler three-quarters full of rapidly boiling water, 2.5 metres of string and ¹/₂ cup (75g) plain flour close by.

Wearing rubber gloves, dip prepared pudding cloth into boiling water; boil 1 minute. Remove cloth from water, squeeze excess water from cloth. Working quickly, spread hot cloth on bench, rub flour into the

centre of the cloth to cover an area about 40cm in diameter; leave flour a little thicker in the centre of cloth where the "skin" on the pudding will need to be thickest. Place cloth in medium bowl, place pudding mixture in centre, gather cloth evenly around pudding, avoiding any deep pleats. Lift pudding out of bowl, pat into round shape with hand. Return pudding to bowl; tie cloth tightly with string as close to mixture as possible. Tie loop in string to make pudding easier to lift from water, leave long ends of string free. Pull ends of cloth tightly to make sure pudding is as round as possible.

Gently lower pudding into boiling water. Tie free ends of string to handles of boiler to suspend pudding. Cover with tight-fitting lid, boil rapidly for 6 hours. Replenish boiling water as necessary. There must be enough water in the boiler for the pudding to be immersed at all times.

Untie pudding from handles. Place handle of wooden spoon through loop in string, lift pudding from water. Do not put pudding on bench; suspend from spoon by placing over rungs of an upturned stool or wedging handle in a drawer. It is important that the pudding swings freely without touching any surface. Twist wet ends of cloth around supporting string to keep away from pudding. If pudding has been cooked correctly, the cloth will begin to dry out in patches within a few minutes.

Leave pudding to hang 10 minutes. We prefer to remove a boiled pudding from its cloth before refrigerating or freezing. This prevents mould from forming on the pudding which often occurs when pudding is hung at room temperature especially in humid weather.

Place pudding into bowl; cut string. Carefully peel cloth back a little; stand 5 minutes. Invert pudding onto plate, then carefully peel cloth back completely.

Soak cloth in cold water overnight, wash, rinse well; avoid using detergents.

Wrap cooled pudding in plastic

## Cinnamon brandy CUSTARD

*Recipe can be made 2 days ahead
Recipe can be reheated gently; do not allow mixture to boil*

**6 egg yolks**
**$1/3$ cup (75g) caster sugar**
**2 cups (500ml) milk**
**300ml cream**
**10cm cinnamon stick**
**$1^1/_2$ tablespoons brandy**

Beat egg yolks and sugar in small bowl, with electric mixer until thick and creamy. Combine milk, cream and cinnamon stick in medium pan; bring to boil. Remove from heat; remove and reserve cinnamon stick. Gradually whisk milk mixture into egg mixture. Return mixture and cinnamon stick to pan, stir over low heat, without boiling, until custard thickens and coats the back of a metal spoon. Discard cinnamon stick; stir in brandy.

☐ SERVES 12

***Storage*** *Covered, in refrigerator*
***Freeze*** *Not suitable*
***Microwave*** *Milk mixture suitable*

wrap, then seal in freezer bag or an airtight container. Refrigerate up to 2 months or freeze for 12 months.

**Thawing pudding** Thaw frozen pudding 3 days ahead in refrigerator. Remove pudding from refrigerator 12 hours before reheating.

**To reheat steamed pudding** Return pudding to steamer and prepare as for cooking method. Steam 2 hours according to cooking instructions, left.

**To reheat boiled pudding** Remove plastic wrap and tie clean, dry, unfloured cloth on pudding. Boil 2 hours according to cooking instructions, left.

Hang hot pudding 10 minutes. Remove cloth. Stand pudding at least 20 minutes for skin to darken.

☐ SERVES 12

***Storage*** *Covered, in refrigerator*
***Freeze*** *Suitable*
***Microwave*** *Not suitable*

## ORANGE liqueur hard sauce

*Recipe can be made a week ahead*

**125g butter, softened**
**$1/2$ cup (80g) icing sugar mixture**
**2 tablespoons Irish cream liqueur**
**2 teaspoons grated orange rind**

Beat butter in small bowl with electric mixer until light and fluffy; gradually add sifted icing sugar; beat well until smooth. Add liqueur and rind; beat until combined. Spoon mixture into serving bowl. Cover, refrigerate until mixture is firm.

☐ SERVES 12

***Storage*** *Covered, in refrigerator*
***Freeze*** *Suitable*

Quick-mix Christmas pudding, *above left*
Orange liqueur hard sauce,
Cinnamon brandy custard, *left, from left*

# terms
## *and techniques*

**Almonds**
*Blanched*: skins removed.
*Flaked*: paper-thin slices.
*Ground*: also known as almond meal.
*Slivered*: small lengthways-cut pieces.

**Artichoke hearts** the centre (heart) of globe artichokes. Available from supermarkets and delicatessens in bottles, cans and in bulk.

**Bacon Rashers** also known as slices of bacon; made from pork side, cured and smoked.

**Bake blind** baking a pastry case without a filling. Lift pastry into required pan, cover with a sheet of baking paper, fill cavity with uncooked rice or dried beans. Bake as required, carefully removing paper and rice or beans halfway through cooking time.

**Baking paper** also known as parchment, silicon paper or non-stick baking paper; not to be confused with greaseproof or wax(ed) paper. Used to line pans and can also be used to make piping bags.

**Baking powder** a raising agent consisting mainly of 2 parts cream of tartar to 1 part bicarbonate of soda (baking soda).

**Bamboo shoots** the shoots of bamboo plants, available in cans.

**Bean sprouts** also known as bean shoots; tender new growths of assorted beans and seeds germinated for consumption as sprouts. Those readily available are mung bean, soy bean, alfalfa and snow pea sprouts.

**Beef**
*Boned rolled sirloin roast*: trimmed, flavoursome cut from the sirloin; when sliced, known as New York cut.
*Minced*: also known as ground beef.
*Scotch fillet steaks*: eye of the rib roast.

**Bicarbonate of soda** also known as baking soda.

**Biscuits**
*crumbs*: crushed plain, uniced biscuits (cookies).
*Sponge-finger*: also known as Savoiardi, Savoy biscuits or ladyfingers; Italian-style, crisp biscuits made from a sponge-cake mixture.

**Black bean sauce** made from fermented soy beans, spices, water and wheat flour.

**Black-eyed beans** also known as black-eyed peas.

**Bok choy** also called pak choi or Chinese white cabbage; has a fresh, mild mustard taste and is good braised or in stir-fries. Baby bok choy is also available.

**Bran, unprocessed** made from the outer layer of a cereal, most often the husks of wheat, rice or oats.

**Brandy** spirit distilled from wine.

**Breadcrumbs**
*Packaged*: fine-textured, crunchy, purchased breadcrumbs.
*Stale*: 1- or 2-day-old bread made into crumbs by blending or processing. Use white or wholemeal bread.

**Butter** salted or unsalted ("sweet") butter; 125g is equal to 1 stick.

**Buttermilk** low-fat milk cultured with bacteria that give it a slightly sour, tangy taste; low-fat yogurt can be substituted.

**Butternut cookies** biscuits made from sugar, flour, rolled oats, butter, coconut and golden syrup.

**Cajun seasoning** a blend of paprika, basil, onion, fennel, thyme, cayenne and white pepper, used in Southern (USA) cooking.

**Capsicum** also known as bell pepper or, simply, pepper. Seeds and membranes should be discarded before use.

**Cayenne pepper** a thin-fleshed, long, extremely hot red chilli; usually purchased dried and ground.

**Cheese**
*Blue-vein*: mould-treated cheese mottled with blue veining; we used a firm, fairly strong-flavoured variety.
*Bocconcini*: small rounds of fresh "baby" mozzarella, a delicate, semi-soft, white cheese traditionally made in Italy from buffalo milk. Spoils rapidly, so must be kept under refrigeration, in brine, for a maximum of 2 days.
*Brie*: originating in France, this buttery soft cheese with a downy white edible rind, is now produced by many countries, including Australia. The interior should be quite runny when ripe.
*Cream*: commonly known as "Philadelphia" or "Philly", a soft milk cheese having no less than 33% butterfat.
*Cheddar*: use an aged matured variety which is hard and has a pronounced flavour.

*Fetta*: Greek in origin; a crumbly textured goat's or sheep's milk cheese having a sharp, salty taste.
*Gouda*: a hard cheese with a creamy texture and nutty flavour. Originally produced in Holland, it is now made in several other countries.
*Gruyere*: Swiss cheese with small holes and a nutty, slightly salty flavour.
*Mozzarella*: a semi-soft cheese with a delicate, fresh taste; has a low melting point and stringy texture when heated.
*Parmesan*: a sharp-tasting, dry, hard cheese made from skim or part skim milk and aged for at least a year before being sold. The best quality is Parmigiano Reggiano, from Italy, aged a minimum three years.
*Ricotta*: a sweet, fairly moist, fresh curd cheese having a low fat content.

**Chickpeas** also called garbanzos or channa; an irregularly round, sandy-coloured legume used extensively in Mediterranean and Hispanic cooking.

**Chillies** available in many different types and sizes, used fresh and dried. Rubber gloves should be used when seeding and chopping fresh chillies to avoid burning your skin. Removing seeds and membranes decreases the heat level.
*Flakes*: crushed, dried chillies.
*Mild sweet chilli sauce*: a comparatively mild, Thai-type, commercial sauce made from red chillies, sugar, garlic and vinegar.
*Powder*: the Asian variety is the hottest, made from ground chillies; it can be used as a substitute for fresh chillies, assuming that $1/2$ teaspoon chilli powder is equal to 1 medium chopped fresh chilli.

**Chinese barbecued pork** available from many Asian food and specialty stores; ready to eat when bought.

**Chocolate**
*Dark*: eating chocolate; made of cocoa liquor, cocoa butter and sugar.
*Melts*: available in milk, white and dark chocolate. Made of sugar, vegetable fats, milk solids, cocoa powder, butter oil and emulsifiers, these are good for melting and moulding.
*White*: eating chocolate.

**Cinnamon stick** dried inner bark of the shoots of the cinnamon tree.

**Coconut**
*Cream*: available in cans and cartons; made from coconut and water.
*Desiccated*: unsweetened, concentrated, dried shredded coconut.
*Flaked*: dried flaked coconut flesh.
*Milk*: pure, unsweetened coconut milk available in cans.
*Shredded*: thin, unsweetened strips of dried coconut.

**Coconut macaroons** small biscuits (cookies) based on coconut.

**Corella pear** miniature dessert pear up to 10cm long.

**Corn chips** packaged snack food that evolved from fried corn tortilla pieces. Can be flavoured or plain.

**Cornflour** also known as cornstarch.

**Coriander** also known as cilantro or Chinese parsley; bright green leafed herb with a pungent flavour. Leaves and roots are edible.

**Cranberry sauce** a packaged product made of cranberries cooked in sugar syrup; its astringent flavour goes well with roast poultry and meats.

**Cream**
*Fresh*: also known as pure cream and pouring cream; has no additives. Minimum fat content 35%.
*Sour*: a thick, commercially-cultured cream. Minimum fat content 35%.
*Thickened*: a whipping cream containing a thickener. Minimum fat content 35%.

**Curry powder** a blend of ground powdered spices used for convenience when making Indian food. Can consist of some or all of the following in varying proportions: dried chilli, cinnamon, coriander, cumin, fennel, fenugreek, mace, cardamom and turmeric.

**Custard powder** packaged vanilla pudding mixture.

**Daikon** a basic food in Japan, it is also called Chinese turnip or Chinese white radish.

**Dried currants** tiny, almost black raisins so-named after a grape variety that originated in Greece.

**Dried mixed herbs** a blend of dried crushed thyme, rosemary, marjoram, basil, oregano and sage.

**Eggplant** also known as aubergine.

**Essences** also known as extracts; generally the by-product of distillation of plants.

**Fish sauce** also called nam pla or nuoc nam; made from pulverised salted fermented fish, most often anchovies. Has a pungent smell and strong taste; use sparingly. There are many kinds, of varying intensity.

**Five-spice powder** a fragrant mixture of ground cinnamon, cloves, star anise, Szechuan pepper and fennel seeds.

**Flour**
*Chickpea*: made from ground chickpeas; also known as garam flour or besan.
*Plain*: an all-purpose flour, made from wheat.
*Potato*: is made from cooked potatoes which have been dried and ground.
*Self-raising*: plain flour sifted with baking powder in the proportion of 1 cup flour to 2 teaspoons baking powder.

**Food colourings** available in liquid, powder and concentrated paste forms.

**Fruit mince** also known as mince meat.

**Garam masala** a blend of spices, originating in North India; based on varying proportions of cardamom, cinnamon, cloves, coriander, fennel and cumin, roasted and ground together. Black pepper and chilli can be added, to make a hotter example.

**Gelatine** we used powdered gelatine. It is also available in sheet form known as sheet gelatine.

**Ginger**
*Fresh:* also known as green or root ginger; the thick, gnarled root of a tropical plant used extensively in Asian cooking and, to a lesser degree, throughout the West. Unused ginger can be kept, peeled, covered with dry sherry in a jar and refrigerated, or frozen in an airtight container.
*Glace:* fresh ginger root preserved in sugar syrup. The sweetmeat crystallised ginger can be substituted if rinsed with warm water and dried before using.
*Ground:* also known as powdered ginger; used for making cakes, pies and puddings but cannot be substituted for fresh ginger.

**Glucose syrup** also known as liquid glucose and corn syrup; a sugary syrup obtained from starches such as wheat and corn and good for use in making fondant and jams because it helps control crystallisation.

**Golden syrup** a by-product of refined sugarcane; pure maple syrup or honey can be substituted.

**Gow gee pastry** packaged sheets of pastry used to enclose various fillings; wonton or spring roll wrappers can be substituted.

**Green ginger wine** alcoholic sweet wine infused with finely ground ginger.

**Green peppercorns** available in cans or jars, pickled in brine.

**Herbs** when specified, we used 1 teaspoon dried (not ground) herbs as being in proportion to 4 teaspoons (1 tablespoon) chopped fresh herbs.

**Hoisin sauce** a thick, sweet and spicy Chinese paste made from salted fermented soy beans, onions and garlic; used as a marinade or baste, or to accent stir-fries and barbecued or roasted foods.

**Horseradish cream** a creamy paste of grated horseradish, vinegar, oil and sugar.

**Hummus** a Middle-Eastern dip made of chickpeas, tahini, garlic and lemon juice.

**Instant lasagne** wide, flat sheets of precooked durum wheat pasta ready to be assembled, with no need for boiling in water.

**Jam** also known as preserve or conserve; most often made from fruit and sugar.

**Jelly crystals** fruit-flavoured gelatine crystals available from supermarkets.

**Kumara** orange-fleshed sweet potato.

**Lemon grass** a tall, clumping, lemon-smelling and tasting sharp-edged grass; the white lower part of each stem is chopped and used in Asian cooking or for tea.

**Lemon pepper seasoning** a blend of crushed black pepper, lemon, herbs and spices.

**Lentils** many different varieties of dried legumes, often identified by and named after their colour.

**Liqueurs**
*Cointreau:* citrus-flavoured liqueur.
*Creme de cacao:* chocolate-flavoured liqueur.
*Creme de menthe:* mint-flavoured liqueur.
*Grand Marnier:* orange-flavoured liqueur based on Cognac-brandy.
*Irish cream:* we used Baileys Original Irish Cream, based on Irish whiskey, spirits and cream.
*Kahlua:* coffee-flavoured liqueur.
*Malibu:* coconut-flavoured rum.
*Tia Maria:* coffee-flavoured liqueur.

**Maple-flavoured syrup** also known as pancake syrup but not a substitute for real maple syrup.

**Maple syrup** distilled sap of the maple tree; a thick, sweet syrup used in cooking and as a topping for pancakes, waffles and the like.

**Milk**
we used full-cream homogenised milk unless otherwise specified.
*Evaporated:* unsweetened canned milk from which water has been extracted by evaporation.

**Mince meat** also known as ground meat, as in beef, pork, lamb or veal.

**Mirin** a sweet, low-alcohol rice wine used in Japanese cooking.

**Mushrooms**
*Button:* small, cultivated white mushrooms having a delicate, subtle flavour.
*Dried Chinese:* also known as donko or dried shiitake mushrooms; have a unique meaty flavour.
*Oyster:* also known as abalone. Grey-white mushroom shaped like a fan.

**Mustard**
*Dijon:* a distinctively sharp French mustard.
*Powder:* finely ground mustard seeds.
*Seeded:* a coarse-grain mustard made usually from crushed mustard seeds and Dijon-style French mustard.
*Seeds:* can be black or yellow.

**Noodles**
*Bean thread:* also called cellophane; made from green mung bean flour. Good softened in soups and salads or deep-fried.
*Fresh egg:* made from wheat flour and eggs; strands vary in thickness.
*Fresh rice:* thick, wide, almost white in colour; made from rice and vegetable oil. Must be covered with boiling water to remove starch and excess oil before using in soups and stir-fries.
*Hokkien:* a fresh wheat flour noodle; looks like a thicker, yellow-brown spaghetti. Sometimes referred to as stir-fry noodles and best in fast-fried dishes. Soak in hot water before use.
*Rice vermicelli:* also called rice stick; made from rice flour. Must be soaked before using in stir-fries or soups.

**Oil**
*Macadamia:* extracted from macadamia nuts.
*Olive:* a mono-unsaturated oil, made from the pressing of tree-ripened olives; especially good for everyday cooking.
*Peanut:* pressed from ground peanuts; most commonly used oil in Asian cooking because of its high smoke point.
*Sesame:* much used in Asian cooking, made from roasted, crushed white sesame seeds; used extensively as a flavouring.
*Vegetable:* any of a wide number of oils having a plant rather than an animal source.

**Onion**
*Green:* also known as scallion or (incorrectly) shallot; an immature onion picked before the bulb has formed, having a long, bright-green edible stalk.

*Red:* also known as Spanish, red Spanish or Bermuda onion; a sweet-flavoured, large, purple-red onion often eaten raw in salads.

**Oyster sauce** Asian in origin; a rich, brown sauce made from oysters and brine, cooked with salt and soy sauce then thickened with starches.

**Paprika** ground dried red capsicum (bell pepper), available sweet or hot.

**Passionfruit** also known as granadilla; a small tropical fruit, native to Brazil, comprised of a tough outer skin surrounding edible black sweet-sour seeds.

**Pine nut** also known as pignoli; small, cream-coloured kernels obtained from the cones of different varieties of pine trees.

**Port** a rich, sweet dessert wine fortified with brandy.

**Prawns** also known as shrimp.

**Prosciutto** salted-cured, air-dried (unsmoked) pressed ham; usually sold in paper-thin slices, ready to eat when bought.

**Prunes** commercially or sun-dried plums.

**Pumpkin** sometimes used interchangeably with the word squash, the pumpkin is a member of the gourd family used in cooking both as one of many ingredients in a dish or eaten on its own. Various types can be substituted for one another.

**Ready-rolled pastry** frozen sheets of pastry (puff or shortcrust) available from supermarkets.

**Redcurrant jelly** a preserve made from redcurrants; used in sweet-making and served with roast meats.

**Rice**
*Arborio:* large, round-grained rice especially suitable for risottos.
*Basmati:* a white, fragrant, long-grained rice. It should be washed several times before cooking.
*Calrose:* a medium-grained variety readily available from supermarkets.
*Long-grain:* elongated grain, remains separate when cooked.

**Rind** zest.

**Risoni** rice-sized, rice-shaped pasta.

**Rocket** a green salad leaf.

**Rolled oats** oat groats husked, steam-softened, flattened with rollers, dried and packaged for consumption as a cereal product.

**Sago** also known as seed or pearl tapioca, it is from the sago palm while tapioca is from the root of the cassava plant. Used in soups and desserts, often as a thickening agent.

**Sambal oelek** (also ulek or olek). Indonesian in origin; a salty paste made from ground chillies.

**Sausage mince** ground pork or other meat mixed with fat, salt and various seasonings, and sold without the sausage casing; used for meatloaf and terrines.

**Seasoned pepper** a packaged preparation of combined black pepper, red capsicum (bell pepper), paprika and garlic.

**Sherry** fortified wine consumed as an aperitif or used in cooking. Sold as fino (light, dry), amontillado (medium sweet, dark) and oloroso (full-bodied, very dark).

**Soy sauce** made from fermented soy beans. Several variations are available in most supermarkets and Asian food stores, among them are salt-reduced, light, sweet and salty.

**Spare Ribs**
*American-style:* long, curved ribs cut from above the brisket so well-trimmed the sweet meat is almost fat-free; best marinated and cooked on an outdoor barbecue.

**Spinach**
*English:* correct name for spinach; the green vegetable often called spinach is correctly known as Swiss chard, silverbeet or seakale. Delicate, crinkled green leaves on thin stems; high in iron, it's good eaten raw or steamed gently.
*Silverbeet:* also known as Swiss chard or seakale. Cook green leafy parts as required by recipes.

**Split peas (yellow)** dried peas often used for making soups.

**Spring roll pastry sheets** packaged sheets of pastry used to enclose various fillings; wonton wrappers, gow gee or egg pastry sheets can be substituted.

**Star anise** a dried, star-shaped pod whose seeds have an astringent aniseed flavour.

**Sugar** we used coarse, granulated table sugar, also known as crystal sugar, unless otherwise specified.
*Brown:* a soft, fine granulated sugar containing molasses to give its characteristic colour.
*Caster:* also known as superfine or finely granulated table sugar.
*Icing sugar mixture:* also known as confectioners' sugar or powdered sugar; granulated sugar crushed together with a small amount (about 3%) cornflour added.
*Pure icing:* also known as confectioners' sugar or powdered sugar.

**Sultanas** golden raisins.

**Sunflower seed kernels** from dried husked sunflower seeds.

**Szechuan pepper** (also known as Chinese pepper). Small, red-brown aromatic seeds resembling black peppercorns; they have a peppery-lemon flavour.

**Tabasco sauce** brand name of an extremely fiery sauce made from vinegar, hot red peppers and salt.

**Taco seasoning mix** a packaged Mexican seasoning mix made from oregano, cumin, chillies and various other spices.

**Tandoori paste** Indian blend of hot and fragrant spices including turmeric, paprika, chilli powder, saffron, cardamom and garam masala.

**Teriyaki marinade** a blend of soy sauce, wine, vinegar, ginger and other spices.

**Thai green-curry paste** consisting of red onion, green chilli, soy bean oil, garlic, galangal, lemon grass, shrimp paste, citrus peel and coriander seeds.

**Thai red-curry paste** consisting of red onion, red chilli, soy bean oil, garlic, galangal, lemon grass, shrimp paste, citrus peel, salt, coriander seeds and citric acid.

**Tofu** also known as beancurd, an off-white, custard-like product made from the "milk" of crushed soy beans; comes fresh as firm or silken, and processed as fried or pressed dried sheets. Leftover fresh tofu can be refrigerated in water (which is changed daily) up to 4 days.

**Tomato**
*Canned:* whole peeled tomatoes in natural juice.
*Cherry:* also known as Tiny Tim or Tom Thumb tomatoes, small and round.
*Egg:* also called plum or Roma, these are smallish, oval-shaped tomatoes much used in Italian cooking.
*Paste:* a triple concentrated tomato puree used to flavour soups, stews, sauces and casseroles.
*Puree:* canned pureed tomatoes (not tomato paste). Substitute with fresh peeled and pureed tomatoes.
*Sauce:* also known as ketchup or catsup; a flavoured condiment based on tomatoes, vinegar and spices.

*Sun-dried:* dehydrated tomatoes. We use sun-dried tomatoes packed in oil, unless otherwise specified.
*Supreme:* a canned product consisting of tomatoes, onions, celery, capsicums, cheese and seasonings.
*Teardrop:* small yellow pear-shaped tomatoes.
*Tomato pasta sauce, bottled:* prepared sauce available from supermarkets.

**Tortilla** thin, round unleavened bread originating in Mexico; can be made at home or purchased frozen, fresh or vacuum-packed. Two kinds are available, one made from wheat flour and the other from corn (maizemeal).

**Vanilla bean** dried long, thin pod from a tropical golden orchid grown in Central and South America and Tahiti; the minuscule black seeds inside the bean are used to impart a luscious vanilla flavour in baking and desserts. A whole bean can be placed in the sugar container to make the vanilla sugar often required in recipes.

**Vinegar**
*Balsamic:* authentic only from the province of Modena, Italy; made from a regional wine of white Trebbiano grapes specially processed then aged in antique wooden casks to give its exquisite pungent flavour.
*Brown malt:* made from fermented malt and beech shavings.
*Cider:* made from fermented apples.
*Red wine:* based on fermented red wine.
*White:* made from spirit of cane sugar.
*White wine:* made from white wine.

**Whisky** we used a good quality Scotch whisky.

**Wine** the adage is that you should never cook with wine you wouldn't drink; we use good-quality dry white and red wines in our recipes.

**Worcestershire sauce** a thin, dark-brown spicy sauce used as a seasoning for meat, gravies and cocktails and as a condiment.

**Yeast** a 7g ($1/4$oz) sachet of dried yeast (2 teaspoons) is equal to 15g ($1/2$oz) compressed yeast.

**Zucchini** also known as courgette.

# facts and figures

Wherever you live in the world you can use our recipes with the help of our easy-to-follow conversions for all your cooking needs. These conversions are approximate only. The difference between the exact and approximate conversion of liquid and dry measures amounts to only a teaspoon or two, and will not make any difference to your cooking results.

### Measuring Equipment

The difference between measuring cups internationally is minimal within 2 or 3 teaspoons' difference. The most accurate way of measuring dry ingredients is to weigh them. When measuring liquids use a clear glass or plastic jug with the metric markings.

In this book we use metric measuring cups and spoons approved by Standards Australia:

- *1 cup: 250ml*
- *1 teaspoon: 5ml*
- *1 tablespoon: 20ml*

### How to Measure

When using metric measuring cups, it is important to shake the dry ingredients loosely into the required cup. Do not tap the cup, or pack ingredients into the cup unless otherwise directed. Level top of cup with knife.

When using metric measuring spoons, level top of spoon with knife. When measuring liquids in the jug, place jug on flat surface, check for accuracy at eye level.

We use large eggs with an average weight of 60g.

## DRY MEASURES

| Metric | Imperial |
|---|---|
| 15g | $\frac{1}{2}$oz |
| 60g | 2oz |
| 90g | 3oz |
| 125g | 4oz ($\frac{1}{4}$lb) |
| 250g | 8oz ($\frac{1}{2}$lb) |
| 280g | 9oz |
| 315g | 10oz |
| 345g | 11oz |
| 375g | 12oz ($\frac{3}{4}$lb) |
| 410g | 13oz |
| 440g | 14oz |
| 470g | 15oz |
| 500g | 16oz (1lb) |
| 750g | 24oz ($1\frac{1}{2}$lb) |
| 1kg | 32oz (2lb) |

## HELPFUL MEASURES

| Metric | Imperial |
|---|---|
| 3mm | $\frac{1}{8}$in |
| 6mm | $\frac{1}{4}$in |
| 2.5cm | 1in |
| 8cm | 3in |
| 10cm | 4in |
| 15cm | 6in |
| 20cm | 8in |
| 28cm | 11in |
| 30cm | 12in (1ft) |

## LIQUID MEASURES

| Metric | Imperial |
|---|---|
| 30ml | 1 fluid oz |
| 125ml | 4 fluid oz |
| 150ml | 5 fluid oz ($\frac{1}{4}$ pint/1 gill) |
| 250ml | 8 fluid oz |
| 300ml | 10 fluid oz ($\frac{1}{2}$ pint) |
| 1000ml (1 litre) | $1\frac{3}{4}$ pints |

## OVEN TEMPERATURES

*These oven temperatures are only a guide. Always check the manufacturer's manual.*

| | C° (Celsius) | F° (Fahrenheit) | Gas Mark |
|---|---|---|---|
| Very slow | 120 | 250 | 1 |
| Slow | 150 | 300 | 2 |
| Moderately slow | 160 | 325 | 3 |
| Moderate | 180 - 190 | 350 - 375 | 4 |
| Moderately hot | 200 - 210 | 400 - 425 | 5 |
| Hot | 220 - 230 | 450 - 475 | 6 |
| Very hot | 240 - 250 | 500 - 525 | 7 |

*Note: NZ, Canada, USA and UK all use 15ml tablespoons.*
*All cup and spoon measurements are level, unless stated.*

## Make Your Own Stock

Recipes can be made 4 days ahead, store, covered, in refrigerator; or freeze in smaller quantities. Remove any fat from the surface after stock has been refrigerated overnight.

Stock is available in cans or tetra packs. If using stock cubes or powder, use 1 teaspoon of stock powder or 1 small cube with 1 cup (250ml) water to give a strong stock. Check salt and fat content of packaged stocks. Recipes make 2.5 litres (10 cups).

### CHICKEN STOCK

**2kg chicken bones**
**2 medium (300g) onions, chopped**
**2 celery sticks, chopped**
**2 medium (250g) carrots, chopped**
**3 bay leaves**
**2 teaspoons black peppercorns**
**5 litres (20 cups) water**

Combine all ingredients in large pan, simmer, uncovered, 2 hours; strain.

### VEGETABLE STOCK

**2 large (360g) carrots, chopped**
**2 large (360g) parsnips, chopped**
**4 medium (600g) onions, chopped**
**12 celery sticks, chopped**
**4 bay leaves**
**2 teaspoons black peppercorns**
**6 litres (24 cups) water**

Combine all ingredients in large pan, simmer, uncovered, $1\frac{1}{2}$ hours; strain.

### BEEF STOCK

**2kg meaty beef bones**
**2 medium (300g) onions**
**2 celery sticks, chopped**
**2 medium (250g) carrots, chopped**
**3 bay leaves**
**2 teaspoons black peppercorns**
**5 litres (20 cups) water**
**3 litres (12 cups) water, extra**

Place bones and unpeeled chopped onions in baking dish. Bake in hot oven about 1 hour or until bones and onions are well browned. Transfer bones and onions to large pan, add celery, carrots, bay leaves, peppercorns and water, simmer, uncovered, 3 hours. Add extra water, simmer, uncovered, further 1 hour; strain.

# index